Where the Spirits Ride the Wind

Where the Spirits Ride the Wind

TRANCE JOURNEYS AND OTHER ECSTATIC EXPERIENCES

Felicitas D. Goodman

WITH DRAWINGS
BY GERHARD BINDER

Indiana University Press

BLOOMINGTON & INDIANAPOLIS

This book is a publication of

Indiana University Press
601 North Morton Street
Bloomington, IN 47404-3797 USA

http://iupress.indiana.edu

Telephone orders 800-842-6796
Fax orders 812-855-7931
Orders by e-mail iuporder@indiana.edu

The paper used in this publication meets the minimum requirements of American
National Standard for Information Sciences—Permanence of Paper for Printed
Library Materials, ANSI Z39.48-1984.

∞TM

Manufactured in the United States of America

Library of Congress Cataloging-in-Publication Data

Goodman, Felicitas D.
Where the spirits ride the wind : trance journeys and other
ecstatic experiences / Felicitas D. Goodman ; with drawings by
Gerhard Binder.
p.   cm.
Includes bibliographical references.
ISBN 978-0-253-32764-2 (alk. paper). — ISBN 978-0-253-20566-7 (pbk.)
1. Astral projection. 2. Spirits. 3. Trance. 4. Visions.
5. Ecstasy. 6. Experience (Religion) I. Title.
BF1389.A7G66   1990
133.9—dc20   89-45567

7   8   9   10   11   12   11   10   09   08   07

To my companions
who traveled the path of the Spirits
with me,
and whose voices speak through me, page after page,
this work is fondly dedicated.

Contents

LIST OF PLATES

PROLOGUE

It was with trepidation, even fear, that in response to the urgent entreaties of many friends here and abroad I began writing this account of our common adventures. Would our spirit friends, the Surpassing Ones, approve of the endeavor, which was bound to reveal much, perhaps too much, about their secrets? And even more important, had I even properly grasped the nature of the kind of reality into which our hesitant steps had taken us?

Then one night, just before the day was about to break, I had a vision. Snowy white against the grey of restlessly seething clouds, I saw the head of the Bear Spirit emerging. But before I could give in to the feeling of happy recognition, it twisted as if agitated by a mighty wind and, dissolving, became one with the hulking mass of a powerfully pulsing white presence. Driven by the storm, that in turn lifted, and from below it, a bundle of taut, vibrating strands streaked with enormous force into the hugely magnified likeness of one of the pebbles that I had found during the summer of my initiation, bearing the face of the Badger. The wind carried that away also, and a delicate fawn cavorted out of nowhere, twisted upon itself, and was gone. Then all was calm, and nothing was left but a slightly tilted, narrow, empty bookcase, carelessly nailed together from short furring strips with some of them missing, floating, as if suspended forever, in the vacuity of the now immobile greyness.

The significance of the vision and its relation to the project I was agonizing over did not become clear to me until a week later, when on a field trip to Yucatán (Mexico) late in 1986, I once more saw Anselmo preach. In May 1970 this young Maya Indian farmhand and barber had had a vision. During the Sunday service of the Apostolic village congregation to which he belonged, he saw some candles being extinguished, and he heard the voice of the Holy Spirit ordering the Brothers to go out and convert everyone, for Christ's Second Coming was close at hand. The hoped-for event was to occur at the beginning of September of that year. After the failure of the prophesy, what was left of the devastated congregation developed along more conservative lines, while a handful of diehards gathered around Anselmo and built their own House of Prayer at the far north end of the village, independent of any church authority or organization.

Anselmo was still the fluent and effective speaker I had known sixteen years before. But as I sat there in the carefully tended small mud-and-wattle building, listening to him speak about a vision of the Prophet Isaiah, it occurred to me that not once did he ever refer to his own many visions of that fateful summer so many years ago. Instead, over and over again, he lifted the Bible

high and laid his dark and work-worn hand on the white, open pages. That
is where it was, only there. There was nothing else.

There was a sudden chill in the air in that warm tropical night. There had
been a time when Anselmo had known the power of seeing. It still gave wings
to his words. He had been to where, in-ever rolling waves, religion was in a
constant state of being born. He had been propelled during that summer to
leave behind the world of a faith in which all was solid, finished, created, safe,
and had stepped out into a reality where everything was new and scintillating,
a revelation continually rising anew. But timidly, he had stepped back. With
compassion I recalled how during that season of visions the Brothers had
watched him for many days and nights to keep him from killing himself. He
was still fighting that battle, grasping for that security that was destined to
elude him. He now knew that whoever had really been "out there" could
never have that kind of safety again, the security of the ancient revelations,
frozen on the printed page. In front of the altar there stood a man who was
mortally afraid.

And suddenly the understanding of my own vision washed over me like
a mighty wave. The structure in which I had been raised no longer offered
any shelter and protection. I would never again be allowed to flee back to it
when the power of the Outside became overwhelming. That finite world was
but a fragile, empty hull, like the empty bookcase of my vision, that I could
no longer occupy. My small fears were meaningless. For life or for death, I
was committed to that mighty realm of which I was shown a brief reminder,
the world where all was forever motion and emergence, that realm where the
spirits ride the wind.

Section I

THE SEARCH
FOR THE SPIRITS

CHAPTER ONE

The Call of
the Old People

On the eve of my twelfth birthday
I had a severe headache, and it startled me, for I had never had that kind of
a headache before. The next morning, I bled for the first time. I went to my
mother, and she showed me what to do. There was great trust between us,
and because she was not upset, I was not either. When the shock came, it
was in a different guise. My mother took a piece of chalk and drew a little
cross on the bedroom door. "This means," she said, "that we now have an
adult daughter in our house." I puzzled over what that might mean—sex education had not been invented yet—but did not ask her. I always kept the
most disquieting questions to myself.

Very soon I discovered all on my own what being an adult apparently
meant, and confided it to my diary: "The magic time is over." For all of a
sudden and without the slightest warning, I realized that I could no longer
effortlessly call up what in my terms was magic: that change in me that was
so deliciously exciting and as if I were opening a door, imparting a special
hue to whatever I chose. I noticed the curious impediment first with the fresh,
crunchy snow which fell right after my birthday. It was nice, but I could not
make it glow. Bewildered, I began paying more attention to my seeming dis-
ability. The orange glow of dawn streaming through the bedroom window was
the same as before; so was the smell of the horses on the market. But I had
changed.

I believe today that a large part of initiation in the wiser societies, those
small ones that, together with so much else that is worthwhile and beautiful,
are disappearing at an alarming rate in our century, has to do with helping
the adolescent to reconstitute the waning capacity for ecstasy. The harsh stimulation of the nervous system incorporated in many of those rituals, the pain,

the fatigue, the fasting, are designed, I think, to substitute a different, an adult, form for the spontaneous ability to call up that very special trance, the one leading to ecstasy, the passing of which I mourned so deeply as I entered puberty.

Obviously I was living at the wrong place. How gladly I would have submitted to whatever trial if only someone could have told me what it was I was losing, and if there would have been a promise of reconstitution. Actually, I was coming up for confirmation, which was modeled after ancient initiation rituals, but it was cruelly vacuous. I was confirmed in the simple Lutheran church of Nagyvárad, in the Hungarian region of western Rumania, and for some reason I hoped vaguely that it might provide the help I wanted. But after the ritual, the details of which we had had to learn by heart and dutifully performed, there was only a festive meal in the Kispipa, my father's favorite restaurant, and then nothing, absolutely nothing happened. I did not even know what I had expected, but it was very clear to me that I had not received it.

I experienced that frightening emptiness once again when in the convent school I sang in the choir during the induction of a novice into the order. We talked among ourselves about Philomela's hair being cut, and about how she would be given a wedding band that from then on would mark her as Christ's bride. "Then what will happen?" I wanted to know. "Oh, she can't leave the convent anymore." I knew that already, and it was not what I was after. I wanted to find out what sweet miracle would engulf her once she went back to be alone in her cell. But no one had an answer. I imagined Philomela in her lonely, empty room, and the vicarious anguish nearly tore me apart.

The question is, why did I even hope for "something" unimaginably wonderful to happen in conjunction with a ritual? After all, I was brought up in a Western-type society where such expectations were certainly not taught, in school or out. Neither did I have any source of information about other types of tradition—no radio, no television, not even a public library; only a few books borrowed from friends here and there. But that was perhaps how it happened. Everyone had books of Hungarian tales, legends, and myths, which I began reading even before starting grade school. Stealthily, those stories insinuated a knowledge and a yearning into my childish world that were to shape me for the rest of my life.

Because what to me was so precious was inexorably slipping further and further away, I finally came to the conclusion that I had to do something to save what was still left of it. Its fading had clearly been associated with entering adulthood, so I decided that I simply would refuse to become an adult. Wisely, I kept that decision a secret. To everyone around me, I was a normal teenager. I developed strong physically. I was at the head of my class in school. I enjoyed swimming and ice-skating, and I fell in love with a boy whom I had known in grade school and for whom I embroidered a fancy handkerchief. But I had a secret chamber deep within; I could retire to that hidden place, and working with desperate concentration, I could cheat adulthood out of a victim and stay a child and have the familiar trance wash over me once more.

As the years went by, though, the occulted ecstasy became less and less accessible. There was college, professional work, love, and marriage. I bore and suckled three children. The Second World War burned over Europe, and when it was over, I went to America with my family.

I arrived in this country as countless immigrants before me, starving, beggarly, all my belongings in one cardboard box, and deeply scarred by the blood, gore, and death of the war. For years, I woke up at night barely able to suppress the urge to scream. The floor of reality was a thin crust of slag; I had to walk over it ever so gingerly in order not to break through and fall into the merciless darkness of the void below. Caring for my children and my professional work were my only safety, my escape. Do not look left, do not look right, and especially never look up at the sky, for it too was endless and void.

Seven years after my arrival in this country, I had a new baby, the world around me became less threatening, and I began feeling safer. I even started writing again, poetry, and then a novel. Yet I could not escape a feeling of pervasive despondency. This world was entirely different from that of my childhood, where I could always feel the comfort of invisible presences around. All was deserted, empty around here. No matter how wide I opened the gates of my inner being, there was nothing asking to enter.

My new daughter was still quite small when it happened that we took a trip to a national park in neighboring Kentucky. Lying in the grass, I rediscovered the sky. It was dotted with fluffy cirrus clouds, and as I watched, an endless procession of white bundles came drifting across the blue, like Indian warriors laid out for burial, the feathers of their war bonnets trailing behind them in the wind. We later stopped at a historical marker, which spoke of Kentucky as "the dark and bloody grounds," home of the frontiersmen who, I recalled, notched their rifle butts to keep count of the Indians they murdered. Perhaps those cloud biers were of the Indians' spirits, forever reenacting their sorrowful exit after the white men had killed their people and had raped the land. Were the spirits dead now too? There seemed to be no answer, and I felt even more disconsolate than before.

Then in 1960 friends from Ohio State University invited me to spend my vacation with them in their new home in Santa Fe, New Mexico. I had never before been to the Southwest, with its vast spaces and sepia and magenta flat-top mountains, dotted with patches of green junipers and pinyon trees, and alive with a thousand lacy rock carvings created by wind and sand and shimmering golden in the sunlight. Most of the time the madonna-blue sky above the land was brittle and clean. But sometimes, ample cloud breasts would drip the blessing of rain from their nipples on the thirsty earth, and the misty Feathered Serpent humped over the ridges in the morning, celebrating fertility.

There were still other impressions. After walking over the Indian arts-and-crafts markets with their celebration of beauty, so appealing to the senses, I came away with the feeling of having been touched by an almost palpable presence, a special, undefinable quality. Was this the land to which the spirits had fled from the dark and bloody grounds? Nowhere in Europe had I ever experienced being overwhelmed by such a magical quality except when I was very young and still knew ecstasy, and it filled me from the start with an intense yearning. For what I did not know, perhaps for that secret recess of childhood, a world that used to be sweet, holy, and inviolate.

It was the month of August, and my hosts took me to see the Corn Dance that took place every year at Santo Domingo, the largest of the Rio Grande pueblos. The dance is an ancient Indian prayer ritual asking for an ample harvest for all people. Well over a thousand Indian men, women, and children in colorful native attire danced this prayer from the forenoon until sundown to the songs of the men's choir and the rhythm of the large drum, the tone of which resounded in the desert like the heartbeat of the earth. I was totally overwhelmed by the bewildering beauty of this new and strange world.

The night after the dance I had a dream, or more likely a vision. I saw three old Indians in front of the window. They were dressed in the colorful shirts and slit pants of the choir, and one of them carried the big drum. With his drumstick, he knocked on the window, and when I looked up, he waved for me to come along. The experience made me unaccountably happy. I did not know the ethnographic literature about the Pueblos at the time, but it seemed to me that what I had seen was the spirits of the "Old People" of the pueblo I had heard about, and who had come to invite me to this, their land. And so I decided, like a sleepwalker choosing the right corner to turn, that no matter what, I was going to acquire some small piece of land here. Then I would be able to say to those kindly old spirits, "You see, here I am."

The search took nearly three years; land was—and still is—very scarce in the Southwest. Finally, in 1963, my real-estate agent found not the modest five acres that I thought I could afford, but a large spread, nearly three hundred acres, which the Forest Service had rid itself of some years ago, and which its present owner wanted to sell off at a suitable profit. My lawyer counseled adamantly against it: "Don't waste your money on that," he wrote. "We call it the Pojoaque Badlands." But after all, I was not intending to grow alfalfa, and I knew the beauty of the Pojoaque Valley from my previous visit. I was not going to be disappointed.

This "badland" was on all sides surrounded by Indian pueblos, which in part had retained their old Tewa names—Tesuque, Pojoaque, Nambe—and by Santa Clara and San Ildefonso. In the east, the Sangre de Cristo range turned wine-red at sundown. To the west, the property was protected by the fortress wall of the Jemez Mountains, where, according to Indian legend, humans emerged from the crowded and dark third world to this, their fourth one under the arc of the rainbow. Its loose sandy terrain was crisscrossed by arroyos, deep cuts caused by water erosion, but each one a picturesque world of its own. A million years ago, the volcanoes of the Valle Grande, thirty miles away, spewed glinting, many-colored pebbles on its softly rounded hills. Yellow rabbit brush bloomed near a juniper by the fence, and on some barren hillsides Indian paintbrush flamed red among the rocks. At night, the coyotes laughed from across the ancient river bed of the Cañada Ancha, and the spirits haunting the pueblo ruins by the river whispered in my dreams. Of course, I could not make the despoiling of the earth go away that rolled on greedily on the highway down in the valley day and night, or the threat of the final holocaust that glowed in the steely lights of Los Alamos, the "Atomic City" toward the west. But at least here among these gentle hills, the world was still at peace. I signed the contract for the land, and never regretted that the decision committed me to much sacrifice and many years of hard labor.

In the summer of 1965, after days of hiking, we—that is, a helpful relative, my young daughter, and I—located a spot suitable for building. It was like a tongue stretching outward from among the hills, affording a view of the Sangre de Cristo toward the east but surrounded on all other sides by protective ridges. I had a well drilled, and men on horseback brought in electricity from the region's electric co-op. We knew next to nothing about how to build a house from the local sun-dried bricks, the adobes. But if we got stuck, we went to our Hispanic or Indian neighbors for advice, or to the ever-useful builders' supply store. People would make expansive fun of us. "Look at that, here they come again from the Rancho Grande," they would say. But actually, everyone was friendly and helpful, and also curious about what a woman was doing there, homesteading pretty much on her own.

It was hard. We could not use our tent, because scorpions and six-inch orange centipedes with dragon heads made it their home. Besides, it kept collapsing in the violent storms that were our frequent visitors. In the cruel heat of midday we crawled instead into the sparse shade of the junipers. During the cloudbursts of the summer's rainy season, our only safe haven was the cabin of the pickup truck. Our camp stove gave up in the persistent wind, so I had to cook on an open fire. It rained, our firewood got wet, and we had to eat sandwiches. There was no money to hire a backhoe, so armed only with pick and shovel, we dug all the ditches for the foundation. We laid the heavy cast-iron pipes for the rough-in of the plumbing and finally built the walls for our first room.

The summer was nearly over when we finally nailed the tarpaper on the roof and hung the door. I had registered for graduate school at Ohio State University, and two weeks before school was to start, we were finally ready to leave. We loaded everything we had borrowed on our pickup truck, the wheelbarrow and the sawhorses, the scaffolding, and Baba, our faithful goat, to take back to the neighbors in the valley. As we rolled out, I turned back for a last glance. Our flat little house was shrinking into insignificance in the glare of the noonday sun, its adobe walls becoming one with the sand and the clay. Had the Old Ones, the spirits of this land, even noticed that I had come? Did some of them live in these hills or did they have to be invited? I had no idea of how to invite spirits, and after all the big problems and small triumphs and successes of homesteading, it seemed to me that I had left the most important task undone. Perhaps next summer, I thought hopefully. After all, I was now on the right path. I did not realize then how long and arduous that path would turn out to be.

CHAPTER TWO

Getting in Touch
with the Spirits:
The First Discoveries

In the Protestant Christian tradition in which I was raised, it was held that the only way in which a human could communicate with the beings inhabiting the alternate reality was by prayer. But in the view of the vast majority of other traditions, speech, as the mode of communication of ordinary reality, is singularly unsuited for this purpose. It is but a hardly audible knock on the very thick wall separating humans from the spirit realm. In fact, humans have to make a truly heroic effort to be noticed on the other side. Merely talking, falling into a worshipful mood, feeling "transcendent," "numinous," or "oceanic," or whatever other pompous words are listed in the dictionary, simply will not do. Instead humans, if they have the urgent necessity or desire to squeeze through the chinks in that wall, need to change the very functioning of their bodies in the most radical way. The term summarizing these changes is *religious trance*, one of a large group of altered states of consciousness of which humans are capable. It is termed religious because observation shows that it is the one occurring in religious context, that is, when contact is made with the alternate, the sacred, reality. (For the problem of defining "religion," see Goodman 1988.)

Before the worship service on the particular evening in the Apostolic church in Mexico City which I want to describe here, I had only read about this kind of trance; I had never actually seen a person experiencing it. I had come to Mexico City in hopes of finally observing this nonordinary behavior, the presence of which, I was fervently wishing, would clinch a scholarly argument I had advanced in a paper for a seminar in graduate school.

It was the summer of 1968. Around me in the crowded bus there were brown-skinned passengers going home from laboring in offices and factories, girls in fashionable dresses, men in bedraggled work clothes. Women boarded with baskets or shopping bags filled with vegetables and fruit from the market, a mother with her sleeping infant slung across her back in a scarf. My destination was the Colónia Pro-Hogar, a rather poor section of the city, and I had wrapped my tape recorder in newspaper so it would not tempt any would-be assailant. As the bus rumbled and lurched over the narrow back streets of the vast metropolis, burping Diesel fumes, I thought about the circuitous search that had brought me here to Latin America from the classrooms of Ohio State University.

My initial university training, a diploma (master's degree) in translating and interpreting from the University of Heidelberg in Germany, had certainly not prepared me for what I was now interested in. Neither had my professional career in the United States. For many years after immigrating to this country, I earned a living as a multilingual scientific translator in the fields of metallurgy, biochemistry, and medicine. But I was never quite happy in my work. So when my children were old enough and gone the greater part of the day, I decided to go back to school in the fall after we had completed our first building in New Mexico.

This was in 1965. I was fifty-one years old, and the concept of the "mature scholar" had not yet been invented. I recall how shy I felt about having to present my diplomas, which in the meantime had acquired a telltale yellow hue. But I had the good fortune of encountering an understanding dean of admissions at Ohio State University and was accepted into graduate school as a special student. I elected to major in linguistics, for languages were really the only subject I felt I was competent in. Despite dire predictions to the contrary from friends and relatives, studying came easily and after the first quarter, I was upgraded to "regular" status.

As it turned out, it was a propitious time to embark on linguistics. This was no longer the old-time philology, the endless search for roots and relationships of words in musty documents written in long-forgotten tongues. Everything was being questioned, turned upside down, and put together in new and interesting ways. There were the acoustics of speech sounds, the physiology of the way we produced them, and the psychology of language usage. Language behavior was being tied in with human evolution and with culture. Much of it, such as Noam Chomsky's ideas about a deep structure in our mind, which he thought of as a black box full of grammatical rules that "generated" what we said out loud, was new and controversial. It was great to see all this innovation happening right before my eyes. Yet I kept feeling that this was not what I had come to the university for, and as the quarter wore on, there arose an undercurrent of doubt and uncertainty about what I was doing that I could not staunch.

It was in this mood that in the second quarter of my graduate career I registered for a course offered by Professor Erika Bourguignon of the Department of Anthropology, entitled "Religion in Native Societies." I had never been interested in the Protestant philosophy of religion or in theology generally. But there was something in religion as a topic that seemed to tease me. I had read, widely if unsystematically, everything from Robert Graves's *White Goddess* to Bronislaw Malinowski's *Magic, Science, and Religion*. The title of the course seemed to carry a promise, as if to say, "There *is* something to all of this," an allure like the distant jingling of a shaman's staff.

Dr. Bourguignon's lectures began putting some order into the jumbled mass of information on the religious systems of small, non-Western societies that I had gathered on my own, and this alone was most gratifying. But there was an added bonus, for she also introduced us to her own ongoing research. For a number of years she had been heading a project, funded by the National Institute of Mental Health, the aim of which was, as she explains,[1]

> a multifaceted analysis of what appeared to be a widespread psychocultural phe-
> nomenon, about which, however, curiously little of a systematic nature was known.
> The phenomenon with which we were concerned was the religious evaluation . . .
> of a psychological state variously termed "dissociation," "trance," or more recently
> and more generally, "altered states of consciousness." (1973:viii)

I was instantly captivated especially by two lines of thought that Dr. Bour-guignon presented. One was that such "altered states of consciousness" or "trances" were entirely normal. I had read my share of learned disquisitions about the psychotic nature of religious experiences, especially of shamans. My reaction had always been one of angry disbelief: a *táltos*, the Hungarian shaman, mentally ill, a schizophrenic, or an epileptic? There had to be an error in judgment somewhere. Here then was someone who agreed with me. The second idea that I found enthralling was that such behavior, which added excitement, color, and drama to otherwise humdrum rituals, was institution-alized in many societies, part and parcel of a large number of religious ob-servances. So this was the magic ingredient, the lack of which I had felt so keenly as a child! All these new insights were not only exhilarating. It was also deeply satisfying to discover that my thinking had all along been in line with bona fide behavioral science. The graduate-school adventure was finally taking on a truly thrilling aspect.

And there was more to come. Soon after I joined Dr. Bourguignon's course, she hired me on as a translator for the foreign-language material to be included in the large-scale statistical study she and her staff were working on. Eventually that study was to provide proof that religious trance behavior was not some oddity reported by a few observers, but was so widely spread that we could find virtually no small society of the kind that anthropologists are typically interested in that did not have some institutionalized form of it. I felt happy and somehow personally vindicated by these findings.

Neither was the linguist in me to go empty-handed. In the course of my work for the project, I frequently came across references in the foreign eth-nographic literature to the fact that during religious trance rituals, those par-ticipating also uttered a strange kind of speech. It was called *glossolalia* in linguistics and was known also to Christians as "speaking in tongues." It is a vocalization that usually consists of syllables that carry no meaning, such as "lalalalala" or "?ulalala dalala." (The ? indicates a consonant called a "glottal stop," a catch or closure in the throat.) It was often referred to as gibberish by Western observers, "something not worth recording," but to my mind, if it was part of a ceremony, it had to have some significance, and therefore it merited a second look. When, after earning my master's degree in linguistics, I took a course in anthropological linguistics with Dr. Bourguignon, I decided to do a paper on the phenomenon.

Dr. Bourguignon provided me with a number of sound tapes recorded by members of her project during fieldwork with various Pentecostal-type congregations, where glossolalia is institutionalized. A linguistic analysis of the tapes revealed some intriguing features. The people uttering these curious sequences of syllables were all English speakers, although they used a number of different dialects—Caribbean black, Appalachian, and American middle-class English from Texas. But as soon as they switched into "tongues," their utterances exhibited a number of characteristics that certainly were not to be found in these variants of English. This speech was rhythmical, "scanning," as it were, with a continually repeated regular accent pattern, as though it were the recitation of traditional nineteenth-century poetry. In addition, each syllable invariably began with a consonant. Most striking, however, on all the tapes there was the same intonation pattern: It rose to a peak at the end of the first third of the utterance unit and then sloped gradually toward the end. I began measuring the pattern with a stopwatch: there was no mistaking it. Years later I analyzed the same tapes in the phonetics lab using a level recorder, and the electronically traced curves were exactly the way I had heard them during that initial scrutiny.

The agreement struck me as strange, because after all, the congregations which had provided the tapes were geographically distant from each other, so there could have been no imitation, especially in light of the fact that they did not even belong to the same denomination of the general Pentecostal movement. What was even more surprising was the regularity of the pattern. Not even poetry was as regularly accented, and certainly intonation was never that monotonous. In natural language, we vary intonation endlessly in the service of communication. The message conveyed by "*John* is in the garden" is different from that conveyed by "John *is* in the garden" or "John is in the *garden*." Something, it seemed, was interfering with normal speech behavior. Remembering that people spoke in this nonordinary way during religious observances that, as those anthropologists reported, included trance behavior, I speculated that this "something" was certain changes that occurred in the body during trance.

There were some nagging doubts, of course, about the validity of this assumption, as always when one hits on an entirely new explanatory hypothesis. So I sent the first draft of my paper to a Canadian linguist who had published a number of papers on glossolalia. I thought he would find my thesis intriguing, and might perhaps offer some additional conjectures. Instead I got a letter back the gist of which was, now, now, young lady, there is no such thing as trance, and even if it did exist, we would not want to make people unhappy by suggesting that they experienced a weird state of some kind.

It was a stinging reprove, and after getting over my disappointment, I decided to fight back. There had to be a way to counter this man's objections, and the best way to do that, it seemed to me, was to discover whether those curious patterns were peculiar to English speakers only. Did the glossolalia of Spanish speakers, for instance, exhibit the same or possibly quite different characteristics? If what I had discovered occurred also elsewhere, I had a better base from which to argue that this peculiar vocalization behavior was not merely a psychocultural one, but carried within it a hidden factor deriving from biological processes. One could think of them as part of the content of a "black box," different from the grammatical one, but in the case of glossolalia equally acting as a generating "deep structure" in the Chomskian sense.

To me, showing that actual physical changes were involved in the religious trance, that it was not all "just imagination," imbued the experience with a never-hoped-for, tangible reality. What I did not realize at the time was that with a search in this direction I was in fact joining a larger movement toward the view that behavior had a biological basis, as well; it was not determined exclusively by psychological motivation. In the decade of the seventies, this movement resulted in a revolution in the treatment of so-called mental illness, away from analysis and toward biological psychiatry.

What I wanted to find out in Mexico City, then, was what the glossolalia of Spanish speakers sounded like. I looked for some branch of the Pentecostal movement, for instance, for the Apostolics, because there, speaking in tongues was expected of every worshiper. It was believed to be the manifestation of the Holy Spirit, of its baptism, without which no one could enter into heaven. The telephone book listed a number of Apostolic congregations, among them one in the Colónia Pro-Hogar, which was not too far away from where I was staying.

The modest rectangular temple was a nondescript building on a side street. Its single room was painted pale blue and was lit by a solitary naked bulb hanging from the ceiling. A podium served as the altar. There were vases with bright flowers and a rostrum with a hymnal and a dog-eared Bible. The worshipers were the same kind of people I had seen on the bus, tradesmen, laborers, maids, washerwomen, housewives, who curiously scrutinized the foreign intruder. But I had explained my purpose to the minister on the phone, so he introduced me and said that I had his permission to record, film, and take notes. Although still uneasy, the congregation settled into the usual routine of the service.

I attended a number of these evening gatherings, hopefully setting up my tape recorder next to me on the yellow wooden bench, but nothing happened.

However, during this particular service, the ice was finally going to be broken. I had arrived earlier than usual and before the service had a long conversation with Juan, a professional soldier and one of the deacons of the church. Turning on my tape recorder, I asked him to describe his conversion and some of his experiences when he had spoken in tongues. He told how he had prayed for years for this "manifestation of the Holy Spirit," but it kept eluding him. Finally one day, the bishop of Juan's church laid his hands on Juan's head and prayed for him:

> And after this Brother prayed for me, I continued praying, beseeching God for this gift. And my tongue locked itself, and immediately I knew nothing, I knew nothing at all, but I did feel this impulse to speak. I wanted to stop talking, but my tongue was in this way impulsed. I have noted since then, on other occasions, that I would be praying, but I would insist that I would not talk. But then I'd hear my own words, but no, I don't understand them, but yes, I do feel my tongue impulsed to speak. Afterward, I felt serene, and well, and all my problems were forgotten.

The minister was occupied elsewhere that evening and had left Juan in charge of the service. As was customary, he was conducting it standing on the podium, behind the rostrum with its embroidered white cloth. The service had gone on as usual, with prayers, hymns, and the reading of Bible passages. Then came the altar call, when people came up to the podium and knelt to pray. The minister had told me that speaking in tongues usually occurred then. "How do you know?" I asked. "Pues, that's easy—it isn't Spanish!" was his surprised answer. But all I had heard until then was a low jumble of voices that I also knew from tapes I had worked with at home in Columbus.

Juan had kept the service rather low-key up to this point, but it seemed to me that at the second altar call, perhaps stimulated by our conversation, he was beginning to "drive" his congregation harder with clapping and occasional loud shouts, addressing God and the Holy Spirit. Then his voice dropped for a phrase or two, and all of a sudden, from the middle range, he went into a rising glossolalia utterance, "sió, sió, sió, sió . . ." My field notes reflect how startled I was:

> On the tape, the onset is easily discernible, but upon hearing, it came upon me as a tremendous surprise, because here I was, right in the middle of a true glossolalia. . . . There was a constant pulsing, curve after curve.

The event was not lost on the congregation:

> As the realization of a true manifestation broke upon the people, the trance swept through them like a fire. Another man went into trance, much less intense than Juan's, but with the same pulse, "sió, sió. . . ." A woman at the right had her hands folded, holding them about breast-high and moving them up and down very rapidly.

At the start of the altar call, Juan had knelt down behind the vases filled with gladiolas, but now he suddenly jumped up.

He had his knees slightly bent forward, his body a bit inclined toward the back, very rigid, his eyes closed tightly, his face extremely tense but not distorted, his arms outstretched, his hands alternately clenching and opening with the rhythm of the pulses. After a steep decline in his voice, his arms dropped, his eyes opened. He happened to catch my glance, and an expression of total, questioning bewilderment passed over his face. . . . Then, practically without a pause, he passed into (natural) language and, calling on the Holy Spirit, knelt down again.

Here now for the first time I had actually seen a man in trance, the tight muscles, the flushed and sweaty face, the light tremor, and the cramped hands. I was to see many more examples, men and women, in the course of that summer, in numerous gradations from hardly noticeable to very dramatic changes involving the entire body. And as I had surmised from the analysis of the soundtracks, they were, just as Juan had been, visibly in trance *while* they spoke in tongues, exactly as I had predicted. As he had said in the interview, "I knew nothing at all, but I did feel this impulse to speak."

I subsequently analyzed Juan's glossolalia and that of many other speakers in tongues, and the patterns I had discovered were once more evident. The next summer, I went on to do fieldwork in Yucatán, with a Maya congregation of the same denomination, and recorded the glossolalia of speakers of this Indian, that is, non-Indo-European, tongue. The results were always the same. In fact, after the publication of my book about speaking in tongues,[2] colleagues sent me numerous other tapes recorded during their fieldwork in such faraway places as Ghana in Africa, the island of Nias in Indonesia, the northern edge of the island of Borneo, and Japan. The busy needle of the level recorder continued to trace the same curve. No matter where people spoke in this nonordinary manner during a religious ritual, their bodies apparently underwent the same telltale changes, a wondrous confirmation of our common biological heritage.

The Canadian linguist continued to insist for years that there were no bodily changes involved in glossolalia. Perhaps his consultants, whom he recorded in his office, I was told, had spoken in tongues so long, the physical changes they underwent during their glossolalic prayers were not readily observable anymore, although the level recorder would still have detected the glossolalia pattern. I analyzed a number of such samples from my own collection, and the telltale curves, although somewhat flattened and elongated, were always there.

In the meantime, since the spring of 1968, I had been teaching linguistics and anthropology at Denison University, a private liberal-arts college in northwestern Ohio. In my lectures, I frequently mentioned my fieldwork, especially my observations on the religious trance, how important it was to uncounted societies, that it was a learned behavior, and how well and happy people felt after a trance ritual. I also showed my students the film documentary I had put together from footage I had taken in Yucatán. In previous decades, the topic might have created no interest. But these students were of the generation of the fabled sixties. They were fascinated by the unusual; they talked of "expanding the mind." They were eager for adventure, for experience. "Could you teach that trance to us, too?" they wanted to know.

I pondered their request for quite a while. It would have been impossible and of course quite inappropriate to try and recreate a Pentecostal service for them. Besides, they obviously did not want to experience glossolalia. Would it be possible to dissect the behavior, as it were, and to induce only the underlying physical changes? I finally decided to abstract what to me seemed the salient features for trance induction, leaving out all those factors that I had observed to lead to speaking in tongues. There had to be the expectation that the nonordinary state of consciousness was available to anyone. From their readings of the anthropological literature and my lectures, my students already knew that. Private space was needed, and rhythmic stimulation. We used a classroom at the end of the hall, and for rhythmic stimulation, I chose a gourd rattle of the kind that I had seen during Indian dances in New Mexico. I told my participants that they should do whatever seemed appropriate to them—walk in a tight little circle, stand, sit, kneel, or lie down. Their only task was to close their eyes and concentrate on the sound of my rattle. Initially, I rattled for ten minutes, but after a bit of experimentation that seemed too short, and I went to fifteen.

Experimentation in this form continued with a number of different student volunteers from 1972 until 1976. The experiences they reported clearly indicated that they had achieved a change in the way their bodies acted and also in their consciousness, their perception. They told about noting an increased heartbeat, of feeling hot, of muscles turning stiff, of shivering and twitching. The sound of the rattle might go away, or it turned into light. They saw various shapes, shadowy figures, or a long-forgotten girlfriend. Afterward they felt joyous excitement and a great need to talk to others about the experience. The world around them looked changed, and when one girl glanced into the mirror after an exercise, she found herself exquisitely beautiful. She was startled; she had not thought of herself as Miss America material. I began noting that their sense of time was off. "Did you really rattle for fifteen minutes?" was an often-heard question. It was also difficult for them to tell things "in the right order." After a trance, experiences would tend to come tumbling out helter-skelter, first things last, last things first, and a jumble in the middle, so to speak. Yet all were lucid, perceptively observing both the physical changes and whatever images came floating past their eyes.

There was one thing, however, that bothered me about what the students observed: Their experiences varied too much. Responding to the same rhythmic rattle sound, should the experience not always be the same? Yet some felt hot, but there were others who became very cold. While there were visions of bright light, these contrasted with the appearance of a black hole. To be sure, I had heard similar inconsistencies when talking with various speakers in tongues. But in their case, their conviction that it was the Holy Spirit that was possessing them provided something like a supporting grid. It did not matter that for one, the Holy Spirit entered through the stomach, for the next it came up the backbone, and that still another felt it like gentle rain on his shoulder. But without an absolute commitment to a mythology, as with my students, there was nothing to give any cohesion to the experiences. Yet I could think of no other-manner in which I could proceed with the experiments. I decided there was nothing more to be gained with this approach.

One concern that kept secretly nagging at me, and that I was not even willing to countenance, was whether we had even induced the same physiological changes that underlie an ecstatic experience. Humans are capable of so many different states of consciousness. How could I be sure we had hit on the right one? I could think of no way in which I could test that, other than relying on the similarities I had observed between my students' behavior and that of the speakers in tongues. It seemed a dead-end situation. So to wrap things up and put the matter to rest, I reported the results in 1976 at a meeting of the Ohio Academy of Science. "The trance experience itself is vacuous," I wrote in the conclusion. "If no belief system is proffered, it will remain vacuous. It is a neurophysiological event that receives content only from signals present in the respective culture." Outside the Pentecostal movement and its offshoots, such as charismatic Catholicism, our own main-line culture no longer provided any such signals, and I did not know where else to go.

In the fall of that year, however, a new avenue of research was to open up. Dr. Bourguignon, who had become my dissertation adviser, and with whom I had kept in touch even after receiving my Ph.D. in 1971, had called my attention to an article by the Canadian psychologist V. F. Emerson.[3] He had done research with various meditative disciplines and had found that differences in their belief systems correlated with the fact that during meditation, each discipline employed its own specific body posture. All the functions of the body changed with alterations of posture, Emerson pointed out, the heartbeat, breathing, even the motility of the intestines. This was bound to have an effect also on the psychological level.

I had looked at that article briefly in the spring when I was working on my report to the Ohio Academy of Science. But the full implications of Emerson's emphasis on posture did not occur to me until the fall, when I once more pondered how to go on with my research. Then it hit me like a thunderbolt. How come it had never occurred to me to note that there was this connection? Was it this factor that caused the experience of receiving the Holy Spirit to vary so much? I had recorded the details of how speaking in tongues was taught. But not one of the ministers I had seen in action insisted on any posture. In a few congregations, a special body posture seemed to be preferred, but even in those cases, it was neither taught nor assumed by everyone. I could see why they did not care: All that mattered was that the Holy Spirit put in an appearance. But I wanted to find out something about the nature of the physical changes involved and had to find a reason for why the experiences of my students varied so greatly. I had never even thought to suggest any particular posture to them during our experiments. Obviously, we were all subject to the same blind spot, for neither did I recall any instance in the literature where an ethnographic observer specifically called attention to any particular posture used by the celebrants during a trance ritual.

Here, obviously, a novel way suggested itself for carrying out my experiments. What I needed to do was to teach my subjects distinct postures for use during their trance exercises and then record the variations. But what sort of postures? Luckily I never thought of inventing any. Instead I did what comes naturally to an anthropologist: I turned to the body of ethnographic literature for advice. The authors may not have described any postures, but the many illustrations in their books were bound to contain examples anyhow. I began searching for photographs of native, that is, non-Western, subjects during religious rituals, and when that did not yield very much, I started perusing volumes of aboriginal art, looking for figured representations of a religious nature.

The logic of this new step seems self-evident now. Yet it really was something like the egg of Columbus. According to this anecdote, probably apocryphal, the renowned explorer was sitting at the banquet table at the king's court in Madrid after his famous journey, and one of the grandees challenged him, saying, "I don't think what Vuestra Merced, your grace, did was all that innovative. After all, knowing that the earth is round, anybody could have thought of turning his ships west instead of east to arrive at the Indies." Instead of answering directly, Columbus took a hard-boiled egg from the bowl in front of him and asked, "Who can stand this egg on its tip?" Everyone around the table tried, but no one was able to do the trick. When the egg was handed back to Columbus, he took it and brought it down hard, breaking the shell at the tip. That way the egg could easily be stood upright. There was laughter around the table and shouts that anybody could have done that. "Right," agreed Columbus, "but no one thought of it." The idea of adding a posture when going into trance was suggested by Emerson's train of thought, and taking it from the ethnographic literature was only a hunch, a shot in the dark, much like turning the boat toward the west instead of the east. But it had not occurred to anyone before, and in doing so, I was to rediscover a mysterious, long-lost world.

A brief remark about research methods might be in order here. As will become obvious throughout this account, my approach is not a "positivistic" one, as was described by Rosenthal and Rosnow (1969), for example. According to that paradigm, there are a number of "artifacts" that originate with the researcher and might affect the results, such as the experimenter's expectations and the awareness of the subjects of the experimenter's intent. Intense effort is therefore lavished on keeping the experimenter and the subject separate. However, there was no danger of my producing any such artifacts; except for my expressed expectation that a change in perception would take place, I myself was entirely unaware of what kind of experience might emerge, if any at all. Besides, as an anthropologist, I am much more inclined anyway toward a method that has come to be called the "naturalist" one (see Lincoln and Guba, 1985). In this method the case study is the reporting mode of choice, the experimenter and the subject are "in a state of mutual simultaneous shaping" (p. 38), so that it is impossible to distinguish causes from effects, and the researcher is as much a data-gathering instrument as the subjects. Results are not certain but probabilistic and speculative. Most important, from a philosophical point of view, objective reality is not absolute but relative. Such a method was tailor-made for my present inquiry.

Eventually I indeed found a number of postures that I thought might qualify for my intended research. It was obvious, for instance, that the wood carving of a small shaman embraced from the back by a mighty "Bear Spirit" (pl. 1) represented a religious scene, and the ecstatic smile of the Bear's protégé, so familiar to me from people in trance, seemed to point to the kind of experience I was looking for. Clearly, the late-nineteenth-century Indian carver from the Pacific Northwest had to have seen that entranced facial expression many times to have rendered it so faithfully. And there were a number of other representations of the same quality.

With money from the Faculty Development Fund of Denison University, I

Plate 1

embarked on my new research in the summer of 1977. I recruited some interested volunteers, my two yoga teachers, a number of anthropology graduate students, a sociologist—eight in all. Since they had jobs, they could not all come at the same time, so I decided to work with each one individually, which was desirable anyway, because in this way, they could not influence each other. Instead of taking them to a laboratory, I provided an aesthetically pleasing and sparsely furnished room in my own home. The session started with my showing a drawing I had prepared of the posture, containing no other information. After we practiced it, I once again used a rattle to induce the trance, and afterward, I recorded what each had to tell about what had happened.

I wish I could once more experience that surprise, that exquisite wonder that took hold of me as we began exploring this new possibility. The physical changes still tended to fluctuate, although not as uncontrollably as before. As I was to discover later, a remarkable consistency was indeed there, but at a much deeper level, discoverable only by sophisticated laboratory techniques. But as soon as we controlled for posture, something much more important began emerging: The experiences began falling into place. Within certain generous limits, making allowances for individual style and ability of expression, we found that each posture predictably mediated not just any kind of vision but a characteristic, distinctly different experience. In the one where the Bear Spirit hugged the shaman who held his head back, his hands placed above the navel, and his knees slightly bent, the bodies of the subjects or their heads would split open as if to receive something, a substance, a flow of energy, which was then administered to them. In another one, modeled after a photograph of an African diviner (pl. 2), who sits on the floor with his legs toward the right and leaning on his left hand, his right hand resting close to his left calf, the subjects would start spinning around. This furious whirling would then enable them to "find out" or to "understand."

Let me describe another example a bit more in detail. It concerns a drawing in Lascaux Cave from the Old Stone Age, that is, from about sixteen to seventeen thousand years ago. The cave was discovered near the French village of Montignac in the Dordogne in 1940. It contains a profusion of drawings of animals executed with consummate skill, but also a drawing of a human figure (pl. 3). At a cursory glance, this naked man seems to have fallen over backward, right in front of a huge wounded aurochs. It has usually been assumed that the two images represent an integral composition, that the enormous beast had something to do with the fallen man—that the man was frightened or killed, or perhaps was carrying out some hunting magic. At closer inspection, however, it seemed to me that certain features of the drawing of the man did not fit in with any of these conjectures. In the first place, there was a staff stuck upright into the ground next to the man, crowned not by the semblance of horns, as might be expected if there was a connection to the aurochs nearby, but by a bird. If he had fallen, and it was the intention of the artist to show the accident, would the staff not be lying beside him? Also, the animal and the man were executed in different techniques, the aurochs in color and in exquisite detail, the man in black outline.

Yet there was nothing hurried about how the figure was drawn. His left

Plate 2

elbow was represented as a small circle and that arm was stretched out stiffly, while the right arm was bent; his fingers were longer than his thumbs, and only his left thumb was pointing downward, and he had an erection. He was wearing a bird mask, doubtless an indication of a religious context. Analyzing the drawing with a ritual posture in mind, it occurred to me that in fact it contained what amounted to postural instructions. One of these was to hold the left arm rigid, thumb down and elbow locked. The right arm was to lie in a relaxed fashion, elbow bent, so the thumb would naturally come to be

Plate 3

positioned up. And, very important, something that no one had paid any attention to, the body was not to lie flat on the ground, but was to form one side of a thirty-seven-degree angle.

For our own experiment with this posture, we painstakingly duplicated this thirty-seven-degree angle, using chairs, pillows, sleeping bags, and the like. It was quite comfortable, and my participants expected to have a restful fifteen minutes in that posture. Instead, things quickly became highly dramatic, as the following accounts will illustrate. By the way, as I was to hear innumerable times later, not everyone experienced the entire sequence of events, reminiscent of what happens when a number of people are witness to the same event. Rather, the individual reports frequently needed to be taken together and then formed a cohesive, running description of the total event. The following accounts, all from the initial 1977 experiment, are arranged with that fact in mind.[4]

ANITA: The hand position seemed to indicate polarity to me, and I began to experience that more and more as I went into trance. The left hand that pointed down and was pushing away was getting warm, the right one was cold. This seemed to develop a flow of energy that became circular. The energy wrapped me into a cocoon, and for a while I was floating in this very nice, golden cocoon.

JUDY G.: The energy was rushing around in my body, suddenly converged on the genital area, then started rising upward through my body.

DAVID S.: The excitation went through my chest, and the closest thing I can think of is orgasm. It was like an orgasm in my head, like everything was being squeezed out of me, I was being squeezed out through my head. Now I am cold.

BRYAN: There was something like a giant cookie cutter that was going to work on me, making duplicates of myself. Then something inside of me wanted to get out; even the hair on my body was rising up as this thing was coming out as an exact duplicate of myself.

SUZANNE G.: I saw a path, it took me to a white cloud. Then I was in that cloud and it opened and I came out, flying about in the blue.

In other words, the posture prompted such excitation to arise that in the perception of the participants, a flow of energy was churned, the course of which then became controlled, converging on the genitals; hence perhaps the erection of the Lascaux shaman. From there it started streaming up through the body and into the head, and then, as the astounded participants told so graphically, "I was being squeezed out through my head," or "this thing was coming out as an exact duplicate of myself," and "I came out, flying about in the blue." The agreement with countless tales from around the world was evident. In fact, the conclusion was inescapable: We had rediscovered the ancient art of embarking on a spirit journey.

It took a while before the implications of these discoveries sank in. It was now evident that the altered state of consciousness that was induced by the simple rhythmic stimulation of the gourd rattle was indeed the religious trance, for my participants in the experiment had experienced a spirit journey through the agency of this induction method. Not only that—as a wondrous gift from many nameless native artists, we had begun at the same time to rediscover a system of signals to the nervous system, a complex strategy capable of shaping the amorphous trance into a religious experience. Put differently, *guided by hitherto unnoticed traditional body postures, these "subjects" of a social-science experiment had taken the step from the physical change of the trance to the experience of ecstasy, they had passed from the secular to the sacred.*

The question that soon began to occupy us during these experiments was whether such miraculous perceptual changes could really be brought about simply by physiological signals. "The posture sets the stage," Bryan speculated. "I don't doubt that with some practice I could experience all that even without your rattle helping, just by getting into the posture." As a linguist, I started hypothesizing that perhaps as in a gesture, it was the iconic content, a message that lay hidden in the posture, that my subjects were picking up without realizing it. They had done one posture, of an Australian shaman pointing a bone (pl. 4), in order, according to the ethnographer, to "hit" an adversary with a magic missile, where this might have been a reasonable suggestion. But the iconic interpretation simply would not work, for instance, for the above-mentioned divining posture.

Another idea suggested was that the experiences were structured by arousing the chakras in specific, set patterns. This was the time when all sorts of mysterious experiences were attributed to the influence of those complicated centers in our body conceptualized a thousand or more years ago in India. Their bodily aspects correspond roughly to the thoracic, abdominal, and pelvic plexuses of Western anatomic science, together with the optic assemblage and the brain. I conjectured that perhaps by the postures, my subjects were activating various combinations of chakras, creating, in fact, a different altered state of consciousness for each posture. Mathematically, the full extent of combinatory possibilities would have amounted to 2 to the power of 7 = 128, minus the null set, that is, 127. The conjecture did not seem very reasonable even then, and now, after more than a decade of research, we found only about 30 different postures, not 127, and only a single religious trance. This agrees with the observation of other researchers, e.g., Peters and Price-

Plate 4

Williams, who point out that the experiential aspects of various trance states "are descriptive of *a single dynamic psychological process*" (1983:6, emphasis mine; see also Winkelman 1986).

I should like to anticipate here that I did follow up on my early interest in exactly what happens in the body during the religious trance. The first opportunity for doing the medical research needed arose in 1983, at the Department of Psychiatric Neurophysiology at the Psychiatric Clinic and Policlinic of the University of Munich,[5] under consultation with the head of the department, Professor Johann Kugler. Working with the most modern equipment, we tested four volunteers during the religious trance. The findings were the first comprehensive scientifically obtained body of laboratory data anyone had ever discovered about this type of trance. Other researchers, e.g., Neher (1961 and 1962), concentrated exclusively on processes in the brain.

The instruments registered dramatic changes. In the blood serum, the compounds indicating stress, namely, adrenalin, noradrenalin, and cortisol, dropped, and at the same time, there was evidence that the brain started synthesizing beta-endorphin, the miracle painkiller of the body, which is also responsible for the intense joy felt after a trance. The EEG exhibited not the famous alpha waves, so well known from meditation, but a steady stream of the even slower theta waves, in the range of 6–7 cps, usually seen only in bursts shortly before a subject goes to sleep, or in deep Zen meditation. Most puzzling, blood pressure dropped, and simultaneously, the pulse started racing like a runner's during a hundred-meter dash. Under ordinary conditions, I was told, physicians see this kind of paradoxical behavior of the body only under extreme conditions, such as when a patient bleeds to death or is about to die.

Differences in posture did not affect the results, by the way. The experiments were carried out using two different postures, yet all the parameters examined remained the same. It was gratifying that here at last was the consistency I had been looking for in the underlying trance event. But as to the effect of the postures, the message clearly was that while our instruments could certainly reveal something about somatic processes, this was after all what they were designed to do; they were unable to penetrate the mystery of the ecstatic experience.

In the spring of 1987, I had the good fortune to be able to participate in some additional neurophysiological research. When the behavior was approached from a different angle, its results once more demonstrated the truly magnificent modification the nervous system undergoes during a religious trance. The investigation concerned the extent of the negative charge of the direct-current potential of the brain during the religious trance, and was carried out under Professor Giselher Guttmann at the laboratory of the Department of Psychology of the University of Vienna. With EEG equipment available at only a few laboratories worldwide, which works with direct rather than alternating current, it is possible to amplify a weak signal that the brain gives off during tasks requiring intense attention. Peak values during learning tasks found to date amounted to at most 250 microvolts. With volunteers from my workshops experienced in the religious trance, much higher values, rising to an astounding 1,500 to 2,000 microvolts, were achieved. At the same time, the stream of theta waves continued unabated (Guttmann et al., 1988).[6] Again, however, the results remained unchanged when the posture was varied. For the present, their mystery remains intact.

Returning to 1977 now, the summer's work with the postures had put me into a curiously glowing, magical mood, which continued into the school year, especially as I was writing the paper summarizing our findings. But when I presented it in the fall of that year to the annual meeting of the American Anthropological Association, the polite applause of my colleagues was deeply disappointing. Obviously afflicted by an uncharacteristic attack of megalomania, I think I expected them to throng around the podium, begging also to be allowed to try the marvelous adventure that we had discovered that summer. Instead, they went on to the next lecture, and a mild-mannered young man stopped me on the way out and asked, "Are you now planning to do a structural-functional analysis?" The incongruous question struck me as wildly ludicrous, and I was sorely tempted to slip into the jargon of the sixties and counter, "Hey, man, I was in a magic garden!" But these were no longer the sixties. So I smiled politely and left him standing there. I felt like a sleeper trying to awaken from a profound dream, and somehow the ordinary world of my profession and its concerns was very far away.

CHAPTER THREE

The Old Ones Remember

Without eager company, even magic gardens can be lonely places. So after returning from the anthropology meeting, I bundled up my notes on the mysterious postures and turned to a different topic. It was still part of the same field of study, the religious trance, but this time it concerned the experience of demonic possession.

My interest in this subject had been triggered by news stories about a German university student by the name of Anneliese Michel, who supposedly died as a result of being exorcized. From the American magazine item that had called my attention to the case, I had learned that the girl insisted that she was possessed by demons, but that her psychiatrists maintained that she was psychotic, most likely an epileptic.[1] From the start, I had the impression that this might well be another one of those cases where a religious experience was confused with epilepsy, just as was often done in descriptions of shamans. The German courts decided that the two priests who carried out the exorcism had contributed to her death, and convicted both them and her parents of negligent homicide, resulting in suspended jail sentences.

I was convinced that there had to be an error in judgment, that this was a miscarriage of justice. Demonic possession is an affliction well known all around the world, not only among Christians, and exorcism is the treatment of choice. There are no reports on record anywhere that somebody died of an exorcism (see Goodman 1988). I eventually wrote to the defense lawyer, and as I studied the more than eight hundred pages of court records she sent me, I felt increasingly sorry for the young girl, whose case to my mind had been so poorly handled. She was only two years older than my youngest daughter, and I kept seeing my own child being treated with thinly veiled contempt by uncomprehending psychiatrists as she pleaded for help against the demons that were plaguing her, and being plied with psychoactive drugs that only made matters worse. I eventually wrote a book about Anneliese (Goodman 1981), and during my 1978 summer vacation I really wanted to go to Italy to visit San Damiano, the shrine where her possession had first become public knowledge. But I had earlier promised some childhood friends back home to visit them, and that was a tug at the heartstrings. So although I felt a twinge of guilt for giving preference to personal pleasure, I decided in favor of Hungary.

When planning the trip, I recalled that my mother had often longingly told how beautiful the journey was from Vienna to Budapest by boat. She did not live to take it again, so I would do it in her stead. I flew into the Austrian capital, spent the night in a hotel, and the next morning took a cab to the dock and bought a ticket on one of the comfortable modern excursion boats operated by the Hungarian travel service.

I was the first on deck, but soon a vivacious Austrian lady joined me. It was a hot day and she was thirsty, but she could not make the Hungarian waiter understand what she wanted, so I acted as her interpreter. She was a journalist, on her way to a meeting of economists in Budapest that she was to cover. We quickly warmed to each other, and eventually the conversation came around to my research. When I mentioned Anneliese's case, which had made headlines in Europe, my traveling companion knew a lot about it and animatedly denounced the "superstitious" priests who had obviously done her in. I took the opposite tack, and we became so engrossed in our topic that I never even saw the beautiful landscape we were passing through. The beaded necklace of narrow green islands adorning the blond Danube as it meandered between Hungary and Czechoslovakia, Komárom, the city stretching over both banks of the river and cut in half by an unforgiving border, the towers of ancient Esztergom, see of the archbishop of Hungary, and the mountains of Visegrad, all would have to wait for another vacation.

As we said goodbye upon landing in Budapest, we agreed to exchange information. She would locate newspaper reports for me about Anneliese. In return, I was to let her have copies of my publications about my research on the religious trance. We both kept our promise. She sent me clippings about San Damiano, which I had not gotten to visit, and I reciprocated with my book about speaking in tongues, and with some recent papers. I thought this would be the end of our contact, but instead, later in the fall of 1978, I received a grateful letter, not from my journalist but from an author and former professor of religious studies at the University of Vienna, Dr. Adolf Holl. He wrote that he had "confiscated" everything I had sent to his friend. It seems that the material was valuable to him, because he was working on a biography of Saint Francis of Assisi at the time,[2] and the details of the trance research had provided him with additional insights into the experiences of this famous medieval mystic. All of this referred to my book about speaking in tongues, and I almost forgot that among the papers I had sent him there was also the one about the 1977 posture research.

This lapse of memory was entirely understandable, for in the 1978–79 school year I had other things on my mind than research. Quite suddenly, and entirely out of the blue, forced retirement loomed as an imminent threat. I had been so wrapped up in the challenges of teaching and fascinating research projects that retirement seemed something that only other people had to face. It had never entered my mind that at the age of only sixty-five, in the very middle of my newfound career, my university might want to cut me off. But talk of retirement would not go away, and that five other colleagues were in the same situation was no consolation. I was beginning to feel like a condemned prisoner on death row, who could not believe that the date would ever be set. I protested, but to no avail, and so the last year of my university teaching career was a forlorn and bitter time. I was at a loss as to how to go on.

It was a dank and foggy evening in late November, the kind of night that held out no hope at all that spring would ever come again, when the Old Ones decided that they had to reach out to me once more. But being Indians, they did not come straight out with it, maybe with a thunderclap from heaven or in a burning bush, as other divine personages are reputed to proceed. As I was to find out later when I came to know them better, they were much less obtrusive but full of gentle cunning and a great deal of humor. On this evening they were clearly intent on testing to see if this unreasonable woman could be pulled out of the mire of despair into which she had maneuvered herself. And they chose a most unlikely object for their purpose.

I had a statue in my bedroom of the Virgin of Guadalupe, the patron saint of Mexico, which I had bought during fieldwork. It reminded me of the bejeweled Madonna in the glittering chapel of the convent at home where I was raised. There were always candles burning before that statue, and suddenly feeling homesick, I decided to light two beeswax candles before it to make things look right.

I went to the bathroom to brush my hair, and glancing back I thought how pretty the scene was, the statue lit by the soft candlelight and the green sprig of fir I had placed there a few days before. So when I came back into the bedroom, instead of blowing out the candles, I sat on the bed, leaning against the wall, intent on admiring it all. Soon, however, I no longer saw the statue with the candles, but rather the figure of a slender young woman, her dress cinched with a belt, filling out the triangle under the Madonna's folded hands. She was framed by an orange glow that emanated from the space in front of her. I could not see her face, for she was turning away from me, apparently looking out into a room that was lit by that beautiful golden light. I was hoping she would turn toward me, but it did not happen, and eventually the lovely image faded and there was only the light of the candles.

The next weekend, I went to visit my oldest son. The conversation soon drifted to religious experience, a topic of consuming interest to both of us, and I told him about my puzzling vision. Did he have any idea what it might mean? He consulted his I Ching and set up a small altar from the toy box of his son, a fir tree, and beside it a little figure with a big head. As I contemplated it in the flickering light of the candle he had lit, the plastic figure assumed the appearance of a "mudhead," the sacred clown of the Hopis, whose clay likenesses can be bought on the Indian markets of New Mexico.

We waited. I had no idea what I was waiting for; we just sat there. Suddenly there was the sound of wild scratching at the front door, and the family cat jumped up and ran to the entranceway, mewing and spitting. We followed after, and my son opened the door. A black cat jumped off the landing, cut across the street toward the left, and disappeared between the houses. We could think of no reason why that cat should have appeared before the door and demanded that we open it. The family cat was spayed and never had any male suitors. Perhaps, as my son suggested, the spirit whom we had evoked with our modest ritual needed a body in which to respond to our summons, and a cat was all it could find in the middle of a big city.

Like a twinkling light on a distant mountainside, the mysterious experience beckoned to me through the dark months that followed. In an inexplicable way, it carried a message of encouragement. I decided that come what may, I would continue teaching and doing research, perhaps on my land in New Mexico during the summer. In order to be able to carry out these plans, I engaged a lawyer and founded a nonprofit educational corporation, which was registered with the state of New Mexico as Cuyamungue Institute. *Cuyamungue* is the Spanish adaptation of the Tewa Indian name for the large pueblo that once flourished in our valley, and remains of a small part of it were on my land. It was probably deserted after the 1683 Pueblo Revolt.[3] Roughly translated, the name means "where the stones are slipping," referring to the hill across the highway from us, an ancient landmark where large sandstone plates protrude at oblique angles from the softer subsoil.

For my first summer's teaching after retirement, I recruited six undergraduates for a course in comparative religion at Cuyamungue. They were due to arrive in July, and as living accommodations for them I designed a simple wooden building and had it built from part of my university pension money.

It was in the midst of this construction work that I went up to the gate one day to set up the sign of Cuyamungue Institute. It was based on a logo I had composed from Pueblo Indian designs, representing the hills, the mountains, the earth, and the clouds of New Mexico. I had carved it on a board and had nailed it to two cedar posts. The ground was soft and clayey, and in search of some stones to steady the posts, I started walking farther and farther into the rough terrain. All of a sudden I felt a strange tugging, drawing me as if by a powerful lure in among the junipers and pinyon bushes, almost as if whispering, "Come—step closer—still closer—see what is hidden within— come—come. . . ." I followed the call of the still voice, and it led me to an open area which was strewn with numerous rocks. When I looked more closely, I found to my surprise that the rocks were laid out in a pattern. There were a large rectangle, several lines, and a number of small circles. I could feel that it was holy, and I fervently wished I could find out who it was who had left so much of his sacred essence behind. Reverently, I left the site and found the rocks I needed farther away in a wash.

Next day I asked Gilbert, my Hispanic builder, artist, and all-around handyman, to make me some wooden boxes for transplanting the seedlings I had brought from Columbus. He did not get to it right away, but as I walked by the building site, I saw a weathered wooden planter of the kind I wanted, which had not been there before. Gilbert thought that perhaps his dog had dragged it there. But I had fun playing with the idea that whoever inhabited the area of the design up in the hills appreciated my not having taken any stones and instructed the dog to bring me what I had wished for.

That weekend, a cherished friend came to visit, and when he had to leave, I was very sad. Badly in need of consolation after saying goodbye to him, I walked forlornly to the stone design to feel the comforting Presence again, and raised my palms in greeting the way I had seen an old Indian do in one of the pueblos, when he blessed the participants in a feast-day observation. The simple ritual eased me, but when I left, I was still crying.

I went into the house, sat down by the table, and wondered disconsolately what to do next, when all of a sudden a cricket started sounding its silver bell from up in the vigas, louder than I had ever heard it before, insistent and ringing clear and high. It was so loud, I thought at first that a bird had gotten into the house, although I knew of no bird that had that kind of song. The sound came from the ceiling of the next room, and I went to see what it was but could not find anything. Then it occurred to me: It could not be a bird, it had to be a cricket. So obeying a sudden intuition, I said, "Thank you, little cricket, and see, I am not sad anymore." And when I said that, the cricket fell silent. I continued listening for a while, but there was no more sound.

It was thrilling once more to imagine that perhaps it had been the Presence at the shrine that had sent the cricket to console me, and so I began to ponder what I could give this new friend of mine in return. Pollen would be best; I had read that the Navajos made offerings of corn pollen to the Spirits, but I did not have any pollen. So on the way to the shrine I picked some yellow blossoms, the closest thing to pollen I could think of, and put them into one of the circles of stone. Then I sat there for a while like a child waiting for candy. Would this be the end of it, or would I also receive something in return? All the while, of course, I was telling myself that this was merely a game I was playing, inspired by my loneliness. But when I finally left the shrine, right in front of me on the path there was a fluffy, fresh bird's feather of the kind Indian women put on their headdresses during the Corn Dance, and which are said to represent blessing. Deeply moved, I picked it up and profusely thanked the Presence for its gift.

The next day a boy and a girl came to help me, children of Hispanic neighbors from the valley. They had come on foot and told excitedly that on the way up they had seen a large cat: "You know, the kind that looks like it has its tail chopped off. . . ." They described how the bobcat had been sitting at what I secretly thought of as "my" shrine, and had run off down into the Cañada as they approached. By this time, I was entirely ready to accept miracles. To me, this was the message that the spirit who had possessed the city cat was the same as the owner of the shrine.

As June wore on, my Friend of the Shrine had other gifts in store for me. I began finding strange little pebbles. Eventually there were six of these, showing the White Buffalo, the Badger, the Bear, the Snake, Mother Earth, and the Starry Sky. Such stones are well known in the Tewa world. I felt overwhelmed by the kindness shown me and tried to think of how to reciprocate. Since my Friend of the Shrine was obviously a part of Pueblo culture, I went to an Indian woman friend whom I had known for years, and who was living in a pueblo where the old traditions were still alive. I told her how I had encountered my spirit friend, and I asked her if there was anything that she thought I could properly present to him. Would cornmeal be all right? She said I could do that, but also, if I prepared an item of food, for instance bread, I should take a little of that, in the morning when the sun came up, and in the evening when it set. "And in your own language tell him that he should not hurt you, just as you would not hurt anyone." Then she gave me some hand-ground cornmeal from a small clay jar with a black ornamental design. "Give this to him," she said, "and I will also pray for you."

I did as she had instructed me, and puzzled for a while about her cautionary remark that I should ask him not to hurt me. For in my heart of hearts, I was still a child, only now I was playing in sacred precincts without fully comprehending their powerful and therefore of course also dangerous reality. I had been given presents, I had been treated with the utmost kindness; what could possibly happen? So I became presumptuous. Disappointed by a number of books I subsequently perused about the Pueblos, none of which had any answers concerning the nature of the spirit world I sought to understand, I one day reproached my Friend at the shrine that I had no teacher to teach me. After all, Castaneda had his don Juan, so how come I was not meeting anyone like that? I told him I wanted an Indian Holy Man to come up that road right then and there to instruct me in everything that I wanted to know. I was at least figuratively stamping my foot, acting like a very spoiled child. Wisdom does not come automatically attached to greying hair. The Old Ones took one look at me and decided that I needed to be taught all right. But the initiation they meted out to me very nearly cost me my life.

By this time it was August, and I had taken my students to visit Bandelier National Park, only about thirty miles from Cuyamungue. The guide there showed us a plaster cast of two stone lions, the original of which was at a shrine about six miles away from Frijoles Canyon and the Visitors' Center.

She said that it was a sanctuary still in use. Indians frequently offered antlers there, and sometimes the lions had pigment on their faces, like that used by the Indian dancers. Six miles sounded like nothing at all; I often walked that much just visiting friends around Cuyamungue, and I thought the students would enjoy the hike. So we made the proper preparations and early on a bright and sunny day drove to Bandelier once more. We were given a wilderness pass and a map by the rangers, and at about eight-thirty started out on our trek, two young men, four young women, and I. Each of us had two quarts of water, a sandwich, nuts, raisins, and some fruit. I carried a small first-aid kit, salt tablets, bits of salty fried meat, and two tomatoes. And we started up.

I soon realized that this was not going to be a picnic. It was a tremendous climb just to get out of Frijoles Canyon. Then we walked for about two hours across the top of a canyon, along a barely visible path. It was getting very hot. To divert the attention of the students from the exhaustion they were beginning to feel, I pointed out different interesting plants we were passing—several giant yucca, a bush with aromatic colorless flowers being harvested by very aggressive wild bees, Apache feather bonnets, three lovely barrel-shaped cacti ready to bloom—but got very little response except from Sara, who was born and raised in the Southwest. She called out about a wild donkey grazing in the distance and a doe with her fawn slipping noiselessly into the shadows. But no one paid any heed to that either.

The heat, meanwhile, was getting brutal. Elizabeth, the blondest of the bunch, had rushed ahead with bravado but soon got exhausted, although we rested several times in the shade of the junipers. Finally she gave up. "This is ridiculous," she said. "I am enormously thirsty, half my water is gone; I just had better turn back." She had forgotten her head scarf, so I gave her mine and she left.

By this time it was about noon. We had reached Alamo Canyon and were zigzagging downward, alongside fantastic promontories, with junipers growing on stony hillsides as forbidding as Dante's inferno. I pondered whether I should also give up and turn back—I had become unspeakably weary—but the Lions were supposed to be just across the canyon on the other side. And there was Sara, slim, fit, brown, stepping over sticks and stones on her bare feet like a graceful gazelle. I felt ashamed about my temporary loss of nerve. Perhaps I could catch a second wind. So I continued on.

We went down and down. To the right was a sheer rock wall, at least six hundred feet high, its glistening black veins rising toward the merciless sky. As I looked up at the wall, I suddenly saw that the basalt columns had been parted like folds of a curtain, and high among the strands a huge figure was leaning out of a window. He looked like a koshari, the sacred Pueblo Indian clown, aquiline nose over a full mouth, wearing a loose tunic, and with the two dry cornstalks sticking up from his cap like horns. His massive face bore a peculiar expression, half curious, half friendly concern. "My Friend might look like that," I thought, puzzled by the fabulous rock formation. "Do you see that face?" I called to the students. But they were far ahead of me and did not answer. None of them later remembered the face when I asked them, although to me it was as real as the path, the unforgiving sun, and the junipers around us.

We no longer saw the path, but down below there was what looked like a narrow, dark mountain brook. "Water," I thought with elation and relief. Then we reached it, and instead of water, it was composed of sinister ankle-deep and tinder-dry volcanic ash. It crackled and crunched as we waded in it. Then we saw the trail again; it led out of the creek bed up to the right and lost itself among the boulders on the other side. I looked back up at the enigmatic rock face that was still dispassionately watching us from above, and down at that awful flow of ash, and decided to turn back. Still another canyon wall to climb up, and then the same stretch down again on the return trip was just more than I could face. So I left my small bag with supplies and my rain poncho—the rangers had warned about sudden downpours—with the students, keeping for myself only one tomato, a few raisins, and my Yucatecan bottle gourd which was still half full of water. I also gave them my camera. "Take a picture of the shrine and the Stone Lions for me," I asked. Then I started back in that hellish rivulet of ash, always looking for the tracks we had made.

I found the path marker that indicated the start of the trail up, but felt deeply disappointed. Partly, at least, I had suggested the hike for my own sake, hoping to find something at the shrine, a sign, perhaps, that I had not been forgotten. But it was not to be. It was two o'clock. Furtively, I cast an occasional glance at the rock wall, but the face was gone. Was it because of a change in my angle of vision?

I plodded on and up, very slowly chewing on my tomato. It was getting still hotter. All of a sudden, from a distance, I heard the beat of a Pueblo drum. It was very clear and urgent, faster than the pounding of my heart. There was consolation in it and reassurance. The drum fell silent, then started up again, seeming to come from a greater distance, and then it ceased altogether.

I was getting very thirsty, so I decided to start drinking some of my water, timing the sips every fifteen minutes. Occasionally, I sat down in the shade of a juniper. My legs were getting dangerously tired. How was I going to go on? I calculated that I had at least four more hours to hike. I looked around me, and suddenly I dissolved. I was gone, melted into nothingness.

In the days to follow, I was to ponder over and over again what it was that happened to me in that canyon. Sometimes I thought that nothing happened, nothing at all. But then I knew that that was not true. For in that crushing, awesome, total, enormous aloneness, where there was nothing human except the almost obliterated trail, I sank down within myself to the very bottom, deeper than I had ever been before. I was not afraid, I just sank. And when I reached that deepest point in that abyss of myself, that point of death,

I stopped. I was hit by something that was neither in me nor outside of me. It was not light or emotion; it was, if it "was" at all, a coarse-grained vibration. Its touching was faster than when the tip of a streak of lightning hit the summit of those sacred Jemez Mountains. Then I came up again and rose into my conscious self, suspended on a wave of life.

I looked around me. I was still at that same juniper, and before me rose the zigzag path. Bewildered, I took a deep breath and started climbing once more. But I was getting so tired, I was not walking, I was stumbling on. On and up, on and up, endlessly. My tomato was gone. I could feel the burden I was placing on my heart, so I put some raisins in my mouth for their sugar. But chewing them turned them into a sticky paste that tasted like gypsum. I had to sacrifice a few extra sips of water to wash them down.

Finally, the zigzag path ended. It was three-thirty. The illusion that I was almost at the edge of Frijoles Canyon made me more energetic, but only for a fleeting moment. Although I was now on top of the mesa and no longer had to struggle with the erratic path, the trail continued rising, and I knew that no amount of willpower was going to move my numb legs any farther. I had to rest. I gave myself five minutes under the next juniper, but that helped nothing at all. I could hardly get up. If only I could reach the bush after the next one—but it was useless. I collapsed under a juniper close to the trail, and I could not even sit; I just lay there on my side.

I was afraid that I might become delirious and get confused about directions. So from then on when resting I always placed the gourd away from me, toward the direction where I was going. The heat was so intense that the skin on my arms seemed to be crackling. It would give some relief, I thought, if I took my blouse off, or at least opened it in front. But I was afraid of a sunburn, so I kept it on and buttoned. The conventional wisdom about traveling in the desert crossed my mind: Sleep in the daytime and walk at night. Good thought, but in the dark, I would not be able to follow the faint trail. And what about the canyons intersecting the mesa, with their sheer rock walls hundreds of feet straight down? And the snakes and scorpions and mountain lions all prowling at night? I thought about appealing to my Friend, but for reasons I could not understand, that felt flat, superfluous. So I just lay there and fell asleep.

Half an hour later I woke up, feeling just as weary as before. I have to get up, I told myself, teach the kids, run the institute, write that book about the Anneliese Michel case that I was working on. I must not give up now. So I rose, and after a few steps my feet started moving almost on their own. It gave me a clue: I could make it, I just had to take longer rests. So I staggered on and then collapsed again in some shade. I thought of what it would be like if I could no longer move. The students coming up behind me on the trail would find me. Sara would go get the rangers with their mules. I would wake up in the hospital between cool white sheets and be given gallons and gallons of ice tea. There would be a news flash: "Professor, head of Cuyamungue

Institute, sixty-five years old, found unconscious on trail; age limit needed for wilderness permits." That would not do. On to the next juniper. As I lay down, I looked around. Right in front of me in the yellow dust there was the delicate imprint of a small rattlesnake. I did not sleep there. I had to defecate, and intense nausea shot through me. At the next stop, a fire ant got into my jeans. Taking them off and shaking the insect out consumed energy I could have better expended on walking. Where were those kids, anyway?

A cloud covered the sun, and for a few minutes a cool breeze billowed my blouse. It gave me courage. Also, the path was no longer rising, although it was not sloping either. My water was cool in the gourd, and this time I managed to walk for half an hour. Then the blaze of the sun hit again, and I slumped under another juniper. But things were not so harsh anymore. In front of me, I saw Elizabeth's footprints, so I was still on the right track. Most important, for the first time I caught a glimpse of the Sangre de Cristo range through a gap in the mountain wall. Home! I was not sleepy, just weary, and I rested for a while enjoying a pleasant, wildly unrealistic fantasy of a tiled bathtub I would build under a juniper in front of the Student Building with a continuous flow of fresh water from the garden hose.

My wristwatch showed six o'clock. I started walking a bit faster and no longer stumbled, for Frijoles Canyon could not be very far ahead. Across the range, the water tower of Whiterock gleamed between the distant greenery. Soon, there should be the sign that we had seen in coming, giving the direction for the Lions, and down to the comfortable path leading to the Visitors' Center. Well, it was not soon, but I did not have to rest so much anymore. The sun had sunk further down on the horizon, and eventually, shortly after seven o'clock, I did arrive at a sign. Only it did not say "To the Visitors' Center" but "To Headquarters." Whatever, I did not care, as long as it was down.

That it was, zigzagging so steeply that it would have taxed a mountain goat, steps two feet high, the path often choked with big boulders. With my short legs, I usually had to hug the rock wall and carefully ease myself down, hanging my gourd around my neck so it would not shatter against the stones. Halfway down, there was a bench, and there were Elizabeth's tracks again. I rested only briefly, for way down I could see buildings and a paved road, and I was getting impatient. A few more zigzags down, I drank the last of my water. Finally, the headquarters trail ran into another path, and I could not tell where that led. So I cut across a slope to the paved road. To the left, a family was eating a picnic supper. I had to ask them twice for directions to the Visitors' Center; the first time my voice was so husky, they could not hear me.

I had only a short distance to walk, then I was on the parking lot and was hugged in great relief by my entire crew. Everybody talked at the same time. It seemed that Elizabeth had also found the headquarters trail, as I had surmised from her tracks. She had met a hiker at the bench who gave her some water. None of the group had gotten to the Shrine of the Stone Lions. They had wandered about lost and finally reached the Rio Grande. Once there, they

took a refreshing dip, drank from a mountain brook, and went directly back
to the Visitors' Center, never even attempting to return the way we had come.
So this was why they had never caught up with me. We had agreed to meet
at the car at six in case we got separated. When I did not show up, they
became worried. Sara finally went to the rangers, and they sent a Zuni mar-
athon runner, who was also a ranger, up to the sanctuary. Just before I arrived,
he had informed them on his walkie-talkie that he had arrived at the Lions
and had not encountered me. He must have missed me because in the meantime I was descending via the headquarters trail. If I had any pride left, it
evaporated when I realized that the entire run up had taken him exactly one
hour.

I sat down in the car, and Sara wanted to rub my feet, but there was no
pain and not even the smallest blister. Everybody had waited to eat, and they
were now enjoying the big picnic supper I had prepared, German potato salad,
meat patties, watermelon. But I could not eat a bite, only drank many glasses
of ice water. They were all very solicitous, suggesting, not entirely altruistically,
"Let's cancel classes tomorrow; after all, your hike was twice as long as ours,
and that way you can sleep as much as you want to."

I slept very well that night, consciously drinking in the cool air. I awoke
at the usual time, took a shower, and went up to my Friend's shrine. I was
tempted to ask why I had not been allowed to see the Sanctuary of the Lions,
but with a newfound wisdom thought that perhaps sleeping lions had better
be left alone. The students stayed in their sleeping bags till noon, got up to
eat lunch, then slept again. They were sore and severely sunburned. I put in
a whole day's work and had suffered no bruises, no cuts, no burns except for
a tiny triangle where my blouse had been open at the neck, and no muscle
pain. I had died at that place of power in the mountains. But the Old Ones
also awarded their gift of rebirth during that initiation, and it involved all of
me, my body as well as my spirit.

In the following weeks it became progressively clear how thoroughgoing
the change was that I had undergone. Before, it seemed, I had been on the
outside looking in. Now, as I was beginning to learn step by step, I was
admitted. There was, for instance, the matter of the memorial mass for old
Tom, who had been killed in an automobile accident. Tom was an Indian,
and walking up to my gate on the way to the neighbors who were going to
take me, I thought of the incongruity that his passing should be remembered
in a mass rather than with some native ritual. How painful it must have been
for the native societies under duress to make such accommodations to the
religion of their Spanish overlords. Passing by the Shrine, I thought in a re-
bellious mood that my Friend might want to come along to represent the
Spirits who had been banished by the mailed fist of the Conquistadores. I was
alone, so I said out loud, "Please, my Friend, do come along to comfort the
spirit of old Tom. Attach yourself to my left shoulder and be my companion."

Being new to the path of the Spirits, I was thoroughly shaken when there was an instantaneous response. Coming up from behind, a tremendous ball of force hit me squarely on the left side of my body. But bewilderment soon gave way to a sense of companionship and a delicious feeling of conspiracy, which stayed with me as I walked into the valley down the hot and dusty trail.

Friends and family of Tom filled the first few rows of the church, so I sat farther back. I expected the priest in his sermon to comfort them by painting the kind of delightful picture of the heavenly abode that I remembered from my nursemaid in Budapest. Lisi told about a kindly old man in a white beard called Saint Peter waiting for people at the gate of paradise, and beyond it there was a lovely meadow with flowers nodding by a chattering brook. Instead, for unfathomable reasons, the priest had chosen from the Hebrew Bible the story of Jezebel and her unsavory real-estate dealings. I was appalled. I just hoped that poor old Tom was no longer around, but had in the meantime safely found his way down the ladder to the Corn Mothers by the lake in the lower world, where the departed passed their days singing and dancing. Then I noticed that while the priest was monotonously talking away on the pulpit at the left, a steady wind coming from the right began persistently and noisily to flap the pages of the big, ornate Bible on the altar. A window may have been open, but for the wind to come up just at that moment seemed to me a marvelous joke perpetrated by my Friend against the insensitive priest.

And there was another surprise to come. Like fairy godmothers at the cradle of the newborn, the Old Ones had readied a truly precious gift. One night that August, shortly after all the students had left and I was totally alone on the land, I woke up around two-thirty or three A.M. from a startling feeling of a vibration, as if my womb had been touched by a live electric wire. I suffered it for a while, then had the intuition that if I guided that excitation from the depths of my body up to my eyes, I would be able to "see." And that was exactly what happened. Images of lustrous clarity began forming before my eyes, a village street, a garden, all bathed in an orange glow, beautiful, but nothing that I could identify. So I just watched and tried to understand what this was about.

Then back in Columbus, around Christmas of that year, at about the same time at night, there appeared against a dark background with tinges of reddish-orange the face of a man. Just the head, nothing else. He had a white untidy cloth on his head, he was swarthy, and his mouth was open almost to a square, with an expression of violent, intense rage. As I came to, I thought, "He does not belong in my world!" A day later, there came news of the Soviet invasion of Afghanistan and pictures of the tribal chieftains opposing the Russians, wearing those untidy-looking white turbans. Soon afterward, early in the new year, I began "seeing," always several days ahead, salient events of the hostage crisis in Iran. Patiently, step by step, my invisible Teachers taught me to trust my visions by using details that could easily be checked against reports in the media. I was being trained as a seer. I understand now the classical Greek tradition that the god Apollo "raped" Cassandra, thereby endowing her with the gift of prophecy. For the experience did start with an arousal around the genitals, and then became conscious as it traveled upward, eventually taking shape as imagery.

It soon became obvious that these visions, although frequently difficult to interpret by someone as ignorant as I, were uncannily accurate, for I kept track of what I saw by writing it down in the morning. They took many different forms. Often, as happened in the case of the hostage crisis, what I saw presaged events to come. Thus, early on October 19, 1983, there appeared a gateway, two uprights and a crossbeam, with a small, triangular, limp banner attached to it. As I watched, a bright round ball something like the sun burst in the exact center. It can't be the sun, I thought, it's more like an explosion, for a rush of air came toward me and made the banner flutter wildly. Looking closer, I saw a cartoon of President Reagan's face on it. On October 23, just four days later, on a suicide mission, someone drove a truck full of explosives into the headquarters of our Marines in Lebanon, and more than two hundred young men died. I wondered afterward whether I should have phoned a warning to someone. But it would have been no use. Old King Priam of Troy did not believe Cassandra either, and he was probably much more intelligent than politicians are nowadays.

It is curious to live in this way. I have gotten used to it by now, although the wonder of it never ceases to amaze me. The river of ordinary life keeps flowing on, yet there is also another one rippling alongside, sometimes hardly visible, at other times foaming up, or glowing as if hit by a sudden beam of light. An Indian friend appeared in my room one night. I did not see her face but recognized her from her skirt, and I was surrounded by the warmest, sweetest, most exquisite love. Then she was gone. A few days later I received a letter from her family: The vision came on the fourth day after she died.

In another case I could not attend the funeral of don Liborio, another special person in my life, who guided me through the maze of Mexico City when I was doing fieldwork there. I did not even know when or where it would take place, but I saw many details of it at the exact time, as if I had been a guest among guests, because I fell unaccountably asleep just then. Except what the guests did not see was that don Liborio was present too. I saw him clearly, floating above his grieving family and friends, wrapped comfortably in a silk cloth, his favorite crunched-up hat on his face, the way he liked to take a siesta. However, one detail I could not understand because I could hear nothing: Why were those present handed grey and broken bones caked with sand? It could not have been food. As I was told later, don Liborio was taken back to his small hometown to be buried there in his father's grave. Unbeknown to the family, apparently some poor people, having no money for a cemetery plot, had lifted the granite slab and interred their corpse in the secure sanctuary. The bones of the stowaway were handed around during the funeral and later replaced.

In still another instance, the grandfather of my host family in Japan died when I was there in 1982. Good old Ojiisan liked to make fun of my figure, because being a size sixteen I looked considerably more ample than the wispy Japanese ladies; he said that I could be a Sumo wrestler. I had helped with his taro and rice harvest and loved to photograph his beautiful old face and slender, nimble hands. While his ashes were still on the altar in his home before burial forty days later, I burned many sticks of incense before it, and kneeling and bowing in the proper manner, I wished him a good journey to the beyond. When I left for America, I was given a beautifully packaged box of bean confection, but with the caution that I alone was to eat it. Gifts tied with yellow and black strings, the sign of mourning, could not be passed on.

Back in Columbus, I soon had a series of strange accidents. I stumbled painfully, a burning piece of wood unaccountably jumped out of my stove and burned a hole in my cherished Chinese rug, a wine glass fell out of the cupboard and shattered on the floor, and there were others. I finally decided that Ojiisan had possibly hitched a ride on the bean confection. Even cherished friends can cause harm once they become restless ghosts. So regretfully I placed the pretty box in the fire and burned it. That night I had a vision. Ojiisan appeared, but he wore a mask, a white hood with holes for his eyes. Reproachfully he said that he enjoyed being with me, and that it made him sad that I was ordering him away. Then he disappeared. There were no more accidents, but sometimes when I think of him, I feel a twinge of remorse.

Not always are the visions concerned with death. My beloved consultant and field assistant in Yucatán, Hermana Us, a wise and motherly old Maya peasant woman who taught me how to survive in the cruel tropics, had to undergo a serious operation. I saw the threat to her life, brief but specific details of the operation, and the happy outcome long before the letter came.

Sometimes it is the life of a total stranger that for a fleeting moment appears in the waves of that ghostly river. Once I "saw" an accident. A young man in tight motorcycle garb, but without a helmet on his black, rather long hair, lay on an incline, sprawling face down on the highway. Weeks later I bought a bag of green peppers from an old man down the street. He had a sign on his lawn: "Jim's Lawnmower Repair." "Are you Jim?" I asked, for our lawn-mower needed an adjustment. No, Jim was his son, but he was in the hospital paralyzed from a motorcycle accident. I did not even connect the remark with my vision until the man began describing the scene of the accident and mentioned that his son had worn no helmet. The young man spent many months in the hospital, but against all odds he finally did recover. He does not know me, but sometimes I see him around his father's house, and it is as if there were a slight breeze coming toward me when I catch sight of him. It makes me wonder: Did I merely see the accident, or did I have a task to perform, perhaps protecting him against being killed? I remember nothing except for that brief scene, so I will never know.

Principally, however, the gift of seeing was apparently intended as a kind of channel so that I could be reached when need be. Remembering the vision under the Virgin of Guadalupe's hands, I think it was surely meant to be a message of encouragement: I was that woman looking out into the mysterious glowing room, the alternate reality that I was soon to enter. And there have been many other instances. The Old Ones showed me how to make a prayer stick that by way of its feathers takes the requests of humans to the spirit world. "Red and green on black," they kept repeating, quite severely, I thought. But then, I had really botched my first prayer stick. And the vision described in the Prologue was another teaching session. The Spirits can be demanding instructors: It took me a long time to puzzle that one out.

The gift of the Old Ones is still with me, but I cannot call it up at will. Neither can I teach it to others, and so it is safe from laboratory probing. In the meantime, however, there was a promising new development concerning the postures. In the summer of 1980 there was a letter from Vienna in the mailbox by the highway in Cuyamungue, from Adolf Holl.

CHAPTER FOUR

A New Path Opens

The letter from Adolf Holl concerned my paper about the discovery of the trance postures, which had aroused so little interest at the 1977 meeting of the American Anthropological Association, and which had been in the packet I had sent to his journalist friend. Holl asked if I would be willing to repeat those experiments with European participants. He was preparing a miniseries on world religions under contract with the West German educational television system, the so-called Second German Program. My research, he felt, would demonstrate to the viewers the common experiential base that all religions shared.

It had been a source of great regret to me during the intervening time that there seemed to be no way in which to continue working with the body postures and related trance experiences. So I was understandably elated at Holl's suggestion and consented with alacrity. Soon after, however, I was beset by serious doubts. With only one series of experiments, how could I be sure that the same results would be achieved again? What if we would both be embarrassed by failure? But feeling that, after all, I had some powerful friends in my corner, I consented anyway and flew to Germany in April 1981.

The first item on the agenda was a preliminary discussion with the private television firm working for the Second Program in Heidelberg. Patiently the director listened to my requests while his secretary took notes. We were going to work in a hotel, so I wanted a quiet conference room away from hotel traffic, preferably at the end of a hallway. It was to have wall-to-wall carpeting, and all furniture was to be removed. We should have some pillows or mats so we could sit on the floor, and a wall clock. A vase of flowers would be nice on a small table, and perhaps some incense. In other words, I was trying to recreate the conditions that had worked so well in Columbus. I assumed that when we arrived at the hotel, nothing would be in place, and we would have to waste a day trying to create even a semblance of the congenial environment that I considered necessary.

I had seriously underestimated German efficiency. By the time we all assembled around Easter at the luxury hotel on the shores of Lake Starnberg near Munich—Adolf Holl, the participants, the producer and his assistant, the former English and the latter German, and the sound man—everything was in place. Only the flowers were missing. So without much ado one of the girls climbed out of the window of the conference room, which was on the ground floor, and broke a few branches off the forsythia bushes in full bloom in the hotel garden. The little scene made me feel at ease. Obviously, these were not the stodgy young people that I remembered from my own German college days. They were the "alternative," the counterculture, children of the same decade that had shaped my graduate-school career. And indeed, their gay abandon and eagerness for adventure were to carry us easily through our unconventional undertaking. I placed incense in my burner, and we could go to work.

The group of participants that Adolf Holl had recruited consisted of three medical students, Uwe, Irmi, and Ingrid, an advertising copywriter by the name of Franz, who was also a long-time Zen practitioner, Kurt, a psychology student, and Doris, a secretary. Later workshops would show a similar composition: young to middle-aged, from the middle twenties to the early forties, both men and women, medical people, psychotherapists of various persuasions, usually academically trained, and quite generally those people in and out of these professions who had a keen interest in and some experience with what is generally termed consciousness-altering techniques. "We, the seekers," said a young German physician.

Understandably, everyone suffered from considerable performance anxiety. It did not exactly help that Tim, our English producer, kept assuring us, "If nothing comes of this, we can always interview the participants about why they volunteered for a crazy project like this." Actually, I was worried only about the content of the experience, not that "nothing" would happen. I knew there would be trances. After all, I had seen over and over again in fieldwork with what ease people experienced a religious trance, given the expectation and with the right stimulation, provided they concentrated properly.

Actually, concentration was a key issue. There had been one participant in the Columbus group who simply could not do that. Her mind was always on her next shopping trip, on her children, on her new husband, on everything but the task at hand. So she never experienced anything. It is a problem that preachers in Pentecostal churches also have to contend with. Those that I had observed teaching speaking in tongues had often warned that one should "think not of the matters of the world, not of whether the milpa would yield or if there would be enough money for tortillas, but only of the manifestation of the Holy Spirit." As insurance against failure due to lack of concentration,

I therefore introduced an innovation in the form of a breathing exercise. At the outset of the session, everyone was to take fifty relaxed, normal breaths, in and out, in and out. Only during inhalation could one feel the air passing over the septum; it was not perceivable when exhaling. This alternation was what the participants were supposed to observe. It was a natural, soothing rhythm, and I hoped that in addition to putting them at ease, it would also narrow attention to a single signal and thus be a suitable preparation for the subsequent rhythmic stimulation by the beat of the rattle. Experience has borne out this expectation, and we still use the exercise today. As added insurance, I also did the first session before breakfast. Fasting is a time-honored adjunct to the trance experience.

Because this was the first time I had worked with a group, it was a surprise to me how much more intense the trance was than when I had worked with each individual separately in Columbus. In addition, I also saw the participants during the time between the sessions, and we had our meals together. As a result I noticed various aftereffects of the trance that I had not observed before. There was a kind of electric, prickling excitement in the group. No wonder the early Pentecostal congregations that used trance behavior were called "enthusiastic." We laughed a lot and talked with a certain verve, casting aside as if by collusion inhibitions present under ordinary circumstances among casual acquaintances. We began sharing little confidences, experiences not usually told to outsiders. On the second morning, for instance, while we were doing the posture of the *Singing Shaman*, my heart began pounding and I saw the rattle in my hand turn into a hard-working, plump little middle-aged lady, busily bending up and down, "doing her thing," her short skirt flying. It was such a curious experience, I mentioned at breakfast afterward that the rattle had turned into "my aunt," and "aunt" it remained from then on, everybody referring to it that way, with an occasional sly wink.

There developed an urgent need to be close to each other at all times. One afternoon after a session, for instance, there was only one table for four available in the crowded dining room of the hotel. Borrowing chairs here and there, eleven of us simply squeezed around that one small table and thought it a great joke. "The hardest thing to report, though, because it is the most subtle," I wrote in my diary, "is the rapidly blossoming, the almost exploding affection of everyone toward everyone. I truthfully don't think that anybody was excluded. A pattern of hugging and kissing emerged, totally devoid of sexual overtones. It had something innocent, almost childlike, about it. It was like the dawn, the touching of fingertips in the early breeze, the converging and parting of playful waves."

Some of the hidebound and obviously very affluent tourists took offense and complained to the management. But we knew they could not throw us out; we were there on "official" business, and anyway, we did not care. We had rediscovered the exhilaration of the celebrating community, and we would not let anybody take it away. As the assistant producer told me later, when we moved to Munich for the taping, "You know, in that hotel we all lived as if under a protective glass bubble; now I have to break out of it and work, and this is all so different, cold and even antagonistic. I wish there were a way in which I could keep alive some of what we experienced."

I felt that loss also when all was over, and I found myself in the hotel lobby, totally alone again, thinking that the same miracle could not take place a second time. But I need not have mourned its passing. For every time we have a workshop, particularly if we also share meals and living accommodations, as we do at various institutions in Europe and especially at Cuyamungue, we are caught up in the same magic once more.

There was another aspect of the group trance experience emerging that I also had seen evolve in the Apostolic congregations that I knew from my fieldwork. The shared trance shapes a ring around the community, keeping the members in and closing others out. Anthropologists speak of paranoia. But that is not the heart of the matter. The group is forged into one body, as it were, by the heat of ecstasy. We had a demonstration of this when one morning Tim, our English director, instead of merely listening to the tapes in his room as he had done before, accompanied the sound man to our session. We were doing a diviner's posture, and afterward Tim did not just listen but started asking questions. He wanted "media-effective statements," he said. It was a painful intrusion, and by the time we assembled for lunch, those of us in charge had a revolt on our hands. We finally came to the conclusion that we would ask Tim not to come to the sessions again, but to rely on the tapes as he had done before. When the decision passed around the lunch table, everyone broke out into relieved, resounding laughter. We had performed an exorcism.

It was easy to understand why Tim was worried. He did not have a clear understanding of what we were doing and desperately wanted to have some back-up material in case we "fell flat." I had also been worried initially, not about the occurrence of the trance itself but, as mentioned before, about whether the curious regularity would once more appear that I had observed in Columbus, with each posture mediating a different type of experience. However, my anxiety dissolved as I continued listening to the reports during the sessions, for the agreements with what I had recorded in Columbus became more and more evident. As during those initial experiments, the overlap certainly was not restricted to somatic changes only, to the perception of heat during one posture, of cold in another, or to the distortion of time, what one of the Columbus group had called "the total collapse of the time perspective." What was actually even more striking was once more the agreement in the distinctive experiential content of the various postures. Despite a great deal of individual variation, the stability of the general character of each posture was unmistakable.

Of the diviner's posture, for instance, Anita of the Columbus group had said, "The energy went up to my head generating heat in a circular motion and creating a halo effect in the back of my head. . . . It was as if I was trying to pierce a veil, or to see the light at the end of the tunnel." In West Germany now, Ingrid was telling us that "the rattle turned into a mill wheel in my head, and I was a balloon being jettisoned outward from the wheel." The overlap could hardly be more perfect: Anita's "circular motion" as against Ingrid's mill wheel, the halo and the balloon, and wanting to pierce a veil and being jettisoned outward.

Or as another example, during the posture of the *Bear Spirit*, Bryan of the Columbus group related, "Suddenly my heart started pumping, and there was something like a passage opening up in me, a stairway or something. . . . I was just a stairway, I was nothing at all, almost like that was all I was; I wasn't even a body anymore." Compare that with Ingrid finding herself reduced to a small beetle in a very large bottle where she looked up through a narrow neck far above her. The further we progressed in our workshop, the clearer it became to me that the power of the postures was indeed overwhelming.

After three days of strenuous work, on Easter Monday, we had to leave the hospitable shores of Lake Starnberg behind and moved to a hotel in Munich, close to the large studios of the Second Program. When on Tuesday morning we went for rehearsal to the studio, I was taken aback. It was cavernous, drafty, impersonal, cluttered with cameras, platforms, booms, and huge lights dripping from the ceiling. For the television show, Adolf Holl and I had decided to do the posture from Lascaux Cave. I wondered how the ancient shaman, whose presence I had felt so keenly in Columbus, would feel about being transported from the intimacy of his cave to these frigid walls. But when we got to see for the first time the platform that the craftsmen had assembled for our program, I was mollified. We were told that it had cost the studio more than three thousand dollars to construct. It was round, about fourteen feet in diameter, padded with foam rubber, and covered with grey corduroy. While Holl and I introduced the program, the participants would sit on the platform on pink cushions. For the exercise itself, it would be cranked up to the all-important thirty-seven-degree angle.

While Holl and I rehearsed our comments and figured out where we should stand, our "experimental persons"—the "kids" by now—got acquainted with their platform. It was cranked up for them, and instead of using the ladder, they were soon exuberantly climbing all over it like so many monkeys. The footrests were too narrow, but that was remedied while we had lunch in the studio cafeteria, and afterward, we had another rehearsal.

Although the studio by now seemed less formidable, the kids still asked about the incense, which I had always lit during our earlier sessions, and which I had hoped would form a sensory bridge between the conference room and the studio. I took the matter up with the producers. They had extremely sensitive smoke detectors at the studio; smoking was allowed only in certain closed-off areas. But after some arm-twisting, I did obtain the promise that they would turn the equipment off and let us light the incense.

The show was taped the next day. I brought all the incense I had left and arranged it in water glasses on the floor around the platform. I figured the studio was so large, if the kids were to perceive the fragrance, it had to be more massive than in the conference room at the hotel. Then we watched the superb collage of scenes from previous parts of the miniseries that had been prepared by the studio staff, and which was to serve as an introduction to our program. After that, Holl and I taped our own opening segment. We had to do it twice, because there was some disturbing noise on the tape. They finally hooked a new transmitter to my belt under my skirt in the back, which cleared up the problem.

Understandably, there was general apprehension about the trance scene itself. In order not to induce the trance inadvertently, I had simulated the rattle signal by arm movements during the trial runs. But there was a scene after Holl and I finished the introduction where the participants were to demonstrate the other postures. It was visually very appealing, the platform still in horizontal position, the pink pillows, and each one of the young people in a different posture. But they had me rattle for it, and although the scene took not even a minute, some of them started going into trance. Then something went wrong, and we had to repeat the scene. There were also repeated noisy altercations in the studio, because the cameramen kept quarreling with the cable movers. At one point, the entire operation had to be halted for twenty minutes so that, because of a complicated union rule, a man could be called from someplace else in Munich to move a boom.

I had impressed on Tim that we could do the scene only once, that it could under no conditions be repeated except several hours later, that we had to have absolute silence, that no one was to move, open doors, or make any other kind of noise while I was rattling. This was of paramount importance, because although the video was to show only three minutes of that scene, we of course had to go through the entire fifteen minutes, for after a brief recovery period, Holl was going to introduce the experimental subjects and was then going to ask them to report their experiences. The tension was heightened because as before, I had given them no clue whatever about what type of adventure the posture was likely to mediate.

Tim was in charge and worked with marvelous precision. He did not just give his instructions to the crew via earphones. He came down from his perch and in remarkably good German gave a little speech repeating what I had told him, and emphasizing that absolutely nothing could go wrong or else. The platform had been cranked up, and the participants in posture lay very still in their places, an eerie twentieth-century replay of the venerable Stone Age scene. Somebody lit the incense, Tim gave me my signal through the bug in my ear, and we were off.

Half a minute later he had to stop everything. Absolutely no sound came through the equipment. "How long will it take you to fix it?" Holl wanted to know. Tim was noncommittal. "You know how technology works. You get hold of the end of a string and you can't tell how long it is." Luckily, the string was short, and once more I started rattling. It was harder than usual; fifteen minutes is awfully long even under ordinary circumstances, and here I could not see any clock. Doggedly I rattled on. At one point Irmi, stretched out at the apex of the platform, started jerking uncontrollably. Panic swept through me: Would the footrest hold? Kurt, positioned at the lower left, said later that he had perceived that Irmi was in trouble and had tried to "send help" to her. After a while she calmed down. I rattled on and on. Just before I received the signal to stop, Irmi's motions ceased.

Holl bridged the ensuing pause with a few comments on our experimental sessions, introduced the participants, and then asked each one in turn about his or her experience. He started with Ingrid, and I listened with mounting excitement:

> There was a tremendous wave of heat that moved from my feet to my head. When it arrived there, my head turned into a mountain peak. That peak kept growing higher and higher, giving me the feeling that I was the highest mountain peak in the world. The entire world stretched out before me, infinitely far and limitless, and I could see it all. Not only the earth was without boundaries, but also the sky, the entire cosmos, as it opened up above me. Then I could feel the heat no longer, and from the tip of the mountain, I fell into this infinity. A soft wind carried me through the eternal expanse. There was no distance, neither toward the horizon nor into the depth. I could allow the wind to waft me where it pleased, and it was exceedingly beautiful.

What the others had to tell was equally fascinating, each in his or her own way:

> Doris: I also started out feeling heat, but it did not come from my feet. It started around my kidneys and streamed into my entire body. Then I had the feeling, it can't flow through, it can't get through, it is backed up in my body. I became scared; I thought I could burst. At one point, I must have opened my mouth. After a while I finally had the feeling that the heat was flowing through, and that was pleasant. I can't say that I was streaming out with this warmth, but I sure had the feeling that I was flowing away.

Uwe, apparently, had not discovered the release that opening her mouth had brought for Doris:

> For a while I was very quiet, then my entire body began vibrating very strongly. There was a strange pulling sensation coming from my ears and going toward my mouth, and a severe cramping of my face. Even after the rattle stopped, I had an awful time trying to open my mouth. It seemed to be locked and sealed.

Irmi, on the other hand, felt herself expanding like Ingrid had and then splitting open:

I was as if spread out and stretched. Then I had the impression that the rattle appeared behind me, so that I heard two rattle sounds. This being spread out gave me the impression of great space. When I started moving involuntarily, this was converted into being split lengthwise and growing upward.

For Franz, the change was very subtle but still recognizable:

I experienced entering the trance twice, and the image plane moved behind my eyes. I perceived a milky circulation. The second entry was much more intense. I suddenly heard a second rattle, which had an entirely different tone. And although I had the impression that I had fallen back out, I found myself on a vastly different plane afterward.

And finally, Kurt experienced a clear and impressive exit:

I felt a wave arise in me. It came from the extremities and was blocked here in my chest. It was a tremendous struggle, for I knew it had to rise up into my head. That was what I was struggling with, trying to open this blockage in my neck and get through into my head. I then felt a tremendous pressure in my head, and no longer perceived my body at all, only my head. I began hearing the second rattle noise, which became circular. Suddenly there was this picture; I saw this energy exiting from my head in the shape of a circle. After that, I was totally relaxed.

The cameras stopped rolling. Despite all the problems and the interruptions, the experience had come through crystal-clear. I thought the old shaman might have been pleased, just as he probably had been when so many millennia ago he had taken a piece of charcoal-and-tallow crayon and had with such sparse lines and yet so expertly drawn that figure, saying, "All right, now look here, this is what you'll have to do." And his young apprentices had settled on the hillock and, holding their hands and arms the way he had shown them, had gone on a spirit journey.

I had the urgent desire to hug the kids, but all of a sudden, I found myself surrounded by everyone in the studio, the cameramen, the man on the boom, the producers, the "picture mixer" from upstairs, and even some other technicians usually hidden in the caverns housing the controls. Immediately, right then, they also wanted to try what we had just done. Their disappointment was obvious when I pointed out that, after all, the "experimental persons" had worked with me for nearly a week; they had learned to concentrate, they had had a number of other experiences, all in preparation for this one culminating event. "See, I told you," the woman who had done the picture mixing said, as on a cue from Tim, all went back to their places to tape the concluding section that Holl and I still had to do. "Do you realize," Kurt said to me afterward, "that you just witnessed a miracle? These people here in the studio are a thoroughly jaded audience. You should have heard their snide remarks when we were getting ready to tape. All about one more circus and on like that."

"After that, all was painful dissolution," I wrote in my diary. But our story did not end there. We are still in touch, some as friends, such as Doris and Irmi. Ingrid Mueller organized the medical research in Munich, mentioned before, in conjunction with her medical doctoral dissertation. Franz and Uwe were two of the four subjects who volunteered for those tests. And Kurt's enthusiastic reports brought the first participants to the ensuing workshops which I have continued on a regular basis in Europe every spring.

Going on with more workshops was actually the most important development that came out of our television project. The idea originated with Franz. He was the cofounder of the Buddhist Center in Scheibbs (Austria). On the day before the taping, as we were all walking through Vienna, laughing and munching strawberries, he suddenly turned to me and said, "I'd like you to give me copies of those drawings of the postures that we used. Maybe in Scheibbs I could do a seminar like we just had." Then, before I could even answer, he laughed, put his arm around me, and, switching into his earthy Austrian dialect, continued, "Naw. . . . Actually, why should the little smith do it when we can have the real smith?"

CHAPTER FIVE

The Way of the Spirits

The first workshop that Franz organized in the Buddhist Center in Scheibbs (Austria) took place in 1982. He published the announcement in the schedule of the center, and a few of the regulars became interested. Others had seen the television show. Kurt, also of the television workshop, told friends in Vienna about his experiences, and they came to Scheibbs to find out more. Yolanda of a later Scheibbs workshop was from Switzerland. The next spring, she got some friends together, they rented suitable quarters in a mountain resort, and we did a workshop there. A stop in Switzerland has become an institution since then, part of my yearly spring tour, which at this writing covers five European countries.

In this country, the development of the workshops took off slowly. For several summers in a row, I taught anthropology courses at Cuyamungue Institute. However, with the connection to Denison University, my home institution, weakening with the years, recruiting undergraduates became more and more difficult. Increasingly also, that was really no longer what I wanted to do. It was at this juncture that summer workshops comfortably fitted into the premises already available there.

The participants in both Europe and this country represent pretty much the same groups. For many of them, what they are learning in the workshops is simply yet another step on the path to finding out more about themselves. "Esoteric tourists," as one of my friends calls them, are a characteristic feature of our waning century. Others, especially those in the health-care professions, often make the postures and the trance part of their therapeutic activity. Still others give workshops of their own. But the workshops spread acephalously, as anthropologists would say, that is, without a head. An inexpensive newsletter published by the institute announces my program and reports on ongoing research, keeping the lines of communication open, but there is no organization collecting dues or issuing certificates for teaching activity, which is beginning to blossom in a number of other places. The institute itself is a research-and-teaching institution concentrating solely on trance workshops. For many participants, however, Cuyamungue has developed into something of a place of pilgrimage, and taking a workshop has become a highly prized experience.

The grounds of Cuyamungue are an informal wildlife refuge, open to outsiders only during workshops. The house we built over a number of years is now occupied year-round by members of the institute who act as administrators for the workshops and issue the newsletter. The wooden Student Building that we were working on during the summer of my initiation has served us well ever since. It has a long dining table and benches, showers, and a kitchen corner, a thickly insulated roof, mimicking the bushes and the rocks of the arroyos that dispense such cool, protective shade, and a double wall with cracks between the boards, so the wind can waft in and out and keep it fresh. Tiny flycatchers and bluebirds have come to nest between the boards in the spring, and the big-eyed desert mice have discovered the crawlspace underneath, as has their nemesis, the ever-hungry bull snake. A thieving pack rat, recently moved in, has been less welcome. Some summers ago I had a Dutch visitor, a Shinto priest with a passion for shaving his head every morning. The pack rat stole his razor, and he was reduced to borrowing the small safety razor one of the girls used to shave her legs.

Outside the Student Building, I started a vegetable garden. Its mention brings a resigned smile to the lips of my Hispanic neighbors, who helped me plant the fruit trees, and who are expert gardeners themselves. Whoever heard of letting the weeds intentionally take over a garden? For in my garden, the wild ones are invited in. The chiles and the tomatoes and the leaf lettuce and the variety of herbs without which I cannot cook grow topsy-turvy, doing the best they can between Indian tea and mullein and mountain sage, Mexican hat, primroses and bluebells, and dozens of other plants the names of which I have not yet learned that have settled in, brought by the birds and by the ever-singing, ever-driving wind. And from the moist and sheltered place, their seeds now travel outward and are beginning to recolonize the hills about, cruelly denuded by many decades of overgrazing.

We also have some other structures on the land now, a shaded arbor in the back of the Student Building, a favorite of the hummingbirds who come to suck syrup from the feeder there, a shed built in the Hispanic style we use for storage, and a large rectangular adobe shell, the Library, where we can set up our cots when we need to get out of the rain, and where I present an occasional puppet show to the children of the region. It looks out on the land with its two front windows set high, the masked face of a kachina. But the true heart of the land is the kiva.

I no longer remember when exactly it occurred to me that what I needed as a classroom was a kiva. One day, I simply found the suggestion "in my head," like one would a melody, or a poem, a gift from the other, the sacred side. Since white people are barred from entering these sacred buildings of the Pueblo Indians that are still in use, I went around to prehistoric ruins, trying to figure out how the people of old had created their round, semi-underground structures. And then I designed one like them. Only ours has an entrance from the ground level for the greater safety of the participants, not the traditional one with a ladder through the roof. Just like the traditional kivas, ours has no electricity, getting its light from two windows and the panes flanking the door.

From the start, the kiva was special. One summer a workshop participant swore that when she got up in the Library one dark and starless night to go to the bathroom in the Student Building, the empty kiva was lit from the inside, an orange glow suffusing the entire building.

"Did you look through the window to see what was going on?" I asked.

"Oh heavens no," she said, "I wouldn't have dared."

There are those who like to sleep in the kiva, because it is a warm and closed shelter, and the dreams are mysterious and easily remembered, but not everyone is welcome. A German friend, a writer who shall remain unnamed here, came only to visit and wanted no part of any trance experience. "The idea that you might put me into trance," she protested, "makes my soul roll up in fear like a hedgehog." The first night she slept in the kiva, a big drop of water splashed on her face. She moved her cot, and another drop hit the mark. She moved again, then went back with her flashlight to examine the puddle that should have formed on the floor had there been a leak, but could not find any. Another guest, a relative on a tour of the Southwest, heard a mouse run across the ceiling and then slap noisily on the flagstone floor. "The fall must have broken every bone in its body," he remarked. "But this morning, I could not find any dead mouse."

The most dramatic kiva story happened to my friend Hans Peter Duerr, a German anthropologist and best-selling author, who came to Cuyamungue in June of 1981. He later told about it in a small volume of occasional pieces entitled *Satyricon*.[1] A few days before Hans Peter's visit, I was sitting in front of the Student Building with a friend from Albuquerque. Suddenly we saw a large predatory bird circling over the hills toward the west. As it came closer, we recognized that it was an eagle. I had never seen an eagle in our area, and I marveled at its size and the majestic circles it was now describing directly above us. When Hans Peter arrived, the eagle was still very much on my mind, and it was one of the first things I talked about. To our mutual surprise, he had just had an encounter with an eagle himself, at the Sun Dance of the Cheyenne Indians.

Hans Peter had been invited to the Cheyenne by Dr. Schlesier, a German ethnographer doing fieldwork there. As he was sitting among the guests watching the Sun Dance, he closed his eyes for a moment and suddenly saw a bright light on the horizon. As it came closer, he realized that it was an eagle. It finally stopped directly before him and turned its head as if wanting to look him over. The eagle was so close that Hans Peter saw every detail of the bird's eye as it was steadily scrutinizing him. Startled, he said to Schlesier, "Hey, look what came by!" Needless to say, Schlesier saw nothing, but he suggested that Hans Peter go to the Arrowkeeper, the Cheyenne Holy Man, and tell him about his vision. The Arrowkeeper explained to him that the whistles the dancers were blowing were made from eagle bone and that it signaled great good fortune that the Eagle Spirit had chosen to appear to him. The Eagle Spirit, he said, was very powerful, and it did not matter that Hans Peter was a white man, he would still be blessed.

We both felt that the eagle that my guest and I had seen had announced Hans Peter's arrival, and that indeed, the Eagle Spirit had taken a liking to him. I asked him whether he had properly thanked the Eagle, perhaps by a small gift of tobacco? After all, I argued, Hans Peter being an anthropologist, he should realize that he had been invited into a world of reciprocity with his vision, where each gift merits another one in return. But Hans Peter procrastinated, and I did not press the point.

We spent some pleasant days together; there were guests, we went sightseeing, and the return gift to the Eagle Spirit had obviously been forgotten. On Saturday morning, as always, we were using the adjoining bathrooms of the Student Building, and Hans Peter asked through the thin board wall whether I had removed the lid of his soap dish. He was sure that he had put it on tightly to keep the mice from eating the soap, and several times, he had found it off. I had not been in his bathroom, so I said, "Who knows, perhaps the Spirits are teasing you because there is something important you haven't done yet, like presenting a gift to the Eagle."

This time, to my surprise, he was apparently quite eager to carry out the small ritual. We walked together up to the ridge, where I usually say a blessing before sunrise and after sunset and scatter some cornmeal. He not only offered the Eagle his due, but even had a pinch of meal for my Friend, leaving me still to wonder about the reason for his change of heart. On the way down, he suddenly asked, "Tell me, the kind of rattle you use, is that available locally?"

"Yes."

"Do you have one here?"

"No, I left mine in Columbus and have not gotten around to buying another one yet."

Then the story came out. After our dinner guests had left the night before, Hans Peter had retired to the kiva to go to bed, closing the door behind him. He was wide awake, listening to the concert of the crickets outside. Suddenly he heard a loud rattling in front of the door and thought that I was trying to play a practical joke on him. As he tells in the *Satyricon,*

> I got out of my sleeping bag, opened the door, and checked. I could see the entire area clearly in the bright moonlight, but saw no one, not even a rattlesnake on the

ground. The rattling had stopped, and I crawled back into the sleeping bag. I felt very unwell, and the only thing that I could think of was to "call" the Eagle Spirit. Suddenly, the cot began to jerk violently three times in succession at an interval of several seconds, and I thought, "How in the world am I going to get out of this situation?" Then I had the feeling that the Eagle was there, in the kiva, spreading his wings over me. (1982:84–85)

During all this time, the noise of the crickets had stopped, and there was a deathly silence outside. Just as suddenly, all was over, the crickets went back to their music, and Hans Peter fell asleep. He was quite shaken by it all. "And to think," he writes, "that twenty years ago I officially left the Church!"

I think the reason Hans Peter was treated so roughly in the kiva was that he had shown disregard not only for reciprocity but also for ritual. But why should ritual be so important to the Spirits? Because ritual is the means of communication for them, as important as speech is for us. In fact, there can be no religious ceremony without ritual. This is a simple fact, known to all religious communities the world over. Ritual is the rainbow bridge over which we can call on the Spirits and the Spirits cross over from their world into ours. The question is, of course, why would they even want to? Because they are so much wiser than we. They know something that we in the West all too often forget, namely, that the ordinary and the other reality belong together. They are two halves of one whole. Only their joining will make a complete world, a world worth living in. The existence of humans is empty without the Spirits, but theirs is equally incomplete without involving us, and the world about us. Although they are so much more powerful than we are, in this sense they need us.

As an anthropologist, I of course knew all of this in theory. But being a recent immigrant in an unfamiliar country, I too had to learn many new rules, so to speak, from the bottom up. Dimly at first, as when I asked the Spirit of the Shrine to accompany me to the mass to say farewell to Tom, I began to understand that these Beings were standing ready to be our helpers and our friends. All we had to do was ask them, and they responded instantly and in startlingly tangible ways. I had experienced this many times before, but never more thrillingly than at a workshop I offered at the *Volkshochschule*, an adult education institution in Salzburg (Austria) in the spring of 1984.[2]

It had snowed on this day in April, and the snow continued to fall gently as the group of more than thirty people assembled for a session in the large hall on the second floor. We were doing the posture of the Singing Shaman (see Chapter 11). At my suggestion, the participants started singing to the rattle, and soon the initial open *a* vowel (as in *father*) began to increase in volume under the effect of the trance, and the many voices united in a powerful chorale, with the many pulsing glossolalia phrases rising from it like so many sparkling flames.

That morning, before coming to the session, I had leafed through a new

German publication on shamanism,[3] and I noted a section where the author quoted the Hungarian folklorist Vilmos Diószegi. It seems that during a trip to Siberia, Diószegi visited an old shaman, whom he found lying on his cot, weak and chronically ill. When the folklorist began asking him about his past shamanistic activity, though, the old man became animated and visibly gained strength. At this session now, as the group in front of me was beginning to sway lightly, and some were trembling under the effect of the trance, and I felt the wave of energy that started streaming toward me, I suddenly thought of something. If what I was perceiving had any sort of reality, it should actually be possible to gather it up, to concentrate it like ball lightning, and to dispatch it to an old shaman like the one Diószegi met, to console him and to heal him. So while rattling on, I spoke to my Friend and asked him to be our messenger. Idly I was thinking of the surroundings of a shaman in Siberia, the endlessly undulating low shrubs on the dark and mucky tundra, the snarling dogs, his black felt tent dusted with snow, when all of a sudden I was startled by my rattle slipping in my hand and leaning over to the left. Brought out of my reverie, I grabbed hold of it. But a minute or so later, the rattle did it again, this time jerking noticeably to the right. I was puzzled. Had we actually sent out something and, like an echo, it was being returned to us?

At the conclusion of the rattling, the participants settled down on the rug, and since the group was so large, I did not call on everyone but asked for volunteered comments. I did not mention the favor I had asked of my Friend, or the strange behavior of the rattle. I felt that that was my secret, which I was not obligated to share.

There were the reports expectable for this posture—how they had felt extremely hot, how the muscles of the chest had become stiff, and how the singing had seemed to become independent of volition. Some talked of their hearts beating fast and of weeping. There was nothing that I had not heard before, and my attention flagged a bit as I looked out through the window on the soft snow that in the dusk was continuing to fall, when to my left a young woman started to speak. "Actually, nothing remarkable happened to me," she said. "I think I probably continued in the ordinary state of consciousness all the way through. And then there came this very large yellow butterfly, and it settled here on my left upper arm, and I could feel exactly how its legs affectionately pressed around it."

It all sounded so commonplace that I smiled and answered, "Oh, I see, and all that happened while you were in the ordinary state of consciousness!" Then what she had said sunk in. It took my breath away, and tears came to my eyes. Not only had our missile reached its goal, but we had also received a greeting in return.

A week later I conducted a workshop at the Forum in Freiburg. I had given the introductory lecture, and we had held the first trance session. The meeting room was in the front of the building, and the traffic noise seemed to distract the participants, so their concentration was not as complete as I had wished. At any rate, I was not too happy with the results. That at least was the explanation that occurred to me. Or had the fault been mine? I decided to give it my all during the next session.

Once more, we did the Singing Shaman. I started rattling. Usually I keep my eyes open, because I want to observe the participants. But this time, I closed them in order to be able to concentrate more fully. As soon as I started rattling, something truly surprising happened. As if drawn by a crayon of gold, an old man appeared in front of a wall of fog, but only the upper part of his body. His deeply creased face was serious, inwardly directed. It showed Mongolian features, almond-shaped eyes and high cheekbones. His grey hair, which was short and waved in the wind, hung down on a crumpled collar. He did not look at me but up at the sky, and he held his arms extended as if in prayer. If I could only see him long enough so that I'll remember everything, I thought, as I desperately tried to keep my rattling even. But in an instant he was gone, the image wiped away, and I was left with only that ephemeral sweetness that often followed an ecstasy.

What had been discovered by serendipity soon became a new ritual, namely, always asking my Friend to participate in the sessions. And just as I had done it the first time, I expressed such requests when I started rattling and with the barest movement of my lips. As I became more experienced in ritual matters, it also felt appropriate at the outset of a workshop to invite all the Spirits that I felt were hovering about to come and be our guests, by rattling toward the four directions, as well as toward the earth and the sky, and then to scatter a pinch of cornmeal as an offering of welcome.

That the latter ritual was proper and, in fact, expected was brought home to me some time later. This was in Cincinnati, and I had a group that included several psychiatrists, a Protestant preacher, and a Catholic priest. I felt that it might be tactless under these circumstances to confront the group with something that would be "unscientific" to some, and most certainly "pagan" to some of the others, so I skipped the opening ritual.

After the first morning session I felt unaccountably tired, and in the intermission, I settled down on the rug and tried to sleep. Instead of sleeping, however, I immediately slipped into a brief vision. I was holding a small object and eagerly hid it under my pillow. Touching it gave me an indescribable feeling of joy and yet also yearning. I knew that what I had hidden was something that I needed in order to resolve a situation. But when I came to, I could remember neither what "it" was nor what the problem was that I needed it for. So I went over my notes before the start of the next session, and then I understood. Ordinarily when I invite the Spirits, they announce their presence with a gust of wind that one of the participants feels. Not once had it been reported this time. Obviously, they expected to be invited, and I had neglected to do so. Humbled, I stepped into the center of the room before the next session and went through the requisite ritual. I knew all was well when Jill, the Protestant minister, told about seeing the "Wind Spirits" dance during the following posture.

This particular workshop was a learning experience for me also for another reason. After not carrying out the ritual that was expected of me, I made a second mistake. I taught the group a posture that was unfamiliar even to those who had worked with me before, the *Calling of the Spirits* (see Chapter 11). It is somewhat similar to another one, that of the *Feathered Serpent* (see Chapter 13). For the Calling of the Spirits, I usually ask my Friend to help us achieve the experience. In the case of the Feathered Serpent, I appeal in addition to that mighty source of life and fertility directly. Perhaps because of a brief lapse of attention and the similarity of the two postures, I made the mistake of calling on the Serpent. No sooner had I spoken the wrong request than I noticed it and corrected myself, apologizing to the Venerable Ancient One for troubling her inappropriately.

When it came to the telling of the experience, I called on Diane first. It was a random choice, but this young psychiatrist had done a workshop with me previously, and I knew how gifted she was. I expected her even at the first try to turn into a tree or something similar, as happens during this posture, and to see the Spirits approaching. Instead, this is what she told:

> My mouth became very large and dry, and then snakes started coming out of it, very many snakes, and I don't even like snakes. Then a very large snake followed, and my mouth and throat became white, as if coated with clay. After that, some Essences arrived and started making a hole in the roof, so that the snakes would be able to leave.

Diane was the only one who saw the Serpent, and she clearly helped to guide the snakes out. The incident taught me an important lesson about the power of a conjuring ritual. I also comprehended once more that this was a gentle world. No lightning struck my stupid head; there was only the indulgent wagging of a finger. I could almost hear my Friend say, "It's all right, but try to be more careful next time."

As far as postures were concerned, I initially taught only those that we had explored in Columbus during my various courses. In fact, I was under the illusion that the postures that I had discovered were peculiar to the particular societies who represented them in their art, the Indian fishermen of the Pacific coast, for instance, or the Nupe of sub-Saharan Africa. Actually, there had been a faint signal that this was the wrong view, but I did not understand it. For soon after we did the TV show, a friend pointed out that the thirty-seven-degree angle was not peculiar to the Lascaux Cave shaman. It appeared in Egypt as well, although about twelve thousand years later. With an altered position of the right arm, which is stretched upward, it is at this angle that the god Osiris rises toward the heavens (pl. 5). According to classical Egyptian tradition, Osiris's twin brother Set dismembered him. His mother, together

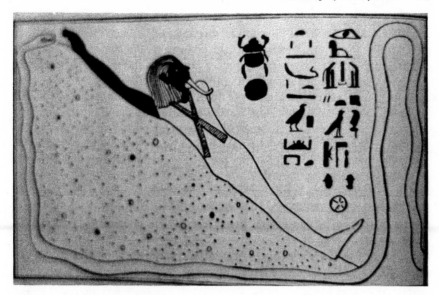

Plate 5

with his sisters, put him back together again, and whole once more, he was
then ready to join the other gods in their sky home.

The divine twins, the dismemberment, and the reassembly, as well as the
spirit journey to the world above, are all shamanic elements, known from the
Mediterranean, from Siberia, and from the Americas. We may therefore assume
that originally Osiris was a shaman, for the figure contains elements of this
role and seems to point to the fact that shamanism in this form once predominated around the Mediterranean, from southern France all the way to
Egypt. What is remarkable is that these elements were preserved in northern
Africa over such an enormous time span, especially in light of the fact that
we are dealing with two different cultural types. The shaman of Lascaux was
without a doubt a hunter, like everyone during that period. Osiris, on the other
hand, changed into a god of the much more recent agriculturalists on the Nile,
without, however, losing his original character. Nor indeed did the Egyptians
lose the knowledge about the correct posture, especially about the proper
angle for ascending to the sky world.

I took the agreement to be an engaging coincidence and was too dull to
look any further. What is even more chastening is that it took me two more
years to realize the significance of the fact that here we had a revealing,
completely independent confirmation of the experiences reported in connection with this posture. My participants had risen to the sky world, too, without
any prior knowledge whatsoever of the connection to Osiris's resurrection,
body posture, and angle of ascent.

As to the wide-ranging occurrence of the postures, I was not to remain blind much longer. Friends from various workshops began looking around in museums and in books of "primitive" art, and they realized what I had not seen. A number of the postures we had done also appeared elsewhere, and there were others, perhaps equally potent but unfamiliar to us, that occurred over and over again in various parts of the world. Clearly, we were dealing not with a few curious, isolated local ritual patterns but with a behavior and no doubt an attendant knowledge having a worldwide distribution. Not only that, this very frequent occurrence also meant that most of the thirty-odd postures which we eventually identified had to be extremely old. Actually, we knew this intuitively. I recall hearing the well-known American flutist Herbie Mann speak about playing a three-thousand-year-old Maya flute, and of the thrill he felt as the moisture of his breath activated the fragrance of the ancient clay. That was exactly what we experienced as we went on exploring these various postures. The Old People began to talk to us, awakening anew in the unfathomable depths of time.

Gradually, as I was seeking to put order into the seeming chaos by identifying just which societies were involved in the phenomenon, I began to understand that here was a cultural complex that the ancient hunter-gatherers did not just know about but of course must have invented eons ago. It became apparent that the Lascaux Cave shaman was only the most ancient example we had been able to find of the pictorial or sculptural representation of an important feature of ancient religious rituals, of a way to establish contact with another dimension of reality. It was then brought to full flowering by the horticulturalists, the hunter-gardeners that followed the hunter-gatherers and who gave us so many telling representations of the postures in their art.

For important cultural reasons, there was an occasional crossover between distant cultural types, as in the case of the Lascaux Cave shaman, the hunter, to the Egyptian agriculturalists' god Osiris, illuminating some historical accident, but these instances were relatively rare. Instead, a few postures remained for various reasons the exclusive property of the hunters in the course of historical development, while others passed on to the horticulturalists and there were retained unaltered, as happened, for instance, in the case of the Bear Spirit (Chapter 8) or the Singing Shaman (Chapter 11). Or new ones were enthusiastically elaborated, as in the case of those leading to metamorphosis (Chapter 10). The entire complex vanished with the advent of full-scale agriculture. This insight was very useful; it meant that we were not facing the almost unmanageable task of searching all the records of art, but had to consider only those found in these types of societies.

However, despite the obvious antiquity of the postures, what made work with them so enjoyable from the start was the fact that they mediated experiences that we moderns could relate to. It was easy to celebrate with the Singing Shaman, to go on a spirit journey with other postures, or to open up to healing. One reason, as I saw it, was that we still possessed the same nervous system as those humans that lived so long ago. So basically, although surely not as masterfully, we could do what they were able to accomplish. The other reason was that horticulturalists were cousins to the agriculturalists, from whom we descended. But there were two postures, one that apparently had never made it into horticulture and another one that did, where the cultural gap was so pronounced that when we tried them, we felt like strangers in a strange land.

One of these postures was that of *Bone Pointing* (pl. 4), mentioned briefly in Chapter 2. It is an Australian posture which for obvious geographic reasons could not spread outward from there. The aboriginal societies practicing it believe that only the deaths of young children and of the old are due to natural causes. When mature adults die, it is as a result of murder by "magical" means. Bone pointing is used to take revenge on the murderer by hitting him with an invisible but deadly missile.

In order to carry out this execution, the avenging shaman folds his right leg under him, while his left leg is upright and bent at the knee. His left hand holds the bone, with his arm resting against his left knee, and his right hand touches his left wrist and serves for sighting. My participants, who were generally unaware of the ethnographic context, usually experienced a tremendous flow of energy which seemed to come from the earth, course through their bodies, and explode out of the end of the stick they were holding in lieu of the bone. Othmar, of the 1984 Scheibbs group, related,

> It was amazing how my left hand kept vibrating more and more as if supercharged with energy. Then that stopped, and I saw a small tree with its branches hanging down. They had slender thorns on them. To the left of the tree there was a small being, something like a dwarf, who remained motionless. The landscape was that of a steppe; the ground was brown, and there was a puddle of water which reflected a white skeleton. In the distance, the grass was burning, animals fled by me, and then I saw a man, but only his legs. Then I saw the tree again.

In this experience, Othmar did not just conduct the energy but was himself the invisible spear that emerged through the stick, the surrogate bone, and went in search of his victim. The Australian landscape is surprisingly complete—the color of the plain, the grass fire, even down to the puddle of a water hole and the thorny vegetation—except that it is the Australian outback in the alternate reality, as indicated by the motionless dwarf and the skeleton reflected in the water, foreshadowing the deadly intent. However, Othmar does not have murder on his mind, so when he comes upon his quarry, the attack is aborted; he sees only the legs. Whoever it was he encountered remains unharmed, and he is taken back to the tree. No wonder that Franz, who did the posture several times, eventually refused to repeat it, as he said, because he was afraid that he "might do too much," that is, actually carry out the aggressive act and hurt someone in the alternate reality. We know of many societies where it is believed that such injury can cause illness and even death in ordinary reality.

Plate 6

The second hunter's posture is one frequently represented. Once we started looking for it, we found traces of it on the Northwest Coast (pl. 6), pecked out on rocks in California (pl. 7a), painted on a jar in Cochiti Pueblo (pl. 7b), and cut into a menhir in Sweden (pl. 7c). It was known in prehistoric times in Florida and Peru, in the Sahara, in New Guinea and islands of the South Pacific. Gerhard Binder, an artist from Austria and the illustrator of this volume, and I explored it one summer in Cuyamungue.

The posture involves standing with legs apart and knees somewhat bent, although some stick figures also stand straight, which was what we elected to do to make things easier on ourselves. The arms are raised to shoulder height; the elbows are bent, so that the lower arms are nearly at right angles to the upper arms; and the fingers are spread.

The following is my journal entry:

> Cuyamungue, 29 August 1985
> This morning after the sunrise ritual we decided to go to the kiva for a session. We had not done anything for several days, and felt that special yearning of wanting to "go home." I suggested that we do that petroglyph posture that looks almost like a child's drawing in its simple directness, and which neither one of us had tried before. I had taped my rattling, so I was also able to participate.
> After the breathing I turned on the tape, assumed the posture, and closed my eyes expectantly. But as soon as the rattle sound started, the tape began behaving so outlandishly that I thought that either the recorder was malfunctioning or the batteries had gone berserk. First the signal was extremely loud and fast, then it slowed down and became almost inaudible, and from then on it kept going up and down like a roller coaster. I wanted to turn toward the tape recorder to see what was going on, but found myself frozen in the posture and unable to move. Finally, the tape settled down, but by that time, the fifteen minutes were nearly over. I had a searing pain in the shoulders which later dissolved. I had not seen anything, but felt as if I consisted of nothing but enormous hot, radiating palms.

Gerhard had also heard the tape acting strangely and described exactly what I had heard, but since he did not feel responsible for the equipment, he simply screened it out, and concentrated on his experience instead:

> The sound of the rattle started off with a bang. A line passed through my body; there was power that entered into my hands. My hands started getting bigger, and that power flowed through them. I felt that I was passing over into a simpler form; a round hole opened in me that reached down to the ground. Then I became amorphous. A sheaf appeared; I embraced it with tremendous force. It was very

bright, yellow, then turned bluish-white. I fell on the ground with it in my arms and rolled on and on over the stubbles on a field that I knew from my childhood. It used to be a field, it isn't anymore. The sound of the rattle was very loud, like a tremendous roll of thunder, and I seemed to be making powerful sounds myself. At that point I started turning toward you. I can still feel it in my belly how strongly my energies were stimulated.

The feeling that we had experienced something extraordinary persisted throughout the day. My hands felt like sieves; they were leaking my life force, energy, I didn't know exactly what.

In the evening, we were sitting in the Student Building, and Gerhard was working on a choker of porcupine quills. I had spotted the animal on the shoulder of the highway near the Mescalero Indian reservation some time back. It probably had been hit by a car and was still warm when I pulled out its quills. I used them later to make necklaces for my marionettes. There were some trimmed quills left over when Gerhard had finished the choker, so I said, "Keep those, too, really, I can always get more." I had no idea how; I had not seen any porcupines in our area.

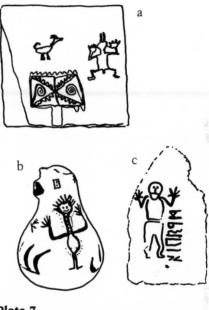

Plate 7

We both felt the urgent need to get some answers about the puzzling posture, so we decided to do the posture of the *Tennessee diviner* (see Chapter 7) before sunup the following day. I woke up before my alarm sounded, and as I lay quietly in my sleeping bag, looking up at the paling stars, I heard a curious sound, "Swush, swush, swush, swush," rhythmical and persistent. Finally it became softer and then fell silent. I was sure there was no insect that sang that way. It was not until I imitated the sound for Gerhard that I realized that I had heard my own rattle. We had had forerunner experiences around here before, where the perception anticipates the event often by an hour or more, so it wasn't so startling, but it still seemed to signal the dawn of a special day.

We went to the kiva, painted our faces as required in this posture, and then assumed it. I had injured my left knee months earlier, but it no longer gave me any trouble. However, unaccountably it now started hurting unbearably. In agony, I tried to change the posture, but at that moment, I reared up and I *was* a wounded animal. It was an unbelievably strong experience, that rearing up, the very pinnacle of ecstasy. Then an overwhelming force pushed me down and I collapsed.

Gerhard had worn the cap of the Tennessee diviner, which I had recreated and which tends to sharpen the images (see pl. 12), and as a result his experience was even more elaborate than usual:

> The cap seemed to make my skull transparent. I saw a bright light when the rattle started and had to turn my head to the right. The kiva had an exit in the back. I was brightly illuminated from the back. Then it turned dark again and I could see myself. That picture dissolved and I asked my question. At the exit the stickman appeared in the posture we had done, except that he had his legs apart and his knees bent. Simultaneously, the sound of the rattle changed. The figure glowed brightly and was gay and pleasant. I climbed into it from the back. In front of me everything was brightly lit, behind me it was dark, and I as the figure was the partition. It all felt very positive, as though I were being saturated with sun energy.
>
> Then I stepped out of the figure, again toward the back. I saw a sphere, and I climbed into that and was being propelled forward like a bubble. I stood on the summit of a mountain and kept calling, "Grandfather Bear, Grandfather Bear." He came and treated me by scratching the inside of my mouth and the nape of my neck. Then the stick figure appeared again; there was a lot of light, but I didn't know if it was day or night. I asked the same question once more and was given to understand that the hunter needed the posture, it was completely clear at the moment why, but now I don't remember it anymore. Then everything turned grey. I was in a teepee at sunrise. An old Indian sat in the tent; he had sparkling eyes, and he wore an animal skin, the skin of a buffalo. Together, we looked out into the dawn. A rug covered the floor of the teepee, once more showing the stick figure, which glowed. He said that he would tell me a story, but then the rattle stopped.

When we stepped out of the kiva, the sky was still pale. The moon had sent all the stars to bed and was making ready to retire herself, but the sun had not yet risen. With Kizzie, my German shepherd, joining us as always, we walked up to the ridge to speak the morning's blessing. Kizzie behaves perfectly during such rituals; she never jumps up on anybody and does not beg to have her ball thrown. She just settles down patiently, her front paws crossed, and waits until we are done. This morning, however, she was restless. She went over the edge of the hill, stopped by a juniper bush down a ways on the other side, and started to growl, her hackles raised. Curious, we followed her, and there under the bush, nearly hidden by the branches, sat a porcupine. It was completely motionless, and as silly as this may sound, I swear it was grinning at us.

I grabbed Kizzie by her collar to save her from harm, for although porcupines do not shoot their quills at attackers as popularly believed, even a sniff at the animal's armor might have turned her snout into a pin cushion. So I took her with me up on the ridge, spoke the blessing, and scattered the meal offering, and then we went down and were afraid to look back for fear that the engaging miracle we had seen would be there no longer. And indeed, when Gerhard went back at noon, the porcupine was gone. Had it been there? We had seen it, but then, we might still have been in a residual trance. However, it was Kizzie who had discovered the animal. What had happened?

Porcupines are no strangers to the Southwest, and being animals that feed mainly at night, it was understandable that I had not seen one on my land before. But the question was, why had it appeared at that particular spot on that particular morning? Going back over what we had experienced, I think that the hunters' posture that we had assumed was one designed to call the animals. We both had stimulated our bodies in trance and broadcast our call through our palms, as an antenna radiates microwaves, so powerfully that it even sent the tape recorder reeling. And we had given shape and direction to that energy by handling the porcupine quills. Perhaps if it had been a deer tail, it would have been picked up by that animal. The porcupine answered our summons, and since it was willing to sacrifice itself, it was probably bewildered and pleasantly surprised that it did not end up on our spit.

Of course, there was, as always, a great deal more that we were taught. For in the trance, we were both hunter and hunted. Gerhard the hunter embraced the sheaf of grain that he had cut as a stand-in for the game and rolled on the earth with it. But Gerhard the kill had a hole in his body and was reduced to a simpler form, and then to the ephemeral state of spirit substance. When we asked the wise old man from Tennessee for clarification by assuming his divining posture, he patiently went over our experience. The wounded animal passes through the ecstasy of dying, he seemed to be saying. The hunter is the partition; before him is the light of life, behind him the darkness of death. But there is renewal of life in the healing power of the mighty Bear. That was the message, as full and round and complete as the bubble that Gerhard stepped into. But the rattle continued on, and our forbearing teacher started the explanation over again, using different imagery this time. In the teepee the stick figure glows on the rug: you see, above it is light, below it one sinks into the darkess of the earth. "We hear you," we are tempted to answer.

Anyone who has read ethnographies of hunter societies[4] cannot help but be struck by how genuine these two trance experiences feel, except that they take us a step further, into the secret heart of the hunter. And indeed I am sometimes asked whether it is not an inadmissible intrusion into occulted secret worlds not our own when we imitate these ancient postures. Obviously, the Spirits do not think so, or they would not have invited us into their world. But these questioners do not know enough history either. For we are not intruding: we are merely trying to find our way home. Once, very long ago, our ancestors were equally hunter-gatherers, part of their habitat instead of its destroyers. Later, someplace along the way, we went wrong and we closed the door on this gentle ancient world. We started conquering the habitat, first by the plow and then by science. That was the Fall. As D. H. Lawrence says in speaking of the Hopi Snake Dance,

> We have undertaken the scientific conquest of forces, of natural conditions. It has been comparatively easy, and we are victors. . . . The Hopi sought the conquest by means of the mystic, living will that is in man, pitted against the will of the dragon-cosmos. . . . We have made a partial conquest by other means. Our corn doesn't fail us: we have no seven years' famine, and apparently need never have. But the other thing fails us, the strange inward sun of life. . . . To us, heaven switches on daylight, or turns on the shower-bath. We little gods are gods of the machine only. It is our highest. Our cosmos is a great engine. And we die of *ennui*. (1934:77)

What D. H. Lawrence could not foresee in 1934 was that in addition to dying of boredom, we may also perish in a nuclear holocaust. Perhaps the secret of the postures was revealed by design. Along with so many other new movements that we see all around us, going in the same direction toward "the strange inward sun of life," it may be one more attempt to turn us around. To that purpose, it seems to me, the postures are uniquely suited. They take us to strange and beautiful worlds. They teach us to divine, to heal, and to celebrate. They comfort us and soothe our fears, better than any of our scientific achievements. And they thrill us with ever-renewed, never-predictable adventure, adding the very stuff of miracles to a modern existence that all too often is drab and unappealing.

Plate 8

Postscript. After the completion of this manuscript, I received copies of two examples of aboriginal and/or folk art, which in the most surprising way confirm our experiences with the porcupine. The first one is a petroglyph composition from South Africa (Holm, fig. 28). A tall shaman, his arms raised in the characteristic manner, is surrounded by a massive school of fish. The heads of most of the fish point in his direction. To the left beyond the fish there are seven small boats, each one manned by a fisherman armed with a long spear, aiming at the fish. One fish has been speared, and the fisherman is making ready to pull it into his boat.

The second picture (pl. 8) is a wall painting from Saora, in the Koraput district of Orissa, India. In Saora, it is customary to hire masters of the art of *Ittal* painting, to paint pictures with rice starch on the clay walls of the houses.

This is done to honor the dead, to conjure up spirits, and as protection against bad luck. Before the master begins his work, he deposits before the picture wall the present he has received for his spirit, so that in a dream the spirit will reveal the subject of the painting. Once the picture is completed, the spirit will through a medium in trance reveal whether it accepts the painting, or whether there are still corrections to be made. Once more, as in the case of the petroglyph from South Africa, there is a close, unmistakable association between the hunters in the "porcupine" posture and the game. All the hunters are shown in this posture. One hunter carries a bow, another one a gun, and they have killed a large reptile, an equally impressive cat, a deer, and several smaller hoofed animals.

Section II

THE POSTURES AND WHAT THEY HAVE TO OFFER

CHAPTER SIX

Going on
a Spirit Journey

What happens on a spirit journey? People fly away on birds' wings, peacock clouds spread their shimmering tail feathers, a woman with stars in her hair guards the entrance to the world below, and humans turned into albatrosses alight on the waves of the ocean. These are some of the tales people tell when they come back. There are several postures that are specifically designed to take us either to the sky, to the middle world where humans live, to the lower world, or out to sea. Although brief sallies or "out-of-body experiences" also happen frequently during other postures, those described below have proved to be the ones needed for a prolonged trip.

The Lascaux Cave shaman's posture. How we happened to try the posture, I told briefly in Chapter 2. Let me recapitulate briefly how it is done. You lie down comfortably on the slanted board (37-degree angle), your legs together, and letting your feet spread apart naturally. Somewhat bent at the elbow, your right arm is placed on the board a few inches away from your body in a leisurely fashion. As a result, your right hand rests on its outside edge, and your thumb is up. Although also resting on the board, your left arm is tensed by contrast, very straight, and your left hand is turned so that its back is turned toward your body, and your thumb is stretched stiffly down. You close your eyes, and you are ready to go.

Since the posture requires a support inclined at thirty-seven degrees, some friends have constructed single boards for themselves inclined at the proper angle and find that it works quite well. But the setup is difficult to procure, and so we cannot always do it during workshops. At Cuyamungue, I had individual boards made that can be hooked onto a stand. We can even move the stands outside, and do the exercise under the blue sky of New Mexico, which makes it very special. In Scheibbs the Buddhist Center had several stands and large rectangular plates that could be assembled when needed. They called the setup Felicitas's launching pad, and it was often the subject of light-hearted levity on the part of novices. As we were gathering for the session a few years ago, one of our participants, a psychologist with the Austrian state mental institution at Gugging, decided to try out the "launching pad" by standing on his head on the footrest. During the session, he of course had his feet down like everyone else. He turned into a bird during the trance, and started happily flying around—but belly up.

In many societies, a spirit journey to the sky is considered to be initiatory; the shaman "dies" during his initiation flight and is "reborn" upon returning. In abbreviated form, this is an experience reported by many who take the trip. Soon after the trance is induced, as if in the agony of death, the trancers experience being split or opened: "I broke in half," or "My belly opened up and there was a gaping hole," or "A flap opened at the top of my head." Frequently after considerable struggle, a being emerges like a butterfly from the chrysalis: The trancers give birth to themselves. "It was as if somebody was pressing me out, like a pea out of a pod," or "I was covered by a black box, there was a light toward the top, and I wanted to get out through that spot. Finally I got out and flew low over the land." This new form of one's being is usually associated with birds: "At the first rattle sound, I saw a huge bird," or "I sat in a tree among hundreds of small birds that were all twittering away, the way your rattle sound seems to twitter." Or what emerges is or becomes a bird or a birdlike being. It will be recalled that, entirely in keeping with such experiences, in the cave drawing the stick figure wears a bird mask, and the stave next to him is crowned by a bird. As Eva D. (Scheibbs, 1983) recalled:

> There was a large bird above me, but I was not that bird. It grabbed me with its talons and flew around with me for the longest time; it was fantastically beautiful. But then I wanted to fly all by myself, and it let go of me. I was very small, more like a woodpecker, and being released produced a tremendous physical reaction, making me twirl downward in very tight circles.

Not everyone goes through all the phases of the experience. The entrance especially is often given short shrift during retelling. As one participant said, "It just went too fast, I don't remember much of it." I recall the same rapid transition from my own first spirit journey, which was, by the way, a rather humiliating affair. I did not experience leaving my body at all. I just found myself a fledgling on wobbly wings aiming directly at a tall rosy wall and thinking all the while, "I really must lose those extra pounds!" Luckily the rattle stopped before I came in for a crash landing. The experience of actually flying is so novel that there is confusion: "I saw a tiny rabbit on the ground and couldn't figure out why it was getting bigger." Others take it in their stride, reporting as a matter of course that they saw large brown mountains down in the distance, or other features of the landscape.

The most impressive spirit journey in this posture is the one that takes people up into the blue sky and beyond (as happened to Ingrid in the TV program):

> ISI (Cuyamnungue, 1986): I was afraid because I was feeling so light, and that I would lose touch with the ground. But by that time it had already happened, and I was in the sky. I saw on the ground below me the shadow of a big bird, and when I moved, the shadow moved too, so I knew that I was that bird. I kept somersaulting backward through the clouds, and saw behind them lots of peacocks, spreading their tail feathers. I kept going higher and higher, I couldn't stop. Finally I arrived at a star, it was really a door, and there was a bright light behind it. I went through the door and saw a sculpture, but it had no head. There was a lot of light all around; people were dancing, and they all seemed very happy.

Spontaneously, and without any prior information, Isi in this case experienced what Australian shamans relate, namely, that after climbing the rainbow up into the sky, one arrives at a door and, upon entering it, is in the company of spirits. Such unexpected emergence of myth fragments during a trance is quite frequent. In fact, there are so many such fragments reported all the time that if they are not identified, it is probably simply because we are unfamiliar with them.

That the statue that Isi saw had no head is another example of this fact. Hunter and especially horticulturalist traditions hold that if humans see the true countenance of a spirit, they die. That is why spirits wear masks. There is a faint memory of this also in European myths, especially in classical Greece, which is still very close to its horticulturalist roots. There is a story of a love affair between Zeus, the father god, and a mortal girl called Semele. Semele nags Zeus; she wants to see his true face. When Zeus finally relents, he appears as fire and she burns to death.

Or take the motif of the miraculous egg seen by another participant. Mircea Eliade, the venerable father of shamanic studies, quotes a Siberian Yakut story,[1] according to which the Bird-of-Prey Mother, which has the head of an eagle and iron feathers, lights on a giant fir tree, the Tree of the World. There she lays a number of eggs, from which she hatches the shamans. The following experience is reminiscent of this legend:

> BENTE (Cuyamungue, 1986): I was slow starting out, then I began spinning through the universe and did not know where I was. A voice said, "I will tell you a story about children." I was sitting in a nest, and when I pushed a button, a maypole rose out of it. From it streamed guardians, in strands of many colors, who formed a cocoon, like a wasps' nest. It opened and a little white slippery dove came out. She began flying toward the sun, and she dried up as she was flying. The sun touched her heart and her belly. She returned to the solar system, laid an

egg, it opened, and a new earth emerged. The earth was very green, and hundreds of children played on it, children of the sun.

A spirit journey does not always take the participant up into the sky, however; it may traverse the middle world of humans instead:

ANN D. (Cuyamungue, 1986): I went out through my left thumb, which I felt was very powerful. I did not leave the kiva right away; I hovered over you first, Cynthia, and patted your hair, then I hovered over Krissie. I tried to find Darlene [another participant] but did not see her. So I thought maybe I should go look for my parents, but there was this voice that said, "Don't, they don't need any protection." So I decided to try and find my friend Jeffie. She was in great pain; I hovered over her, trying to touch her, but could not, so I tried to envelop her to comfort her. But I could not stay with her; I knew my time was almost up. So I turned back, but my thumb had collapsed in the meantime. I was in panic, I thought it was broken. I kept rolling over and over in the air, trying to think of a way of how to straighten out my thumb. All my concentration went into that one thing: how to straighten out my thumb so that I would be able to get back into my body. Finally, only four beats before you stopped rattling, I was able to straighten it out and slipped back in.

Ann had to tolerate a great deal of good-natured ribbing about her thumb later, and we took a picture of her contemplating the offending digit.

Although encountering one's spirit guide is usually experienced in the lower world, it can happen during the trip to the upper world, too. Thus Ewald (Scheibbs, 1985) once more came upon his little Dragon:

As soon as you started rattling, I took off through the window, like a jet engine. But instead of going up, I tumbled down into a hole full of snakes. There was a witch's broom; I took that and fled through the door, and there was my Dragon. We started playing ping-pong together, and I saw you rattling, but your head was that of a white horse.

Lukas (Scheibbs, 1985), a physician, could not avoid his friend the Bear Spirit, the mighty healer, who had taken a liking to him:

I felt effervescent, as though I were becoming gaseous. My third eye popped open, and the Bear appeared. He nodded to me, saying, "Come along." So I went with him and came to a clearing in the forest. I lay down and saw above me a bright spot. I flew away into that, still feeling the prickling sensation, as though I were boiling all over.

And Yolanda (Cuyamungue, 1984), at home in the Swiss Alps, was accompanied on her trip by her Eagle:

My head split open and a spring of water issued from it. Then I felt something pulling me, and when I looked up, there was the Eagle holding me in his arms, and I felt his wonderfully soft, fluffy breast feathers. I did not want to fly, so we

Plate 9

walked up the side of a mountain hand in hand and came to the entrance of a cave. We went in, and I saw a hole in the ceiling, and through it the sky, the world, so much brightness. So we flew through that hole. The Eagle had such enormous wings; I felt embraced by those wings and touched once more by his soft breast feathers. Then I became transparent and flew away on my own.

In my notes about this session, there is the following entry: "While rattling, and of course having no idea what it was Yolanda was experiencing, I saw an eagle feather fluttering down beside her. When I tried to look closer, I saw only her shoes."

By the way, being carried away by a huge bird is frequently reported in this posture, and the motif often occurs in ancient art, too. Yolanda's experience, for instance, agrees closely with the one worked into a gold pitcher by an artist at the time the Hungarians entered their present homeland in the Danube Valley about a thousand years ago (see pl. 9).

Spirit Journey to the Lower World

The lower world offers a much more variegated range of experiences than the sky world. It is a realm as rich as the entire human universe, with its landscapes and towns, its animals and plants, its history, memories, and myths, its many spirits, and its dead. Just like the sky, it is a real world in which the traveler does not only see and act but is also observed and acted upon. Gerhard B. tells of lying supine in a cave, with an eagle sitting on his naked belly, looking him over. And Jackie was carried through the jungle by a troop of ants that made ready to eat her and were disappointed when at the stop of the rattle she escaped.

In many parts of the world, in Siberia, Australia, and South America, the lower world is a place where healing is taught,[2] or where the shamans descend in order to retrieve lost souls, also a curing strategy. In our work with the postures, we found healing to be more broadly based. It can take place in a number of different postures, as we shall see, and it is principally a gift of the greatest of all healers, Grandfather Bear (see Chapter 8).

A Sami (Lapp) posture. A drawing of the posture used by these nomadic reindeer herders of northern Europe was published in Germany in 1673 (pl. 10). The shaman lies prone on the ground. His arms are stretched out above his head, with his right hand reaching somewhat farther than his left. His feet are crossed at the ankles, with his right foot on top of his left. His drum, on which he "rides" to the lower world, is on his back, its handle up, covering most of his head. An assistant provides the drumbeat for his trip. We had no drum of the right size and shape for this posture and ended up simulating it with a wreath of cottonwood boughs or with a pillow. I also believe that the designs on the drum of both the shaman and his assistant, as well as the shaman's garment, have an important role to play in guiding the traveler. We should remember that those are not just haphazardly applied "symbols," a favorite buzzword of Western observers. They are all revealed in trance, and instead of symbols, they are what we might think of as "holes," entranceways into the other reality. However, those were elements we could not supply.

Despite our incomplete rendition of the Sami spirit journey complex, it still mediated a very intense experience. "I must have gone very deep down,"

Plate 10

I wrote in my field record. The following is Barbara's account (Cuyamungue, 1985):

> The images started coming as soon as I assumed the posture, even before you started rattling. I was in a beautiful landscape, similar to the land around here. There was a wall stretching for miles and an adobe house with a door. As I watched, a black insect crawled out of it, then another one. They were followed by an antelope, and then by many dark-skinned people wearing ornaments on their ankles. Ahead of me, there was a dirt road. I followed it and saw the legs of many light-skinned people. A brightly illuminated human figure came toward me. It startled me, and the figure disappeared. I looked up, and above me I saw a beautiful opening into the sky.

When we did this posture in the Netherlands in 1987, almost everyone in that workshop, obviously for important cultural reasons, ended up having something to do with water, as if they had all been taken by charter bus to the same region in the lower world. "I saw nothing; there was only the noise of golden raindrops," was one report; or "I heard water dripping as in a cave, and there were mushrooms growing out of me"; or "There was an intensely bubbling small waterfall, and through it I saw the sun with tiny rays." And according to another one, "I found myself in water, and felt that I was sinking. Then I started swimming like a dolphin." And according to still another one, "I was in the sea, and saw a big animal. It came from below, and I saw its huge spine." Claudia's report was more elaborate (Utrecht, 1987):

> I felt my head getting very heavy, as if there were too much blood in it, and I had problems with breathing. I was a fish, or maybe a whale, very big and massive, and I was swimming in the sea. Before that, I saw a waterfall; there were salmons jumping, and I had fire in my hands. But my hands were not hands; they were completely out of shape.

Other groups scatter, having many different adventures as soon as they reach the lower world, as did the one in Vienna in the spring of 1987. The trancers still sometimes encounter water, although it does not predominate as it does with the Dutch. Thus we hear from Thomas: "As I listen to the rattle, I feel a prickling sensation under my [simulated] drum, and a force is penetrating from above into my body. A wind comes up, and there is a chorus of voices. A curtain is raised, and I am floating above a forest. There is a spring; I dip my fingers into it, and the water feels cool and fresh. I also drink from it. Then I knew that I had to get into the mountain." Or from Isi: "I slipped out from under the drum and slid into the ground, which felt more like water. I saw a a white transparent woman, and she asked me, 'What do you want?' I couldn't think of anything, but suddenly I was floating in the sky and didn't know what was up and what was down." This Viennese group was relatively large, so we added a drum to the rattle, and for some participants the sound of the drum became the dominating stimulus: "The drum ordered me to leave my body. It was very commanding, so I did leave and wondered what I was supposed to do next.''

Animals predominated in the lower world. Sometimes they joined the visitor as companions: "As I arrived below, a hyena joined me and guided me to a cave full of crystals. This was the place where the philosophers' stone was stored, but the hyena said they had no use for it, because they were animals." Or "A raven flew by, and I wanted to fly with it. We flew toward some mountain peaks; they were black, like in the fairytale about the seven ravens." In other instances, the travelers turned into animals themselves: "I was running around on all fours, wondering what on earth I had turned into now. I killed a deer and started feeding on it, but I was not vicious." Or they retained their human shape and wandered about, like curious tourists:

> Sep: I stood on my head, and that way I slipped into the ground. The path led downward, and the noise was always ahead of me. I stumbled over a worm; it was soft and pulled me down into the depths. I ended up in a passageway like in a mine and then arrived in a cave that was a smithy; I could smell coal and iron in the steam.

Or somewhat more ethereally:

> Rosemarie: I fly up to the moon sickle, and on it, I slip down into the swampy earth. I am a being of light and am dancing in the city. There are trees, and I watch them as they are marching out of town while distorted masks stream in.

South American Indian posture. Because of the various difficulties with the intricacies of the Sami posture, we have more experience with a simpler one, suggested by Michael Harner,[3] who presumably saw it used by some of the South American Indian shamans who taught him. The participants lie flat on the floor, face up. The right arm is positioned loosely by the side of the body; the left arm is placed on the forehead in such a way that neither the elbow nor the hand touches the floor. Care must be taken that the forearm puts no pressure on the eyes. As in all postures, the eyes are closed. (See pl. 11.)

With this posture, some people simply find themselves below as soon as the rattling starts. Most of the time, however, there is a clear perception of turbulence at the entrance to the lower world. I was startled when I saw it for the first time: "The entire world was swirling in a massive whirlpool before my eyes," I wrote. It was quite frightening. There is an incident in the Navajo emergence story[4] where the people have fled from the rising floodwaters up into the fifth world, and then, looking down the hole, they see the turbulent water welling and churning below, and they are sorely troubled.

The entrance to the lower world may assume many other shapes also. It may be a cave, and some women see its opening as having the shape of a vulva. For another woman, it was a giant flower. "It had soft petals, and there was a fragrance all about. Further down, it got sticky and dark." An Austrian participant came to a hollow old tree, and there was a girl with stars in her hair sitting at the entrace to the way down. Franz liked to look for "his" bridge.

Once, he told, he could not find it: "I finally decided to visualize it, and it promptly appeared. At the end of it, there was a dark spot, *and then came the real bridge.*" I like to use this example when I am asked about the differ-ence between visualization and a vision of the alternate reality. A visualized image is your own creation; a vision comes about when you see what is "out there," the al-ternate part of reality.

Plate 11

The way down may lead over a slanting highway, down a flight of stairs, or very frequently through a chute, a tunnel, or a similar passage-way. Going down is hardly ever accomplished by simply walking. Some ooze over the earth, "like chocolate," somebody said, or sink into it. There are those who float gently on a magic carpet or a pillow. Others somersault backward and then slip, slide, or tumble downward. Many feel that they are caught in a whirlpool. This is not always comfortable, as we hear in the following account from Judy Ch. (Columbus, Ohio, 1985):

> I felt extreme discomfort, and my arm on my forehead went numb. I heard sounds of spinning, and then I myself was also spinning around in a spiral, rotating faster and faster. I was going in a circle like the clothes in a washing mashine. Then I was in a clothes washer, going round and round and hurting all over. I was glad when it was over.

Clearly, Judy never made it down into the lower world in this session, but her pain dissolved with the last beat of the rattle. She laughed with us about her misadventure in the washing machine, and she has been to the lower world uneventfully several times since, although sometimes feeling "like a dull drill bit."

Once down, the travelers pass through fog or, more often, water. Fre-quently, arrival involves a boat ride, like that taken by the recently dead in Greek myth. "I saw bright circles of light," one told. "I felt a pull in my legs and arrived someplace where there were many dark birds, and I found myself in a boat that was being rowed by somebody." Or "I was in a boat and was slowly traveling into infinity." And "I was lying in a canoe and drifted along. Then I fell headfirst into black water."

Coming back up again is recounted relatively rarely. There are a few reports of floating upward, guided by the sound of the rattle, of suddenly seeing a hole above, or of being back in the kiva and its roof opening up. Some accomplish their reemergence gracefully, as when Fritz E., having assumed the shape of a great white owl, saw the moon through a hole in the rock wall and flew through it into the night sky. But for many travelers the fifteen minutes seem too brief for the journey through the lower world, and they are not quite ready yet to come back when the time is up. Thus there are those who are caught by the cessation of the rattle signal in the midst of preparing for the trip back. Thomas, for instance, had been riding all over that strange world ready yet to come back when the time is up. Thus there are those who are caught by the cessation of the rattle signal in the midst of preparing for the trip back. Thomas, for instance, had been riding all over that strange world sitting on a horse, but facing backward, a situation often described in European folklore. Shortly before the rattle stopped, "something suddenly put me on the horse facing forward." Or in another account, a girl had been hiking about without a head, and when it came time to leave, she put her head back on.

Others do experience emerging, but it is difficult and has to be tried several times, as when Ann B. (Cuyamungue, 1986) tells how, after having turned into an eagle and exploring the lower world,

> I flew into the mountain, and then I was the mountain, I was a dormant volcano storing up energy. Then I erupted, streaming out of the mountain as red energy. Then I was in the mountain again; I erupted, and I was a flame dancing on the rim of the mountain, faster and faster, as the rattle became faster and faster, and I had to watch where I danced, so I would not fall back in again. [By the way, I always keep the rattle signal constant: that it was speeding up was her perception.]

In this posture, too, fragments of folklore keep bobbing up. Thus, in one of Grimm's fairytales,[5] a girl drops her spindle into a well. Afraid that her stepmother will punish her if she loses it, she jumps into the well and finds herself near an oven, where the loaves of bread are done and call out to her, begging her to take them out. She does and later hires herself out to Frau Holle, a principal Germanic deity, whose presence marks the place where she arrived at the bottom of the well as the magical lower world. Ann B. (Cuyamungue, 1986) obviously ended up at the same spot:

> The ground began to shake, then it opened and I fell through, into a world that was green and dark, and there was a fluorescent light everywhere. I went around,

exploring, and came to an oven. I opened it, and the bread inside was done, so I ate some of it.

Those familiar with Greek mythology[6] will in the following tale instantly recognize the entrance to Tartarus, complete with its brooding shadows and its cold fog. Only Hugh (Cuyamungue, 1986) was met not by Charon, the miser who used to ferry the Greek ghosts across the river Styx, but by the generous White Buffalo:

> I was at a cold place; the air was foggy, and there was a dark and eerie light. A White Buffalo was with me, and he came with me when I entered into a boat. On the other side the ground was different, it wasn't solid. I met all sorts of relatives and especially my father. He turned into a bear and we danced, but I felt very cold, so he took me to a fire in a rocky grove, and I began feeling warmer. We danced around the fire, but real slow. Then the White Buffalo came, and we went back.

Here are a few examples of complete reports from this posture. In the first one, the traveler did not make it to her destination, although many different beings, birds, a weeping willow, gnomes, and fish, tried to show her the way:

> MICHELLE (Vienna, 1985): I felt the ground vibrating under me. I became liquid and spread out over the earth. I felt a hot liquid in my abdomen; it opened up, and a golden being rose from it. There were birds above me, and to the left, far above, there was a black hole. It sucked in the birds, but I could not get there. Behind me, I saw a weeping willow; it waved to me. Tiny gnomes emerged from it, and they began dancing on me; it was wonderful. They disappeared in the black hole, too. Then I was in the water; the black hole was the gaping mouth of a fish. Many fish swam toward that black hole. I think I could also have gotten there, but the rattle stopped.

Both here and also abroad, American Indians are often seen in the lower world, as told in this report:

> ELIZABETH R. (Columbus, Ohio, 1985): My face became warm, and I heard a flapping as of wings. I relaxed into that sound and changed into an eagle and was sitting in a tree. There was an Indian family under the tree, a father, a mother, and a small daughter. I flew down to them, and the child gave me part of her meal. In exchange, I gave her one of my feathers, which she stuck in her hair. Then I flew up into the mountains and turned into myself. I came upon an old Indian. He wore traditional Indian clothes; he was small and had snow-white hair, and I instantly fell in love with him. He gave me a necklace made of large green and blue stones. He then took me to the water, and I took off my clothes and stepped in, and it was very cold. He poured cold water over me; I had the feeling that it was a kind of initiation. Then he let me come out of the water, and he wrapped me in furs. There was a brown bear fishing in the water; he gave the old Indian one of the fish. It was night by then. The old Indian made a fire, fried the fish,

and we ate the fish together, and I felt blessed, very grateful, and I began to cry. I asked the old Indian about the pain in my neck. So the Indian and the bear began pulling and shaking me and said that I would be okay. I told them that I did not want to leave, but they said that I would come back again, and that there really was not all that much separation between our two worlds. Then I changed back into an eagle and came flying back, very reluctantly.

Guatemaltecan Indian shamans contend that they possess among their several souls one that is the healer, and during diagnosis and healing this soul enters the patient's body much like the spirit does during a spirit journey. I was aware of this, but it was still startling to hear it being told by a physician in Austria, half a world away, who knew nothing of Central American shamans. Susanna (Vienna, 1985) had not felt well during the session of the previous day, and I did not expect to see her back. But she did come again, and this is what she experienced in this posture:

> I felt the rattle jumping up and down in my belly, and then its beat spread out in waves. Suddenly a tiny green man appeared before me, holding a spear. He jumped into my belly and wandered all about in my body. When he got to my heart, he stuck his spear into it. That felt very good; he had let out all the old air. Then he arrived at my navel and seemed to be pondering what to do next. He slipped out through my navel and became as tall as I. He started wrestling with me, shaking me real aggressively. Then he grabbed hold of my hair from the back and swung me back and forth. He appeared before me, bowed down, then stroked my body from all sides. Then he spread out his arms, gathered up the light, and I found myself floating in that light when the rattle stopped.

While Susanna was given a treatment for what she felt was a bodily ill during her trip to the lower world, Adolf was taught during this spirit journey how to cope with a severe psychological problem, his dread of aging. We all noticed from the start that he had what at first simply seemed like an aversion to elderly women like me, but it soon became obvious that although he was a man in his forties, he was mortally afraid of becoming old. This is what he told:

> My forehead became very hot. Suddenly I found myself in Jerusalem, at the Wailing Wall. Beyond it there was a narrow path among some trees, and I followed that. I did not walk, I was gliding along. Suddenly, I saw next to the path a rabbit sitting in the grass. He looked at me, and I saw that he was a very old rabbit. I was surprised that he did not run away. We were all there together, but we could not see his face.

I never asked him what an "old rabbit" looked like, feeling that a wound was best left untouched, especially when after a number of sessions it was apparently beginning to heal. Two days later we did the *mallam*, the Nupe divining posture (Chapter 2; see also Chapter 7), and I was delighted to hear what Adolf had to tell. It seems that he was taken back once more to the spot he had seen in the lower world:

Once more I saw and heard everything that happened day before yesterday. The path I had seen continued along some fields and then led into the forest. Some lumbermen were at work, cutting down all the old trees. They were even pulling up the roots. It was very sad, because after all, old trees can tell stories to the little trees. I sat down in a clearing, and there were birds around me, and I decided that it was time for me to overcome my sorrow. I looked up and I saw a triangle of light, and from my head, rays of light went in all directions.

After this session, Adolf went for a walk in the forest, and when I came to lunch, he had placed a small bunch of wildflowers in front of my plate. And there were no more snide remarks about elderly women.

Finally I should like to describe a ritual, a combination of makeup and posture that is also a spirit journey, although it has some special and rather curious features. Because of what the women usually experience, we call it the *Albatross adventure*.

In a number of books on American Indian art, I came across photographs of a couple, found in grave C in Etowah, Barlow County, Georgia, made of a marble native to North Georgia (pls. 12 and 13). The man sits cross-legged, his right hand on his knee. His left arm is broken off, but a museum later recovered and reattached his broken-off limb, and he has his left hand on his knee, too. The woman is kneeling with her legs drawn under her body, sitting on them like Japanese women do, but with her knees slightly apart. Her hands are placed on the sides of her thighs, rather close to her hips, and she bends slightly forward. Both figures have protruding tongues, but the man's sticks out farther than the woman's, and both bear traces of striking facial paint.[7] They actually wear greenish-blue painted-on half-masks, the woman's a bit

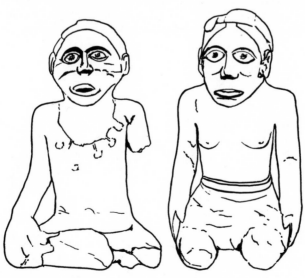

Plate 12   **Plate 13**

shorter than the man's, the lower edge and eyeholes of which are outlined in carbon black.

In April 1985, when I had a group of experienced people assembled in Scheibbs for a masked dance (see Chapter 11), we tried this posture. We painted on the ancient mask, which looked truly spectacular. The following are the experiences of some of the women:

ILSE S.: I was in greenish-blue cold light, somewhere where there was a lot of ice. I was an albatross and flew over the sea; there were icebergs and much water. I landed on the mast of a wrecked large wooden boat. The crew was gone, and there was no one to steer it. I was being rocked back and forth.

MICHELLE: I somersaulted backward and changed into a large white albatross. I alighted on an ancient Greek ship, and there was music from somewhere. I jumped into the blue water and became a dolphin, then I myself turned into water; I evaporated and rose toward the sun. I turned into rain and penetrated the plants and the trees. I was quiet water that started to run as a brook, then as a waterfall. I penetrated into the rocks, then came up to the surface again as a spring in the tropics. Then everything started all over again.

SIGRID: I saw a large number of birds, then my wings began to grow and became longer and longer. I flew up very high into the violet-blue light. Then I descended on the water and began to rock on the waves. That continued for the longest time. The energy began coursing through me; something grew out of my head and began pulling me upward. I became a lake with blooming water lilies.

The presence of water, turning into a bird—sometimes understood to be an albatross—and a rocking motion were quite prevalent. By contrast, the men seemed to be propelled upward by a tremendous force and rushed outward beyond the bounds of the earth:

FRANZ: I took a very fast trip through a long tube in greyish-white, cold light. When I got out on the other side, I was in space, in a different world, on a distant star. There were crowds of transparent people there, as if of glass; they had pointed ears and wore tall caps, and danced in ocher light. Then I had to hurry on.

RUDL: My Tiger appeared, but he said I should go to ask help of the Eagle. The Eagle slipped into my body, and I streaked into empty space in a shower of a thousand sparks, in among multitudes of suns and splinters of more suns. I pleaded that I wanted to stay, but I had to fly on, clear to where the universe started curving upon itself, circles upon circles, space after space. I felt that I could stand it no longer, but then I saw all of you, living, dying, living, dying. Then I heard the Eagle screech, and I was back here.

Listening to the men was quite frightening; they seemed to have "overshot" their goal in this posture. I had had everybody assume the female variant of the posture, so I was concerned that perhaps that had been a mistake. However, even when in a later workshop I was more careful and let the men do the male posture, there was still something exaggerated, an aspect of dangerous abandon, in what they experienced. Thus, Hannes (Salzburg, 1987) told how

> the earth began to swirl crazily; we turned into rockets and started rushing through space, racing by the planets, then back to earth again. . . . I am on the edge of a volcano; it explodes, and I am in a boat, paddling down to the ocean in the lava flow. . . . I find myself in Africa; I am in a hammock, and there are hundreds of snakes, all swaying to the music of a flute. . . . I turn into a monkey, into a gorilla, into King Kong. . . . I become a mosquito and return to the mountaintop and watch as an acorn starts germinating and then grows into an enormous tree . . . but this takes many generations.

We are reminded of Rudl's rush into space and then seeing his friends in the workshop living and dying over and over again; that is, he equally witnesses events that would cover several generations. Is there something wrong with the male posture? The archeologists who discovered the couple reported that they found the two figures tossed carelessly into an open space in the grave, and that was how in all probability the man's arm broke off. Perhaps their contemporaries disapproved of the violence experienced by the men in the posture and discarded the figures for that reason. A woman's figure in the same posture and with the same painted-on mask was found also in Kentucky, but apparently there was no male companion.

In conclusion, I cannot resist sharing a special adventure that has something to do with a spirit journey, although not with posture. The story concerns a group of "little men" from Peru, who were our visitors in Cuyamungue in the summer of 1986. Actually, they were clay replicas of ancient *whistling vessels*. Each figure consisted of two connecting chambers, the back one in the shape of a shell that could easily be held in two hands, while the front one was figured. The figures represented fat-bellied, short-legged little men with curious headdresses, who held various objects on their stomachs— a fish, a parrot, or a lizard (pl. 14).

Plate 14

I am not being facetious in referring to these whistling vessels as though they were personages. They were not simply span-high pieces of pottery, but as we set them up in a circle in the center of the kiva, they exuded a palpable, very powerful presence. So to welcome and to honor them, we hung a tapestry on the wall, actually half of a huipil from a famous weavers' village in Guatemala, intoxicating in its design and riot of colors, and whenever we did a ritual in the kiva, we offered them some cornmeal and the fragrance of burning sage.

These whistling vessels have an intriguing history. They were produced by successive sophisticated cultures in Peru over a period of more than a millennium until the time when the Spanish overran the Inca empire. There are only minimal traces of popular awareness concerning their use or ritual application (see below), so they may possibly have been the property of highly placed priests, who passed on the tradition about them as esoteric knowledge, which was mostly forgotten with the passing of the priestly hierarchy. Archeologists thought of them as water jugs until Daniel Stat, an amateur scientist, bought one at an auction in Pennsylvania in 1972. A careful examination of a number of them, later extended also to broken samples in various museums, convinced him that these various vessels were intended not to contain water but to be blown. He eventually borrowed several other vessels from various museums and worked out a method for duplicating them.

In 1980, Stat and Dr. Steven Garrett of the UCLA physics department ran a number of tests on a sample of sixty-nine bottles and discovered that the high, piercing tone produced on them was confined to an extraordinarily narrow range of frequencies, spanning only half an octave, between 2,000 and 3,500 cps. It was also established that if several vessels were blown simultaneously, a resonance was set up, termed a "difference tone." This tone, although modern physics acknowledges that it exists, cannot be registered by any instrument. It is purely a subjective phenomenon. Speculation is that this difference tone is capable of producing an alteration of consciousness.

Stat carried out a brief ritual with us in the kiva, and owing to the very special acoustic properties of that round subterranean building, the whistle tone was extremely powerful. It seemed to enter into one ear and literally to exit through the other. In addition to the very high, piercing tone, we also heard lower ones that were like a background rustling. As Stat discovered early on, and as others before us who had the privilege of blowing the whistles had found out also, this whistling action did indeed set up a distinct alteration of perception, a trance. As Eva D., one of our Austrian friends present, described it, she felt a strong wind. "It was eerie and filled the entire room. It produced a strange condition, like an intoxication. When we stopped whistling, I continued hearing the whispering and singing for a long while." In a way, we were disappointed, because we thought that with our ample trance experience, we might discover a clue as to what the vessels were used for, but we seemed to have hit a blank wall.

At the time of the visit by the vessels, we were preparing for a masked trance dance (see Chapter 12), and so we did a divination to find out in what way the little men wanted to be involved. We were told that there should be rattling and drumming and dancing. We followed these instructions, and we also made the blowing on the vessels a part of a ritual that we did in the kiva prior to our dance. Apparently, the little men derived some satisfaction from the treatment they had received and, unbeknown to us, had already made preparations to give us a present in return. This is what happened:

As a first part of our masked trance dance, we entered the kiva fully costumed, rattling and drumming, and danced in a circle around the vessels, according to the instructions we had received. After concluding the dance, everyone sat down around the vessels. I fed each one of them a pinch of cornmeal, then handed them to the dancers. I did not notice at the time that Isi, an anthropology student from Vienna, exchanged vessels with Belinda, one of the other dancers. I started rattling, Burgi and David, also of our Austrian contingent, played the drums, and those who had vessels blew on them. Since this was a ritual and not a working session, I did not subsequently ask for a report on what those who had blown on the whistling vessels had experienced. It was not until days later, when we were sitting around reminiscing about the dance, that Isi told what happened to her during that whistling session, and she dictated it to me:

I found myself in the middle of the desert. It was very dry, there were not even any bushes, and everywhere I saw lizards flitting across the rocks. There was a sound, very soft; it was the sound that they made as they were flitting about. Suddenly there was a house before me, a very simple, low house; it had a rectangular opening, but there was no door. A man was standing in that opening; I could not see him very clearly, but I knew there was a man standing there. He did not fill the entire opening, only part of it, so that I realized it was an invitation, that he wanted me to enter. As I stepped in, I knew that he was a salamander. Once inside, I had the impression of being in a cave. It was very moist, dripping everywhere, and the walls were deeply fissured. Everywhere on the ledges, reptiles lay sleeping peacefully. Then he said, "This is where the moisture comes from for the desert."

Afterward, when we replaced the vessels on the floor, I realized that I had been blowing on the one where the little man was holding a lizard in his hands. Belinda had been holding it first; I thought, it doesn't really matter which one I blow on, but then I had the feeling that that was the one I would like to use. Even before I asked for it, when I just looked at it, at the shape of the little man's hat, which was all I could see in Belinda's hand, there was this feeling of recognition that this was the little man who had whistled a few nights earlier, and that I had a special relationship to him.

During the night of August 1, before we went to see the Jemez Corn Dance [our masked dance started on August 5], I had heard what sounded like a whistle or a flute. When I woke up, I thought at first that it was the chirping of the crickets, but then I heard them very clearly, and I thought, what could the whistling be? There was a difference between the crickets and what I was hearing, which was the sound that we had made when we blew on the whistling vessels, and it came from the kiva. It was three o'clock in the morning—I know because I looked at my watch—and the glowing arc of the Milky Way was above the kiva, and the moon was just rising. I had to go to the bathroom, and when I got up, the sound stopped.

I was really glad that I came to have this encounter with the little man of the whistling vessel. Finally, somebody was friendly to me. Other beings always wanted to force me to get going; they frightened me when they started pushing me around. This man did not try to make fun of me, not like the birds, who found my petty fears hilarious, like the one that pushed me across the abyss.

We might speculate, then, that in the trance produced by whistling on this particular vessel, the one that the kindly little old lizard man was in charge of, the shaman could journey directly to the cave where moisture was stored. There he could plead for rain to be sent to his village. Duerr (1984:346) notes, by the way, that many Central and South American societies used to carry out rituals asking for rain in subterranean caves.

Perhaps something of a similar nature was true of the vessel where the little pot-bellied man was holding a fish. In that case, possibly, the shaman sets out to the seashore to ask for a school of fish to be sent. What might be involved with the one holding a bird we have no idea, but recently a friend showed me a rather crudely made whistling vessel purchased in a village in Guatemala. It had only one chamber, which represented a woman holding a tiny baby. The purchaser had been told that the whistle served to "call people to come to church." Who knows, this may be a memory, reduced to a faint whisper over the centuries, that at one time the blowing of that whistle afforded access to a special place where a sacred being would grant a woman the desired child.

CHAPTER SEVEN

The Many Faces
of Divination

Divining is as old as humanity. The hunters developed it as a ritual to discover the location of game, a matter of vital importance to them. As other types of societies arose, divination was adapted to the changing circumstances, but it continued to serve important societal goals. It is regrettable that in the Western world divination has been decried as irrational, antirational, or a fraud perpetrated on the ignorant and the superstitious, because divination is not that at all. It is *sooth*saying, that is, revealing the truth. What the diviner does is uncover to his clients some hidden truth about themselves, or about what is going on around them. There are certainly situations in everyone's life where such insights could be of overriding importance. This is why within and outside the Western orbit, divining continues to play an important role, exposing that which is hidden, soothing anxiety, and aiding in decision making.

In Western-type societies, ours among them, quasi-mechanical means such as tarot cards are frequently employed for "fortunetelling." However, the repository of much of divinatory knowledge is the alternate reality, and access to that treasure trove can best be gained in trance, and in the appropriate posture.

In the course of our research, we discovered three very effective divining postures. One of them is that of the Nupe diviner or mallam (pl. 2), recorded in a photograph from sub-Saharan Africa, and which we have not seen represented in any artwork. It was among the earliest postures we explored (see Chapter 2). As we found out in Munich, where it was one of the two postures our experimental subjects assumed during our medical research project, it was accompanied by a powerful trance. The second posture of this nature comes from Tennessee (pl. 15). It shows the portrait of an elderly man, cut in stone

Plate 15

with outstanding skill. Plate 16 seems to be the same posture, equally from Tennessee, but the figure is not well preserved. The third posture (pl. 17), shown by two female figures from Cholula (Mexico), is similar to that of the Tennessee diviners, except instead of half-kneeling, these women are sitting on a low stool.

The experiences mediated by the above three postures have a number of characteristics in common. Most important, they provide visionary insights about oneself and one's social situation not available in ordinary consciousness. In addition, the trancer may also ask questions in all three postures. In fact, on occasion this is even being suggested, as we see in the following account of a trance experience in the mallam posture:

> EVA D. (Vienna, 1985): I was being twirled in this posture with enormous rapidity. I was above you and saw you all. Then I sank down, and I heard someone say, very urgently, "Ask the birds, ask the trees!"

Curiously, we have found that if on the other hand someone poses a question in a posture not intended for divining, this obvious breach of etiquette will simply be ignored, or one is informed, quite summarily, "This is not the time for that," or something to that effect.

However, there are some subtle differences. The mallam addresses principally social relations; the wise women from Cholula and the Tennessee diviner are more interested in personal problems. In seeming contradiction, however, the old master from Tennessee is also an expert in ritual matters. Another difference concerns the preparatory perceptions, to be detailed below, such as a blue light, and others that characterize the mallam posture. These are lacking in the Tennessee and the Cholula diviners' posture, where the matter at hand tends to be addressed directly, as it were, without any introduction. Still another difference is a certain laconic brevity of the message which is often reported for the Tennessee diviner's posture, so that it can

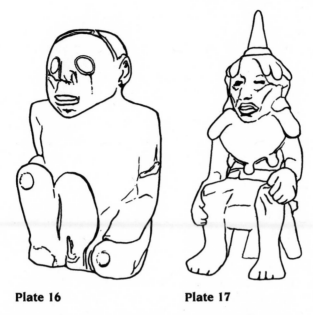

Plate 16   **Plate 17**

happen that if the message is concluded and the rattling is not, the entire vision is replayed, much to the consternation of the questioner.

The Nupe mallam. As described before, this posture requires that we sit on the floor, turning our legs to the right in such a way that the sole of the left foot rests against the right thigh. Because some participants had problems with their knees, we also experimented with a mirror image of the posture, placing the legs toward the left, and it seemed to make no difference. When the legs are to the right, the body leans on the stiff left arm, while the right hand is placed on the lower left leg, at the end of the calf muscle, with all fingers, including the thumb, turned to the front.

Generally, the trancers report the appearance of a vivid blue color in this posture, covering the entire visual field, or more clearly defined in the shape of a light, small spots, or, for Patty, for instance, the vividly blue eyes of a Wolf Spirit. A gyrating motion is experienced, turning on one's own axis, or hearing the "circular motion of the rattle," or the rattle dancing around one; descending into swirling black, orange, and blue colors, or feeling a bright purple light splash on one's face and then swirling; or in minimal form, seeing a white circle of fog, or of arrows. This "cranking up" seems to generate the energy necessary for the successful continuation of the vision. Some then observe how their body or their head splits open, often in the form of a triangle, pointing either up or down. Since many diviners around the world are shown wearing pointed hats (see also the Lady of Cholula, below), we may speculate that this could well be a representation of the triangular split perceived in the divinatory trance, especially because frequently it directly precedes "seeing" or "finding out."

These introductory impressions are usually followed by personal memory content. Thoughts of the past few days flit by, acquaintances, events from childhood or adult life, "like a film." Soon, however, indications of psychological problems may begin to bob up, but significantly for this posture, the personal aspect passes into the societal one. It will be recalled how Adolf's preoccupation with aging, which he had to come to terms with during his trip to the lower world, came up again in this posture. That was how he experienced the importance of the old trees in the forest, because, as he so poignantly observed, they were the ones that told stories to the small ones. Or take the social import of remarks such as "I became sad because I did not seem to be able to reach the people in the room," and this especially wistful comment, "I heard a sound in a canyon but could not find its source." A woman burdened by circumstances at home said, "I saw two figures; they were unsubstantial like fog or smoke. I wanted to rise up, but they kept pulling me softly down." Or from a graduate student who had problems with women, we heard: "I saw the opening to a tunnel; it was pale green, and there was a woman standing in it. She was very delicate, and she was naked, but she wore a shell of hard cold steel; it was like an armor." All of these concern the relationship of the respective person to the social ambience.

Revelations of this sort can on occasion be quite surprising not only to the visionary but also to the group listening to the report. One summer we had a young man by the name of Victor as a guest in Cuyamungue, whom his girlfriend had brought in tow, and who apparently had not been informed that we followed a modified vegetarian diet, using even poultry only minimally, mainly just for seasoning. What we did not know was that for Victor, apparently, red meat was not only a passionately desired food, but its consumption was also a confirmation of his male dominance, which he felt was threatened by our style of eating. All this became clear when we heard him recount his experience:

> There was a warm feeling. I was sitting on the earth outside; there was grass and yellow corn. I walked through it and came to a lonely tree and a rock at the edge of an arroyo. There was a red-and-yellow mountain; I started climbing it and kept going higher; finally I flew. I came to a valley, the mountain was in the middle of that, and in the mountain there was a cave. I flew into the cave and saw a pictograph. There was a man in the cave, he had been hunting, and he had brought in an antelope. He cut the liver out of the antelope and fed it to me. After eating, I flew out of the cave, higher and higher on the mountain; everything became very small, it looked like the region of the Pecos River. I got into another valley; there were bears hunting for fish. I saw a man dancing on a rock. I became that man and carried out a very intense dance. I stopped dancing, went hunting, found an antelope, speared it, took it to the cave, cut out its liver, and ate it. I left the cave, climbed down the mountain, and walked through a cornfield; I got to a creek,

Despite the striking repetition of the hunting episode, unusual for this posture, the trance experience did not rid Victor of his preference for red meat, which clearly had deep-seated, socially informed roots. On the contrary, it made his yearning all the more acute and imbued it with trance-borne legitimacy. Since we had no antelope liver for him, or any other part of an antelope for that matter, he drove down into the valley as soon as this was decently feasible, and under the petroglyph of the local Lotaburger, he consumed a fulfilling quantity of the red-and-yellow mountain of his vision.

Usually we do the mallam posture at the outset of a workshop, and as could be expected, various beings whose home is the alternate reality take the opportunity to look over the new intruders, often with the obvious intent of introducing themselves as possible future spirit guides. In fact, they are very anxious for this role, as Patty found out when the big, blue-eyed white wolf she saw at the outset of the divining session kept coming back in the course of the workshop. Some of the spirits are quite cagey, knowing that Westerners have been estranged from animal garb for many centuries, and so take care not to scare them. Yolanda, who was afraid of spiders, felt only a large, warm, and furry round spot on her leg, and it took a while before the true mask of her gentle friend was revealed. A big white she-bear, who became Elizabeth R.'s trusted companion, did not disguise her shape, but reassured her in another way: "She let me smell her fur and see her back. I thought all animal spirits had wings, but there were no wings there, only energy."

Advice in decision making is also something that the mallam posture can mediate. In the summer of 1984, Yolanda was pondering whether she could leave her three young children for a whole month while she came to Cuyamungue. Her husband had no objections, but she was still wavering.

> Being unsure about what to do [she wrote], I did some rattling for myself in the mallam posture. A big bear came and took me on his arms and carried me up a large mountain, then on the backside of the mountain down again on a narrow path. He set me down next to a structure that looked like a very large beehive and then left. Didn't you tell me that the people around there where you are have ovens that look like that?

The vision convinced her that powerful beings of the alternate reality approved of her plans, and the trip to Cuyamungue became a seminal experience for her.

Finally, the following account tells of an unusual application of the mallam posture, and I want to include it here as a teaser. It is an intriguing mix of ancient knowledge and modern technology, showing how much we do not know about the power of ritual and the effect our trance may have on what surrounds us. During the first workshop I held in the Buddhist Center in Scheibbs, two young women of the group, Eva D. and U., decided to tape my rattling so they would be able to hold trance sessions of their own. A few months after the conclusion of the workshop, I received the following letter from U.:

> Soon after coming home, Eva and I started to try out your rattling tape, and things went very well. There was only this thing that we noticed that there were rooms where it was harder to concentrate. So we of course avoided those. . . .
>
> During the last weeks before Christmas it happened a few times that the tape did not function right, and only with intense effort were we able to hear a very weak rattle sound. The first few times we thought—well, it is not supposed to be today—and the following day, the sound was once more clearly audible. Until one day the sound was gone completely, not only that of the rattle tape but *also* [her emphasis] of all the tapes of the trance sessions in Scheibbs that we had copied. This went on for weeks. I kept the cassettes in my apartment with others I own. The sound of those other cassettes was as normal as before. We then tried to play the workshop tapes on different tape recorders, although we suspected right from the start that perhaps the trouble did not have anything to do with a technical defect. But just to be sure, we tried changing equipment. As expected, unsuccessfully. I then took the tapes to Eva's apartment, which did not help either. I had the intuition that we had let the rattling become a method, and besides, it was not really any part of our workaday culture. Eva and I felt simultaneously awed and helpless. We finally hit on the idea that we should carry out a ceremony of sorts, but procrastinated because we really didn't know how to go about it. After Christmas we then sat down together, and suddenly we knew what to do. We sat facing each other in the mallam posture, and between us we placed two pebbles and a hazelnut which I had picked up during a walk with you in Scheibbs. We stayed there for your "quarter-hour." Both of us had the following very intense insight. Our inner attitude became prayerful, and we understood that whatever power it was that wanted to tell us something, it was not inimical, and that the disturbance had nothing to do with our cultural background.
>
> For half a day more, we left the tapes with the pebbles and the nut where they were, and the tapes completely recovered their former sound. We don't rattle quite so frequently since then, and when we do, it is with a different attitude. (March 11, 1983)

The Tennessee diviner. The beautifully worked sandstone figure of this elderly Indian man (pl. 15) was found in a grave in Wilson County, Tennessee, and is estimated to be about seven hundred years old. Such figures used to be placed into wooden temples on top of earthen mounds, but few escaped the iconoclastic wrath of the white settlers. The second example of the posture (pl. 16) was dug up in the same general area.

The man is sitting on his left leg, which is drawn under him. His right leg is bent at the knee and positioned at a right angle to the floor. Both hands are resting on his knees, which makes him look relaxed, but in reality the posture is quite taxing physically. His head is turned slightly toward the right. A black line is drawn from below his earlobe over the bridge of his nose to his other earlobe, and his tongue is visible between his lips. Since he is nearly naked, it is all the more striking that he should be wearing an elaborate cap.

As mentioned before (Chapter 5), I duplicated that cap, and wearing it had the effect of making the visions sharper and their flow richer.

That this was a trance posture was evident from the start, particularly because the man had his tongue clearly visible between his lips. According to a number of Amerindian traditions, on the Northwest Coast, for instance, but also in Asia, especially in Tibet, one receives power from the spirits by way of the protruding tongue. But discovering what kind of experience it might convey was more difficult. What was the common denominator in observations such as "My ears grew bigger and bigger, until I could hear all your thoughts. Then I slipped into an insect and I could hear like an insect"; and "I came to a fence in the forest and it had an open gate. I kept taking one step forward, one step backward, and could not figure out whether I should go in"; or "I found myself in a kettle with steep, reddish walls. Above the rim I saw a violet-colored landscape. I asked myself: What will I do if I cannot get out of this kettle?"

Soon, however, with the help of the training we had received as we worked with the posture of the Nupe mallam, things began to fall into place. Here we had very clear messages about personal traits and problems—the compulsive curiosity of the first one; in the case of the second, the inability to make use of opportunities as they presented themselves; and the lack of self-confidence of the third. In other words, this was also a divining posture, except that in contrast to the auguries received in the mallam postures, these had nothing whatever to do with social relations.

We soon noted another fascinating difference. The Old One of Tennessee came across very much as a distinct personality, which we never experienced with the mallam. Sometimes, he actually seemed a bit testy. When Christian, an Austrian, was a guest in Cuyamungue, he asked him about a posture he had seen in trance. Which foot was he to put forward? Laconically, the answer came, "The right one." The session could have stopped right there. But I did not have any way of knowing that Christian's question had been answered, so I went on rattling. Subsequently it became clear that the venerable Old One felt that he had said what Christian needed to know, and he was in no mood for further discussion. When Christian persisted, he took him to a deep canyon and had him look at some mountain sheep. "And then," Christian told, somewhat bemused, "I melted into a sheep." I wondered how the Old Wise One could possibly have known that for a German speaker, "sheep" is synonymous with "stupid." His irritation carried over to the next day, when Christian assumed the posture once more, with an entirely different question in mind. The first thing he got was a rather annoyed "And now what do you want?"

When we do the Tennessee diviner's posture in a group, I take the short temper of the Old One into account. I always ask my Friend to summon him in the most respectful terms and afterward thank him for his trouble in the same way, as a granddaughter would a venerated elder. Perhaps the old diviner's impatience can be understood, because telling people about themselves is really just a sideline for him. His true expertise is in the area of ritual. When it comes to those questions, he never tires of providing information down to the most minute detail and on occasion even a brief glimpse of the future, if he deems it appropriate. As we shall see later (Chapter 11), it is for this reason that we always call on him when we plan a dance ritual, and on those occasions, he is our most valuable guide and patient friend.

To give just one example, in the summer of 1986 I needed some advice concerning the location of the sweatlodge we were planning to construct for the masked trance dance ritual we were going to carry out the following month. So I asked two gifted friends, Cynthia and Krissie, to consult the Tennessee diviner for me while I rattled. In both instances, what he told them had a similar content. There was some clarification of a personal nature, as if to say, "Only if your thoughts are pure and clear, unclouded by personal trouble, can you carry out a ritual." In a way, this was on the spiritual level the same as taking purgatives and emetics prior to an important ceremony, so prevalent in American Indian culture. And then there were the instructions concerning the place for the sweatlodge and still other matters our old friend considered important for us to know.

After working through some personal concerns, Cynthia went to quite a bit of effort scouting around for the right spot for the sweatlodge:

> I came to the evergreen tree by the Student Building, and wondered if that was where we should put the sweatlodge, but it burst into flame, so I knew that wasn't it. I passed on to where the kiva is, but I was told, "No, not by the kiva." I started spinning around, but that caused me to be pulled upward. I flew over a snowy landscape, and looking down, I wondered what I was doing there. So I descended into the snow; my legs got very cold, and I was afraid. So I called to Felicitas to bring me back. I did come back, flying very low, and then I saw the spot. It was a flat area, and to the right, a hill rose up. Is it here? I asked. And I knew that it was.

This was not the end of Cynthia's vision, however. She saw a large number of formless spirits hovering about, was told that it would be her task to move them through the sweatlodge during that ritual, and was even given instructions about the costume she was to wear during the dance.

Krissie, too, had to dispense with some personal matters first. Then she reported that she saw crystals all lined up:

> We were at the edge of a drop, and the crystals danced in a circle. They were beginning to lose their moisture. I looked down, and I saw the ground swelling up before me, and there was an aura around the mound. The mound changed into a frog; it was quiet and beautiful. It shrank to its normal size. I looked into its eyes and said, "Grandfather Frog, tell me." And he said, "Include me, include me!"
>
> Then there was a lot of light. An eagle danced, then turned into a flower; I saw the setting sun, a mushroom cloud, and it started to rain.

Krissie was also shown the place where the sweatlodge was to be built. It was on the edge of a drop, which was puzzling, because it seemed to contradict what Cynthia had seen. But we later walked over the land and found the location, which was both a flat area near which a hill rose up and at the edge of a deep arroyo. In confirmation that we had found the right spot, we saw as we looked down into the arroyo a clearly marked flat oval area, and on it, as if laid out on a platter, a large number of granite rocks, perhaps the crystals that Krissie had seen, of the size we needed for the sweat.

Again, as in Cynthia's case, Krissie was given more than just the location of the sweatlodge she had been asking for. She had encountered Grandfather Frog, and since he asked not to be left out, we named the sweatlodge for him. But there had also been a brief preview of what was to come. She had seen us dancing by the sweatlodge, and we were indeed instructed later to do that. While this might be viewed as being within the logic of the situation, the subsequent events were certainly not. A cloud did gather during that dance, but most remarkably only above our sweatlodge. We were indeed rained on, and there was thunder and lightning. After that manifestation of the power of the eagle's "dance," and as we stopped dancing, the whole cloud turned delicately pink, and then, to our amazement, a rainbow girded it from end to end. Truly, the eagle had changed into a flower.

The Cholula diviner. There are two little clay figurines extant in this posture, created about A.D. 1350 in Cholula, one of the important pre-Hispanic religious centers of Central Mexico (pl. 17). Their facial features are quite different, as are their earrings, but both are wearing the same pointed hat and a wide collar with tassels on it. Each is sitting on a stool. They have their eyes closed, their tongues between their lips. Their right hands are placed slightly below the knee, clutching the leg; the left hands are somewhat higher.

Whether the Lady of Cholula is also adept at giving advice on ritual matters, we have not explored yet. She is as competent concerning personal problems as her colleague from Tennessee. But there is a touch of femininity in what she reveals, an element of motherly caring, which is absent in the visions provided by the old gentleman from the South. I consulted her a while ago, because I was quite frightened by the results of a medical test. It took a while before I got through to her, but then I felt surrounded by a number of solicitous elderly women, and one of them said, "Remember, you are our daughter." It was wonderfully reassuring, and the test results turned out to be of much less significance than I had feared. To varying degrees, the theme of loving support was equally evident when we tried this posture in Columbus in the fall of 1987. Even diffuse questions elicit a concerned answer, as we see in this example:

> NORMA: I asked about myself and the rattle was very loud, like it was in my head. I saw the head of a buffalo and mountains like in the Southwest. The buffalo

kicked up a lot of dust, and when I repeated my question to him, he said, "Stay grounded." Then I went to the forest and could feel the forest floor under my feet. I got to the beach; a turtle came out of the water and repeated the same thing, "Stay grounded."

But we found that the Lady of Cholula could also be much more subtle, as when she helped heal old wounds by the visions she gave and then summoned Elizabeth's guide during the same session:

> ELIZABETH: I saw a black panther attacking a man; they killed each other. Then there were scenes from my life, my car slipping on ice; how once I nearly drowned; or how during one delivery I almost hemorrhaged to death. There was a Maya temple and in it an altar for sacrifice, and I thought about just wanting to be comfortable. But my guide appeared and shook me. Did I want to choose death? he asked. "Do you want to sacrifice life?" I said, "No." Then he kissed me.

Problems on the job receive almost practical attention:

> BARBARA: I saw my place of work, and I felt really irritated. There was a stairway and an altar on top. I brought some flowers and put them on that altar. There were two doors on top, and I asked, "May I go through?" No, I was told, there was no more time. Then I saw a raccoon playing with a fish, but it didn't eat it, it let it go. There was a woman flying by wearing a grey crown, and she said, "Stay centered."

Nancy's problems are of a different nature. She works in the health-care field for a large organization of mostly men, and many a day must surely feel lonely and lacking support:

> I saw an electric field that had a lot of broken circuitry. When I started putting the broken ends together, the sparks began to fly. A white buffalo appeared; either she was immense or I was very small, because I nestled in her hair on her head, and her hair was warm and soft. We went from mountain to mountain; I danced on her back. I asked her about what I should do with my clay pipe, and she said, "You'll learn." Then she brought me back, and when I complained, she said, "Stop whining." She kissed me, she did human things, but she was a buffalo.

Belinda and Jan are psychological counselors, and the Lady had some important messsages for them.

> BELINDA: I asked about my health and saw a rusty tube in my throat. Then I heard it said many times, "You push too hard, you push too hard." Bulls came up looking like the astrological figure of Taurus, thousands of them, stampeding. I asked the bulls to stop, and they lay down; all was quiet, and somebody said, "Change the story."

> JAN: My question was, "What about the larger story?" I saw a long caravan that was walking with difficulty. The Bear came and said that with enough energy it

was possible for the caravan to move from country to country, but more helpers were needed. Healing was possible in different countries, but I hadn't paid attention to that, and I wasn't prepared. While we were talking, I saw the instability of ordinary reality, and there were painful memories of the people I work with. Then I saw Belinda in her lion's costume; she was pushing a wheel, and her hands were bleeding. I wanted to help her, but I couldn't do anything. She just kept pushing that wheel, and she was bleeding and I couldn't get to her.

Finally, there was Maxine with her severe health problem, who badly needed encouragement. So the Lady showered presents on her, like an indulgent mother on a sick child:

> Things passed before my eyes very rapidly. All was inky black. In the center there was a black opening, something like a tube. I was supposed to go down; it was like a tunnel. When I slid down, I came to a place down in the earth that was lit in orange light. A huge hawk appeared next to me. It had powerful legs and wore a leather saddle on its back. There were a number of tents, seven in all, and the hawk took me to each one in turn. The first one was full of colors, and I chose blue for myself. The next one had feathers in it, and I chose a large black-and-white one. Then came a tent; there was an old woman in it, and I chose old age for myself. In the next tent there was a big pot with meat stewing in it that I took along. Then we came to a tent with many children in it. I said to the hawk, "I don't want any children." But I had to choose one anyway, so I selected a twelve-year-old boy. After that there was one with all sorts of weather in it. I saw a beautiful plain and mountains with a lightning storm, so I chose that. In the last tent there were innumerable eyes looking at me. I chose a clear blue eye, then I put all my things in a sack, and there was the tunnel again, and I was sucked up.

CHAPTER EIGHT

The Gift of Healing

In Chapter 2, I described the posture of the shaman who is embraced from behind by a huge Bear Spirit (pl. 1). It took some time before I recognized that the trance experience mediated was that of being healed. The posture involves a more or less pronounced inclination of the head toward the back and a positioning of the hands very close to or right above the navel. As I began searching for other representations of this posture, I also came across examples where the hands, although in the same general area of the body, seemed to be placed too far apart. At first I thought we were dealing simply with a variant, but experimentation proved me wrong, and the observation eventually led to the discovery of the *birthing posture*. Although not involved with curing per se, historically the experiences it provided may indirectly have led to the development of the healing posture, and so I am going to discuss it here, in the way of an introduction, although it deals with a different topic, that of the fetus at birth.

In the Western world, women are forced to lie flat on their backs while being delivered. It is a most unfortunate development, doing great harm to the mother, as childbirth activists very correctly keep pointing out. Neither was it done that way in past centuries. In a Berlin museum I once saw a "birth stool" a few hundred years old, with a large hole in the center of the seat for the newborn to emerge. Having just gone through a frightful delivery lasting nearly thirty hours, it seemed to me that letting gravity do part of the work was an eminently good idea. And indeed, in other parts of the world, mothers, past and present, assume postures that are much more helpful, as we see in plate 18. This clay jar, of unknown origin, was most likely created by a woman, probably in Bolivia at a time before white contact. As the artist must have seen many times, the mother is seated for delivery, and a helper in front of her receives the infant as it emerges through her vagina.

What fascinated me in this dramatic figured representation of birth was the woman sitting behind the mother. Not only was this companion supporting the mother's back, but she also had her hands on the mother's abdomen. It was, although vicariously, the "anomalous" healing posture that had been puzzling me. Over and over again, around the world and through the ages, figurines clearly marked as female are shown in this posture, sometimes sitting but most of the time standing (see pls. 19–22). Obeying the conventions of their time, they may be highly stylized, like the European Neolithic figure (pl. 19), about six or seven thousand years old, where slits mark the eyes and rosettas the breasts, and the one from the Negev in the Near East (pl. 20), almost that old. Others are quite naturalistic, such as the Olmec one (pl. 21), created about twenty-five hundred years ago, and the nearly modern one from sub-Saharan Africa (pl. 22). Other examples come from Hungary and Crete (both from 5000 B.C.), and from modern times from New Guinea, New Zealand, Polynesia, and numerous ones from Central and West Africa.

Plate 18

The question is, why would a birthing posture be re-created so persistently? My guess was that most probably the purpose was not to demonstrate the right posture for giving birth, which everyone knew anyway. The reason must have had to do instead with a religious observance, the single most important topic of ancient art, always connected with trance. Thinking along these lines, my conclusion was that representing this posture might have had something to do with the fact that, as I have shown elsewhere,[1] the pivotal, the most significant, rituals of the hunter-gatherers and later of the horticulturalists, who created these figurines, centered around the celebration of birth. Some of these figures are quite large and may well have marked the sacred places where such important rites were celebrated.

In such rituals, which can still be observed in surviving societies of this type in Australia, South America, and elsewhere, the central issue is not the birth pangs of the mother but rather the welcoming, strengthening, and nurturing of the infant. This topic is flanked, as it were, quite logically, by an invocation of the ancestors, whose life is continued in the newborn, and by

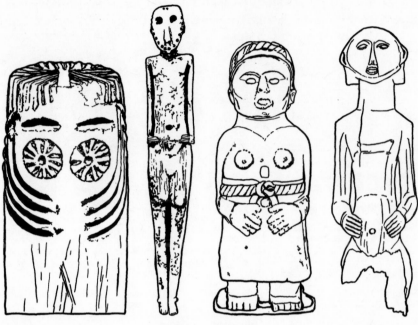

Plate 19   **Plate 20**   **Plate 21**   **Plate 22**

rituals referring to propagation. Surprisingly, when exploring the birthing posture, I found the same to be true of our trance experiences. In fact, the visions
reported by the participants can easily be ranged along the principal sections
of such ancient rituals. The only feature that is more elaborated in the trance
experiences than in the native rituals is the experience of the fetus in the
womb right before and during delivery. Not until that is given its place, too,
the figurines seem to say, not until its sweet mystery revealed in this trance
posture has been intertwined with the communal, the social, celebration, will
the rite be complete.

The posture is quite simple. We did it standing, with our hands flat on
the abdomen, pretty much as shown in plate 20. We tried the posture twice
in 1987, in Cincinnati (C) early in the year, and with a different group at
Camp Agape, Ohio (A), in the fall. The two experiments complement each
other, so I am going to treat them as one.[2] In the analysis, the structure of
ancient hunter-gatherer rituals will serve as our guide. At the outset of such a
large ceremonial, the spirits of the ancestors are invited to participate, and in
the visions, they in fact did arrive. As one of the participants (A) related,
"There appeared faces of old men, with purple beards and white eyebrows."
Or:

> LIBET (A): There was swirling blue light. It moved into the womb; the sound and
> the light became muted. Then the sensation changed. I was in a cave, and there

were seven or eight women around me, wearing dark cloaks and doing some healing. They aged and withered, becoming skulls, but it wasn't frightening. Then there was a lot of movement; they disappeared, but their spirits were still around me.

In the womb, meanwhile—in the "narrow ravine with the winding river" of the umbilical cord—the unborn dream of the world they are about to enter, as it rises from the vapors:

> TERRY (C): I was in a long, narrow ravine, with a winding river, and dense vapors arose from it. I saw lots of clouds; they were light grey. There were also trees and water, but they appeared upside down. The walls of the ravine were cliffs, and along the edge of those walls antelopes could be seen grazing. In swirling colors of purple and black, I saw the eye of a cat, maybe a lion. Lakes with trees appeared, then more eyes, and some more purple. A swan came swimming down the stream, and as I watched, its white color turned to purple. A bear was drinking from the water of the stream. The swan became striped and had strange metallic parts. Then the swan became an eagle, beating its wings. The eagle had totally black eyes, without any pupils at all, and a white stripe down its body. It wanted me to come along, but I couldn't do that. I felt that my head was going to explode, and once more there was that swirling purple and black, and I was it.

As yet, however, birth is not imminent, and the small human-to-be is quite happy inside the womb:

> BARBARA (A): I felt comfortable. I could dimly see a circle of light; it had the shape of a cone, and I could see the rays. I saw the tail end of a manatee; we went swimming with them, we were manatees underwater, and there were caves with double doors. Then something put a necklace on me.

Soon, however, this "underwater" life in the womb is about to end, and the fetus is getting impatient:

> NANCY (A): I felt energy pushing me from my knees to my waist. I was swaying and kept thinking, "I am ready." But there was the answer, "Be patient."

The little being, a bird in the nest, is still confined but will soon be released:

> ANITA (A): There was the image of a huge bird in a huge nest. I felt a strong heat on the left, and that stayed that way. Then the trance became deeper, and I became solid, like a dark column of energy. I was rooted but also wanted to sing. I was pushed to the right, and I became aware of light that was coming from above.

Being born is hard work for the little one in the womb, which is narrow and confining:

> ELIZABETH M. (C): I was in a narrow canyon, walking on and on and feeling very tired. Colors started coming down, black, blue, purple. I felt an arm across my shoulder; there was someone walking with me. I was getting even more tired,

and those colors were still coming down. Then they changed to yellow, and out of it there emerged a human eye. I was so very tired, I was glad when the rattling was over.

Finally, the birth takes place, with the fetus, ready to be expelled, appearing as a blue bud, and then the newborn emerges through the vagina:

MARIANNE (C): I was down in a canyon, and there was a lot of purple. The purple became black and began to swirl. Then, as if looking at it from a bridge, I saw a blue bud coming up out of the canyon. I saw an eagle's eyes, then a slit appeared in the pupil. I thought the slit looked like a vagina, but then rejected the idea. The slit had white figures in it. Suddenly I was cold, there was cold air swirling around me, and I saw more purple.

JEANNIE (C): Everything was in a box, purple and black, changing. I saw a V-shaped opening; it closed and became an eye. I swirled around; there were purple colors, coming and going. I had no hands. I wanted to check if that was true when the rattle stopped.

Now the newborn begins to look around:

LAUREN (C): There were purple and magenta circles of various sizes, and they moved in a rhythm to the rattle. There were presences around the edges of the color, and I was full of apprehension and didn't feel safe. I was standing in front of a column of stone; it was made of coarse material. I saw veils lifting; it felt like layers were being pulled up and back. I touched a mask; it was a painted white cat with whiskers. I was anxious again, my body trembled, but the mask sent a message that I was allowed to go on. So I went behind the cat mask, but no one was there. I was inside the mask, confused, I had no idea what was going on. My body was swirling. I did not want to fall. I wanted to get back into the canyon, but I only had a thin thread of control. I could not do it, and I could feel no answer. I saw the silhouette of a sleeping figure but could not decide if it was a man, a woman, or a child. It was unaware of me but was not resting.

The guests begin to arrive, gathering around the newborn to welcome it: "I saw the face of my white furry bear, and the nose and eye of a cat or a lion," one participant (C) told. They also assume the rule of power animals and impart strength to it:

VILLIE (C): There was pressure on my neck and shoulders. I went down a black-and-white swirling tunnel, further and further down. I saw the face of a tiger with the light behind him. The tiger was waiting. Then there was blackness again; a point of light appeared, and I felt warm. It might have been the sun. Then I saw the whole tiger.

Next, the newborn is placed at its mother's breast, and the purple circles that are the breasts, the nurture, are everywhere:

MAXINE (A): I am sitting by the fire. I am in a cave; the light is coming from above, and the smoke goes up. The back of my body feels cold and it aches. I am surrounded by purple; it is dense, and its edges are black. It comes on as a large purple circle, with several small ones in it. They are all around me, on the fire, above me, and on my feet. A circle of women sits around the fire. Outside the cave, there are overlapping purple circles.

With the newborn safely sheltered by the women in the nurturing purple circles, the ritual now turns to its last act, that of procreation, with the egg entering the body of the woman, and the small fairies, the spirits of other unborn, playing in the "old forest."

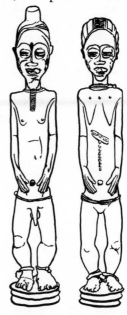

Plate 23

BELINDA (A): I saw a brightly lit hole with antlers on top. I thought it might be the birth canal, but then rejected the idea. There was pressure around my body. I saw an emu swallowing an egg; it went down her esophagus and landed in a nest in her belly. A little fairy came out of the egg and sat on a swing. Then I swallowed an egg. At first a green snake hatched; it came out of my mouth, then it went back in, and I laid it as though I was giving birth to it. I laid an egg through my vagina. I was aware that in the posture my hands were on my ovaries, that is, on my eggs. "What is there to learn?" I asked. The answer was that it wasn't my job to have babies, and I should not be concerned about it. I turned to the right. There was an old green forest. I saw the night and the forest and lots of fairies. They were aware of me because I was different. They were welcoming me, but the rattle stopped, and I knew I would be out of trance, so I asked if I could return. But I was not sure how to get back, because I had lost contact with the fairies at that point.

But the small fairies, "little silver things, containing the memories of the whole race," as Elizabeth R.(A) saw them, have something else on their minds than playing in their secret hideaway. They are hoping for an entrance into a womb, a chamber barred by a gate:

JAN (A): I am riding on the energy of a dying star. When the energy of a star becomes conscious, it can assume form. I am riding on a star, like in a spaceship. Then I am running, racing; my wings are flapping, so I can get through the gate.

The participants quoted for this first session using the birthing posture were all women, but actually there were also three men in the Cincinnati group, and their experiences, although less detailed, materially agreed with what the women told. There were statements such as "Black turned into purple; I was floating and felt like an embryo. I was looking up, through something, and then looking out." Or "There was a muted, generic light and a sense of opening. A wild cat appeared; it seemed coy, rather feminine, brushing its face with its tail." That, in fact, the birthing posture can equally serve as trance posture for men is lent further credence by plate 23, from sub-Saharan Africa, where a man and a woman stand side by side in this manner.

Delivering a woman is essentially a healing. It is quite reasonable, therefore, to assume that in some quantum jump of insight possible in trance, the birthing posture led to the development of the healing one. It is similar, and some of the experiences reported during healing are reminiscent of what happens in the birthing posture. The nurturing purple color appears quite regularly also. However, this is where the resemblance stops, and the sponsorship of the Bear Spirit clearly stamps the healing posture as independent and different.

The healing or *Bear* posture (see pl. 1), as described before, is usually assumed in standing, although there are also some sitting and even kneeling representations (see pl. 24). The feet are about a foot apart, the knees are not locked, the fingers are slightly curled, and the hands are placed on the middle of the trunk in such a way that the knuckles of the index fingers touch at or slightly above the navel.

Plate 24

Judging from plentiful archeological finds, the Bear posture is extremely old and the most widely known of all the postures (see map 1; examples are given in pls. 22–29). In very ancient Europe it seems to be somewhat younger than the birthing posture. However, this impression may be erroneous, given the small number of examples found. That early, representations of it occur exclusively in female figurines. My special favorite is the one created during the brief flowering of horticulture in the fifth millennium B.C. on the Danube near the Iron Gate, at Lepenski Vir (pl. 24); it is the beautifully abstract representation of an ecstatic woman's face, her head tilted slightly back, her hands in the Bear posture, and the triangle of her vulva like an ornamental design on her lower abdomen. By the third millennium B.C., however, the posture is found in Greece in female figures with a phallus in place of a neck and face, possibly signaling the beginning of male dominance over female ritual activity.

As I told earlier, the posture demonstrated by the shaman with the Bear Spirit (pl. 1) was among the very first we worked with. As we began exploring it, and although I was aware that the Bear Spirit was considered a mighty healer in many regions, I was quite generally blind to the connection between tradition and what my coworkers reported about a particular posture. I thought that perhaps the posture was an early one mediating possession, for so many participants reported having been "opened up." Eventually, however, I understood from fieldwork observations of true possession that the latter requires different strategies, and body posture plays no role. I realized that this "opening" was something needed for the curing power to enter, and I began teaching the Bear posture as a healing ritual. Then, whatever nagging doubts I might still have had finally dissolved when I was myself granted a number of cures by mighty "Grandfather Bear."

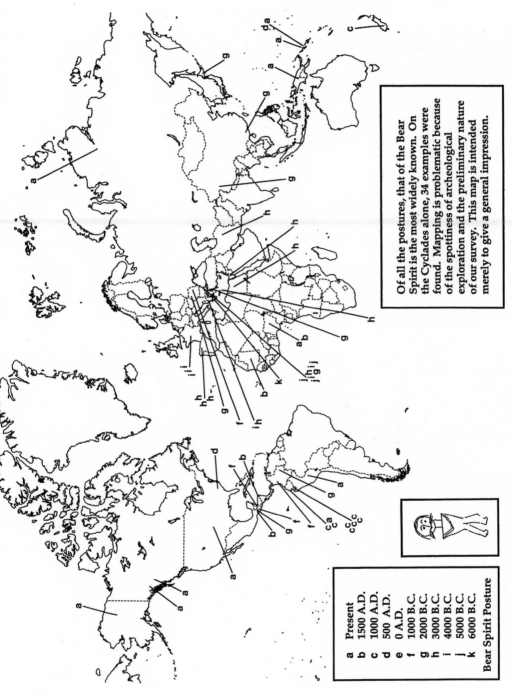

Of all the postures, that of the Bear Spirit is the most widely known. On the Cyclades alone, 34 examples were found. Mapping is problematic because of the spottiness of archeological exploration and the preliminary nature of our survey. This map is intended merely to give a general impression.

a	Present
b	1500 A.D.
c	1000 A.D.
d	500 A.D.
e	0 A.D.
f	1000 B.C.
g	2000 B.C.
h	3000 B.C.
i	4000 B.C.
j	5000 B.C.
k	6000 B.C.

Bear Spirit Posture

Map 1

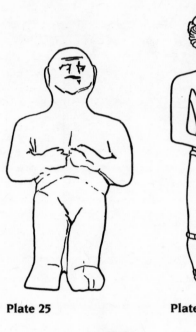

Plate 25

Plate 26

Plate 27

Plate 28

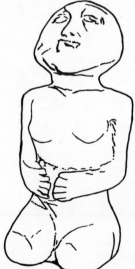

Plate 29

One of these cures involved an aching shoulder. For many years I had been in the habit on my numerous field trips of carrying a heavy shoulder bag made by a Yucatecan village saddler from sturdy deer leather. Finally the maltreated muscles rebelled. Putting anything on that shoulder began to cause excruciating pain; I could no longer sleep on my left side, lean on my left arm, or even turn in that direction. That summer a guest in Cuyamungue noticed that I was suffering and started massaging me. I nearly fainted with pain the first time, but she was quite knowledgeable, and after twelve sessions, when she had to leave, I did experience some relief. She warned, though, that I was not cured by a long shot, that a number of muscles were still bunched into hard knots in my back, and that upon returning to Columbus I should find a masseuse to continue with the treatment.

The massage therapist in the office of my family physician quickly found the same hard muscle knots in my back and after half an hour's work suggested that for those to dissolve I would have to have at least six more treatments. My pain had eased by then, so I foolishly carried a heavy suitcase on my trip to Cincinnati, where I was to do a workshop, with predictable results. By the time I had rattled for fifteen minutes during our first session, I was sure some fiend was gleefully tightening a vise on my left shoulder and pulling on it. We had done the Singing Shaman, and I intentionally slipped into a light trance while rattling, thinking that might give me some relief, but the pain was so fierce, I contemplated calling off the workshop.

At the next session I taught the participants the posture of the Shaman with the Bear Spirit. As I started rattling, I assumed as much of the posture myself as was possible under the circumstances and pleaded with Grandfather Bear to help me. Imperceptibly at first, as though it were stealing away on tiptoes, the pain eased and then disappeared. Nor did it recur during the rest of the workshop.

On the following Tuesday I went back to massage therapy. Try as she might, the masseuse was unable to find those six or seven hard knots that she was going to work on. "I can't understand this," she kept shaking her head, as she worked on me beyond the allotted half-hour. "Obviously you don't need me anymore," she said. "What did you do since the last time I saw you?" It would have been too complicated to tell her about Grandfather Bear, so I lied and complimented her on her good work, while breathing a grateful thank you to my old benefactor. This happened nearly three years ago, and the trouble has not recurred.

An even more dramatic cure happened to me in 1986. I was wearing a pair of lined woolen slacks during my spring trip to Europe. While in Austria, the weather suddenly turned warm, and I began to perspire. The perspiration apparently dissolved the formaldehyde in the lining, to which I am allergic. I developed a burning, itchy skin rash, which soon turned into dermatitis, and I was in agony. So I consulted the Bear Spirit. The attempt was disappointing; I did see his mask, but that was all. Then during the night I heared a voice reverberating through space, "Vinegar water, vinegar water." I was puzzled. Was it a belated message from the Bear Spirit? Besides, where was I going to get vinegar water on a trip? So I did not act on the curious counsel. I gave away the slacks, a physician friend let me have an antihistamine ointment, and in about four weeks, the rash gradually disappeared.

During the early summer, I helped with digging up some plants in Cuyamungue. It was extremely hot, I began to perspire, and as my bad luck would have it, I was wearing a Mexican blouse, which apparently also contained formaldehyde. Within minutes, I was covered with the same rash as before, first where the blouse had touched my moist skin, and soon from my toes up to my neck. As usual, I tried some home remedies first, but to no avail. By evening, I knew what burning in hell was like. To make matters worse, the night was unusually warm. I did not think I would see the dawn. Then I finally remembered that reverberating voice and its strange advice. I went over to the Student Building in the middle of the night, prepared a mixture of vinegar and lukewarm water, and sponged myself down with it. Relief was instantaneous. Within two more days, all traces of the rash had disappeared.

Except in such obvious cases, cures taking place in this posture, performed as we experience it by the Bear Spirit, are difficult to describe, first because, as in all non-Western medical systems, they serve predominantly health maintenance rather than specific cures; that is, they are designed to maintain balance and harmony. So both the body and the soul are treated. Second, the treatments are usually subtle and highly individualized, and frequently concern problems that the patient may be aware of only marginally and the observer even less.

Quite generally, even beginners tend to see their visual field completely suffused with a luminous purple color. They may be supported, shaken, or pushed from behind, gently or quite roughly; they may be caught in a spiraling movement and about to lose their balance. There is heat rising in their abdomens and over their backs, and a heavy weight presses down on their shoulders. They may shrink to a very small size or open up to receive a healing liquid, as we learn from Judy Ch. (Columbus, 1985): "I felt thirsty, so I was instructed, 'Put your head back!' And I felt a nectar of honey trickling down into me." Or from Belinda at the same workshop: "I saw a circular hole and started down. At the end of it there was an enormous glass with ice and a bubbly liquid in it, and that was poured into my head." Some cures are more exotic, as when Jan was fed a generous portion of worms with the assertion that it was good for her.

Without any prompting or prior knowledge, the Bear Spirit readily appears to the participants, visible partially or in his complete mask, either as a furry force holding or warming them from behind, or actually examining his would-be patients, as when Jan's guide took her to a spot in the Big Dipper, where the Bear "assessed my body and energy patterns." In addition, he is often seen to perform cures on others, as when Elizabeth R. watched how, touchingly, he made an incision in a woman's eyes "so she would be able to cry like others" (Columbus, 1985).

Let us listen to a few individual reports. The first one shows how physical perceptions keep merging with experiences that are possible only in the alternate reality.

> KRISTINA (Cuyamungue, August 1984): I was taken up into the Bear, but also saw him. We went flying together very slowly; I perceived a spiraling motion of my feet and also of my spine. There were bluish and purple flowers with yellow centers. I was being pushed back and forth by the Bear, then there were subtle movements all over my body. I felt that I was sinking ever deeper into my body, while at the same time dissolving into nothingness. Then I became conscious of my body again, and it felt okay all over.

For Pij (Salzburg, 1987), the hurt caused by an extremely unhappy childhood begins to dissolve:

> The rattle took me back to a happy memory from my childhood, when I used to roll marbles in a bowl. I saw them rolling around and was very sad when the image dissolved. Then I crawled through a tunnel, and my sorrow and pain were gone. I arrived in the midst of a family of bears; there were thirteen tiny bear cubs, and in the distance, I could see the huge mother bear. I left the bears, and felt very strong. There was a white light to the left of me and blackness to the right; I leaned back and was being rocked, and felt sheltered and warm. A green spot appeared before my right eye. I thought that perhaps it really wasn't there, but it wouldn't go away, and it frightened me. But I felt something black against my back, two heavy paws embraced me, and I was told that I should feed the birds. After I did that, the thirteen little bear cubs all started crawling around on me. I received a white bear skin and turned into a bear myself.

Linda (San Diego, 1985) is helped to resolve a conflict of sexual identity:

> My body was filled with a lot of sexual energy. There was a quick change of scenes; woods appeared as at home in Connecticut. I was a young man. A bear appeared and we danced together. Suddenly my spirit shot out of my face, and I saw a lot of fluffy clouds around me; they were like enormous kachinas, benevolent and powerful. Their energy was reassuring, telling me that I was doing fine. I found myself on a clearing. I was now a woman, and the Bear started teaching me how to dance, and I realized that I was also a bear. The dance had the feeling of a fertility ritual about it. Then I gave birth, not to humans but to many bears. The Bear turned into a she-bear, and she helped me nurse the bear cubs.

Eva D. (Vienna, 1985) speaks of overcoming fear:

> I felt very hot in the back, then I saw a bear skin. Suddenly, the Bear spread it all over me, and I became very afraid, thinking, "What is he going to do?" I was walking as if standing on his feet; I stumbled and fell down. But then I felt how from his skin strength was pouring into me. A fire sprang up before me; I walked

into it, and then I was the fire. The fire split into two fire tunnels and I was in both; I shot into them with tremendous speed, then the two tunnels merged. I once more looked into the fire and I understood. Some gnomes flew by; they wore wild, distorted masks, but I was no longer afraid.

Still others endure parts of their body becoming detached or being torn apart. To hear that was truly amazing to me: Without any preparation and entirely spontaneously, modern Westerners apparently were able to experience dismemberment, which for Siberian shamans is an important phase during their initiation as healers.[3] Apparently, the Bear Spirit especially singles out various kinds of healers for this treatment, which ties these experiences in with the Siberian culture complex. I was alerted to this peculiar coincidence in one of my very early workshops in Europe, when Lukas, a recent graduate of the Medical School of the University of Vienna, reported that the Bear Spirit grabbed him, threw him into a kettle, and started stirring the boiling liquid with him as the ladle. Lukas's body dissolved until only his head and his lungs remained, attached to each other by a thin cord. Suddenly, he was whole again. But while to the Siberian shamans the experience means intense suffering, Westerners do not perceive it that way. Christian St. (Vienna, 1985), for instance, paradoxically found that being manhandled this way by a powerful spirit was great fun, and he laughed about it afterward.

> The Bear put his arms around me, and I felt sheltered as in a motherly embrace. But then he began stroking me with his paws and tore off my head. He ripped open my belly, pulled out my intestines, and I felt the healing power of his paws. Then he looked me over with a serious expression, rent open·my chest, and placed three masks in it, together with some threads. I had a long black penis and found myself at a black lake; I either walked into it or I fell, I don't remember. Then I saw all of you in this room. I wanted to dance. The Bear was here, too; he pissed on Eva, then he kissed Felicitas on her nose, and he was about to rip my head off once more when the rattle stopped.

At the time this happened, Christian was a graduate student in history, and I thought that perhaps my impression that such initiation experiences were reserved for healers had been wrong. However, only two years later, Christian began taking courses in holistic healing and is now well on his way toward his new career as a healer.

On occasion, the Bear Spirit is helped during curing by snakes, and also by various raptors and carrion-eating birds, a fact known from Pueblo Indian myths. "A snake appeared and knocked three times on my forehead," one participant reported. "An eagle came into my body through my forehead. It opened it up." Or as Sharron told (Columbus, 1985): "There was a flicker of fear. I had black plates on my shoulders, head, and back. Then I saw a bird's face looking at me; it was picking at me and tearing pieces out of me, out of that plate." Here is an experience of a similar nature from Switzerland:

URSULA ST. (Sommerau, 1985): I found myself inside a mountain and felt great pain in my shoulders and my neck. I leaned back and felt something supporting me, not only there but on my sides as well. My abdomen felt warm. Dark figures appeared before me; I heard the flapping of wings. I split in half; rags, ribbons, and colors rose out of my belly; my rigid shell dropped away. I felt wonderful, so light. The birds flew away. I saw an eye above me and embryos floating in the light. One fell into the split in my body and turned. I wanted to keep it in there.

The Bear posture can also be assumed if a cure is to be effected for someone else. During the workshop in Cincinnati in the fall of 1987, Dean, one of the participants, complained about sciatica causing severe pain along her right thigh. To help her, I asked the group, including Dean, to assume the Bear posture. After I had rattled for fifteen minutes, everyone gathered around her and touched her, and I continued to rattle for another three minutes to keep the trance going. Healing rituals of this nature are used extensively around the world. The understanding that trance can heal must be extremely old, for modern hunter-gatherers, such as the Bushmen, guardians of the most ancient human traditions, use the strategy simply to keep everyone in their band well and also to heal. Anthropologists tell of seeing the medicine men inducing the religious trance in themselves by singing and dancing, and then touching everyone in their group to this end. Trance healing has survived as "laying on of hands" in Christianity.

After our ritual, Bernie reported that as he placed his hand on Dean, he felt a resistance, and that he was doing "all the work." It was so strenuous, he thought he might collapse. But then his strength came back, and he was back in equilibrium. Another one felt, "not saw but felt," a bright yellow light traveling down her arm and into Dean; or "I saw a large hand; it had a bluish marble on its fingertips, which changed to white and then passed into Dean, a gift to her"; or "I felt pins and needles streaming out of my arm. They were really shooting out; I thought I was going to electrocute her." Dean later reported complete relief.

I should like to add still another example here, for it demonstrates the great power of the Bear Spirit. In this instance, Belinda called on him for help when her mother was discovered to have uterine cancer. The examining physician was convinced on the basis of his tests that the cancer of this patient was extensive and had possibly metastasized. Belinda was desperate. So she and her friends decided to suggest a healing ritual to her mother, and to Belinda's great relief, her mother consented to try it, although she was unfamiliar with what her daughter was talking about.

Belinda and her helpers had her mother assume the Bear posture lying in bed, so that her hands were above her uterus. They then assumed the same posture themselves. The patient felt her uterus start getting very hot. She began seeing small white mice running around in her body and producing more mice. They were busily gnawing away at her uterus, as though they were intent on consuming the uterine wall. After the conclusion of this part of the ritual, one of the healers handed the patient a large crystal which she was to hold on her abdomen above the uterus. The crystal, which had been clear before, showed grey streaks after the treatment and needed to be cleansed by burying it for a while. Going into trance once more, the group guided the "mice" into a bowl of water. This is not unlike what is done by Australian shamans, who, in a ritual which the Australian psychiatrist John Cawte[4] likens to a sacrament, make the illness visible by "sucking" a small object, a pebble or a fragment of glass, out of the patient, thus facilitating a cure.

The subsequent operation proved the physician wrong. It turned up only a small cancerous nodule within a large benign fibrous growth. When the intervention was so successful, Jan, one of the participants in the ritual, joked, "We should have had another week!" I would not go that far, but certainly at least in this case the ritual of the Bear posture proved to be a valuable adjunct to the surgical procedure.

Plate 30

The Bear posture is so powerful that according to some folk traditions, it can also mediate a cure if the patient is too ill or weak to assume it himself. In modern Siberia, for instance, wood carvings of the Bear Spirit in the healing posture (see pl. 30a) are given to the chronically ill. Such carvings are not objects of worship or "idols." After use, children have been observed playing with them, and if the band moves away, they are often discarded.

Even when large-scale agriculture takes over, which usually means the loss of the knowledge of the postures, this particular one seems to endure. This is true of classical Egypt (see pl. 30e), and also happened in the Aztec empire. The Aztec goddess Tlaelquan was conventionally represented in the Bear posture. She bore the epithet of "eater of contamination" (*comedora de cosas sucias*), because she nourished herself with the faults that humans confessed to her, thus freeing them of sin. In other words, there is a memory about psychological healing and the restoration of harmony attached to this posture.

Because of its relationship to curing and health, the posture in other areas of the world has come conventionally to mean "I wish you good health." This at least seems to be the case with the golden jugs from Colombia created by Quimbaya and Chibcha goldsmiths of pre-Inca time (pl. 26). They are decorated with male or female figures in the posture of the Bear Spirit. Such containers were used to carry lime. In many mountainous regions of South America, lime and coca leaves have always been chewed together, contributing to health and well-being, because above fourteen thousand feet, carbohydrates cannot easily be digested without the aid of the active ingredient in the coca leaf.

CHAPTER NINE

Female Powers
of Healing

The forty-one girl knights.
Although the Bear Spirit may on occasion appear in the form of a female bear,
his power seems to be predominantly male. There is another posture, however,
which apparently summons a special kind of female energy.[1] The posture first
came to my attention early in 1985 in a publication about antiquities from
Tennessee.[2] The stone sculpture, created about A.D. 700, represented a woman
who had her arms placed on her chest in a special way, so that her right hand
came to rest above the left (see pl. 31). Subsequently, I saw the posture also
in Marija Gimbutas's book about ancient Europe.[3] The terra-cotta figurine,
once more a woman (pl. 32), was much older (5th millennium B.C.), but there
was no mistaking the position of the hands. I was anxious to explore the
posture, but in neither case was there any indication about the position of the
legs, and I was at a loss about what to do about that.

When I went to Europe in the spring, I took my notes about the posture
with me, however, in order to have some trained people in Austria see what
they could do with it. Given the fact that there were so many standing postures,
I suggested that we try it standing upright. Christian St. subsequently saw
himself in the midst of clinging plants with strange fruit that started wildly
growing about him, and a woman who breathed on his heart. His experience
carried a suggestion of healing, but Eva D. provided no confirmation. She even
became sick to her stomach, and her legs began hurting. Standing, I assumed,
had probably been the wrong choice.

My next assignment was in Budapest. My host, the Hungarian folklorist
Mihály Hoppál, showed me a new book which he had edited about Eurasian
shamanism.[4] There was no time to read it, but I looked at the photographs,
and I was surprised and delighted that one of them showed a modern sha-

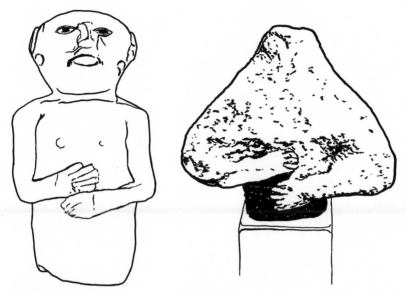

Plate 31   **Plate 32**

maness from Central Asia during a healing ritual in the posture that we had explored in Austria.[5] She had her arms folded over her chest in the way I had seen in the above two ancient pieces of art, and she was sitting with her legs crossed. Here apparently was the answer to our problem.

Once back home in Columbus, I ordered Hoppál's work, and by fall I had it in my possession. We had planned a working session anyway, and so I put the new posture on the agenda. On the day of our meeting, I settled down for a noonday nap but almost immediately woke up again with the curious feeling that I was not alone. The entire room seemed to be crowded with joyously excited entities. I thought, well, a few of our spirit friends are aware that we are going to invite them in this evening, and they arrived here ahead of time. I had much to do before my guests arrived, but I got out Hoppál's book anyway to read something about the shamaness shown in the photograph. But being in a hurry, I could not locate the article in question, so I put the book away again.

We used a tape, so I was able to participate, too, and there were five of us. For reasons to be told later, I am going to give here only three of the five reports:

> JUDY M.: Even while we were breathing, I left my body and went outside. I was floating up high, and looking back into this room, I saw that it was empty. I felt very light and disappeared. I looked down on a desert landscape; there was a dark tunnel with a light at the end, and my spirit guide, a huge stag, appeared next to me. The tunnel ended in a cave with a very high ceiling, and there was a bonfire,

and there were others sitting around it. I stepped into the middle of the fire and started dancing. Then I left the tunnel and became a raindrop; it was wonderful. I smelled the earth and felt all the elements. Then I had to get back into my body, and I didn't like that at all.

JAN: From the start I had the feeling of the room being full of energy. The energy was between my hands; it was so intense, it hurt. Then it became an ear of corn and it burst, and the kernels danced around in a circle. I saw each one of us, living, dying, each one at a different spot. Then we were back in this room. Each of us brought something back; we were a kaleidoscope. Then I went diving down and saw a crystal cave glowing in brilliant colors; I was in the water, then in the air. I shot up to the stars. The energy was still there, so great that my body couldn't take it.

FELICITAS: I was flying rapidly through a glowing, dark-blue world against a night-blue background. To my left, flat images began developing, pitted white surfaces in the dark, like fly-by pictures of the earth taken from a satellite. I reined it in; I didn't want to leave the earth. Then I was sad that I was no longer flying. The vision subsided, and all I still felt was being rocked back and forth and then more energetically sideways by an energy that wouldn't let go of me.

We were struck by the fact that the three of us had all been on a journey to some faraway cold and rainy place. The other two, Belinda and Elizabeth R., equally reported on such a region, and about restlessly dancing, but in addition there were other, curious elements in their tale, something about a totem pole and a white she-bear, and the horns of a mountain goat, which did not fit in with the rest of our experiences. Confident that someday I would understand, I left it alone for the time being. When that understanding finally came, it was one of the biggest surprises of our common journey of discovery, as we shall see later (Section III, The Story of Kats and His Bear Wife). In our discussion we concentrated instead on the dancing multiple energy that had had all of us in its grip, and wondered what its nature might be.

During the following night, shortly before daybreak, I had a vision. A row of curiously shaped masks appeared before a background lightly blushing into rose. They were white and round, delicate like Chinese paper lanterns, yet with their pointed ears they recalled the heads of cats. The place for the eyes was cut out, and inside each one a dark-grey hairy ball was incessantly in motion. Several times I was given to understand emphatically that "we lick blood, we lick blood."

The next morning, I recorded the vision, but except for the restless motion of the grey balls inside the paper lanterns, it seemed to have little to do with what we had experienced during our session the night before. However, that same afternoon, I finally located the report that belonged to the photographs,[6] and I found out that this conclusion was wrong. It seems that in Inner Asia, in the valleys of Uzbekistan, shamanesses ask for the help of a group of spirits called Chiltan when they are called upon to cure. The Chiltan are said to be forty-one young girl knights. No wonder my room had felt so crowded the day before! Their favorite color is white, and in agreement with what I had been told in my vision, the shamanesses smear the blood of sacrificial animals on their tambourines, because the Chiltan spirits like to lick blood.

Now I understood why from the start, even during that first attempt in the spring, where Christian St. was surrounded by clinging plants with strange fruit wildly growing about him, there was the experience of multiple, powerful energy. And in Uzbekistan, obviously, the energy was summoned to aid in healing, as Christian knew when he felt a woman breathing on his chest.

Representations of the *Chiltan posture*, as we are now calling it, have turned up on the Northwest Coast, in Arizona, and with the Olmecs in Central America. In addition to Tennessee, it is known in South America, in ancient Europe, and in modern Africa. A search of the record also turned up a connection between the posture and the cat ears I had seen. It appears that in Colombia, archeologists dug up a tall stone column, about three thousand years old, which shows what appears to be a bearded man in the Chiltan posture (pl. 33). The power animals of the Indian societies of Central and South America, namely, two jaguars with their catlike pointed ears, are carved into the base of the column. The relationship to healing is evident in the snake appearing on the left.

The archeological record also demonstrates that my conclusion about one always having to sit with legs crossed was a hasty one, arrived at with too little experimentation. There are a number of male figures extant that are not sitting but standing in this posture. So in our workshops we now have the men stand, as usual with their feet somewhat apart and their knees soft, while the women sit cross-legged, with the right leg in front.

Experience has shown that the Chiltan spirits can provide a fast surge of energy. In the summer of 1986, for instance, I used the posture to good advantage giving a much-needed boost to a group assembled for the trance dance ritual and tired from working on their masks all day in the unaccustomed heat. Not only did the exercise produce the expected results, but I was once more amazed at how consistently the Chiltan spirits revealed themselves. As during the first time, there was the trip: "I burst forth out of my chest"; "I rode fast through the forest"; and "A tall woman stood by the kiva door; she motioned for me to follow her, and we flew over the land." We heard the endless repetition of experiencing energy, usually in multiple form: "The energy came in waves"; "Lots of energy was lifting me up"; "Whirlwinds twirled me into a cave"; "Lots of energy went through my body and I was getting dizzy; I felt that it was female energy"; and, similar to what Jan had

Plate 33

told during that first session, "I became a green pepper and I exploded." Even the fire kept reappearing, as in "We went across a fire"; or "I sat in the flames and it was healing."

What I found particularly fascinating were the specific references to the blood sacrifice that I had heard about in my vision: "I saw a gorge, in it a river of blood, and a huge sun"; or "I was a leopard. An African warrior threw his spear; he killed me and licked my blood"; and even, "I was covered with the sweet and sticky nectar of a blood sacrifice that the spirits licked off of me." And finally we heard about the militant and possibly dangerous aspect of the girl knights, as in, "We were all spirits in the clouds and were organized like an army."

Here are some examples from other workshops. In rich variation, they play out the different motifs of this posture. One theme, for instance, is the experience of being rocked by the energy of these spirits:

> ELLA (Cuyamungue, summer 1987): I saw pictures like of marbled paper, of earth colors. I was floating and saw an eruption; it was red like fire, but it was also like a flower and a river. I felt movement back and forth, like being rocked, or maybe riding, but I didn't know on what. Was it an animal? I couldn't see it. Suddenly I was flying over a canyon, but I saw only one side of it, and next to it a flat-top mountain. I was riding and rocking again. Then there were unclear figures and a triangle of complicated shape.

Another theme is the multiple nature of the energy. It appears in many different forms, as a group of people dancing, a circle of women all looking alike, and in a vivid burst of visual display, as many multicolored snakes and balls:

> KRISCHTA (Sommerau, Switzerland, spring 1987): I felt warmth in my abdomen and was whirling around. I was supposed to get dressed, and the rattle was my garment. Suddenly I found myself in a dark forest, and it was the forest that was doing the rattling. I got out of the forest, and in front of me there was a huge beak, and gradually an eagle developed out of the beak and vanished into the ground. There was a light from above, and surfaces started moving into each other. I could feel that but didn't see it. Many people appeared. They danced to the rhythm of the rattle; they kept picking up what, I could not see. Then the rhythm of the rattle was a horse, but I couldn't catch it. I was enveloped in an enormous waterfall; its noise was deafening, and there was much movement. I became a stork and flew away into the distance until I was nothing but a black dot.

> KRISTINA (Cuyamungue, summer 1987): There was a lot of talking in the room, and I was wondering what was going on. There was the presence of heavy energy. I was looking down from above, and in the room there were many women; they all looked alike, they were gathered around the fire. The light kept flickering; it got smaller, then larger. I started collapsing and fell to the ground, then I disappeared. I saw a slug or a small snake curling, and I wondered whether I was going to turn into a ring. Suddenly I felt a lot of energy; my spine and my head all became of one piece, and all around me there were peacock feathers.

VRENIE (Sommerau, spring 1987): From my left, there came many multicolored snakes. I landed in a chute. I was very small. I turned into a snake, then into an ant, a flying ant, and flew across a lake. The sun was orange-colored, like a flowerbed. I landed on it and started crawling around; it was very difficult to do, managing the rhythm of the six legs all at the same time. Many green and multicolored balls started coming in from all sides, moving wildly up and down. I fell into a cleft, into a cave, and a multitude of animals started arriving, leopards, deer, snakes, many different animals.

Not only do the Chiltan spirits have energy to give, but they are also healers. Their healing energy may be scattered in the form of gold dust, it may come equally gently carried as honey by swarms of bees, or it may burn as cleansing fire:

JACQUES (Cuyamungue, summer 1987): I saw many animals coming in from all sides, also birds from far away, and many black ravens. They landed and were very strong. A rainbow appeared, and the birds took gold dust and a fan, and scattered the gold dust all over us.

NORMA (Cuyamungue, summer 1987): I became a garden; the earth was moist, there were birds, and bees, and a turtle was sitting on my stomach. There were insects on me; it was pleasant, and the bees dropped honey in my mouth to give me energy. Then the sun became dimmer. It was evening; everything went to sleep, the insects, the birds, and the turtle, too. All were contented.

KATHRIN (Sommerau, spring 1987): For a while, everything seemed to be reversed. Instead of standing, I was lying down, and animals came rushing toward me, a deer, a fox, some birds, many animals, but I could see only their heads. I was a black beetle and could feel my wings in the back, like an armor. Then I was a lion. A white bird emerged from the shadows; then there were many more birds, and their movements seemed to multiply. Finally, a shower of fire rained down on me from the left.

REGULA (Cuyamungue, summer 1987): I saw a wheel turning. I went down into a whirlpool, and masks started coming from all sides and crowded all over me. I heard the drums, and the masks danced around the fire and I with them, and my hands and feet became very warm. Above us, there was a large eagle with its wings spread out, as if standing in the air. Just before the rattle stopped, a large fire sprang up and started burning me.

Finally, the Chiltan spirits are fully capable of taking a novice through a Siberian-type initiation if they encounter a healer worthy of their attention. This is what happened to Hanna, who is a registered nurse:

HANNA (Cuyamungue, summer 1987): I was standing in the desert. As I was looking down on myself, I saw a hand holding a knife that was cutting into my skin. I started objecting; I didn't want to lose my inner parts. But it was useless. The hand took out my heart, my liver, everything; I was left only with my skin, and I started to dance. I was afraid that the hand would cut off my head, too. I said, "Don't do that!" But it happened anyway. I saw myself without a head. The hand put my head into a big pot to boil, and scraped out everything, so my head was completely empty. Then the hand took a totem pole and pushed it through my body. It got bigger and bigger and turned into a medicine man. The medicine man started pounding me into the ground, and I was nothing but rock and sand. The medicine man was an ecstatic dancer; he danced on me, and I was only sand. With every step he took, he began creating me entirely anew; it was like a rebirth. My skin began reappearing, but I was still empty inside when the rattle stopped.

The Couple from Cernavodă. In five- to seven-thousand-year-old arche- ological sites in Europe, but also in much younger ones in Africa, archeologists occasionally come across a male figure seated on a low four-legged stool, his elbows propped on his knees. The folds of his cheeks are pushed up by his hands, which seem to form a fist. He has been called variously the pensive god or the sorrowful god. At one particular dig, however, at Cernavodă near the Danube delta in present-day Rumania, he was found in a seven-thousand- year-old grave together with a female figure, both formed of clay and covered with a brown slip. As luck would have it, the first time I ever saw him was in association with this female companion (see pl. 34). The woman is sitting on the ground. Her left leg is stretched out in front of her, and her right knee is raised. Her hands are resting lightly on her right knee in such a way that her left hand seems somewhat stretched out, while the palm of her right hand is lifted, creating the impression of a paw.

What the man might be experiencing by himself in this posture, if anything, we have not yet investigated. But remarkable things happen when the two of

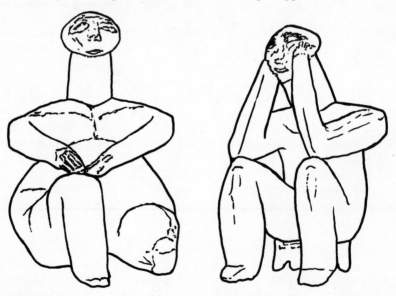

Plate 34

them get together. What takes place, apparently, is a ritual during which it is the female partner who does the shamanizing, while the man's experiences are minimal. Yet he ends up totally exhausted. The reason seems to be that he is the one who provides the energy. "He is the battery," one participant commented.

We tried this combined posture for the first time at a workshop in Switzerland in the spring of 1986. There were only three men facing nine women, and I soon suspected what was going on when I heard the first man complaining that he had felt some shooting pains in his heart, and all he wanted to do when the rattle stopped was to go to sleep. The next one had radiated energy toward the women, which caused him to dissolve, and although he recovered even while still in trance, he was extremely tired afterward: "I started getting nauseated," he said, "and rays issued from my chest, and then I briefly dissolved. After that, I became immensely tall, and there was a lot of light in my head." And Urs R., a physician, recognized the pivotal role of the shamaness when he saw her approaching as a dark mass from which a triangle emerges, which then turns into the navel of the world. However, he struggled in vain to provide the energy needed for her work. That is why he saw the navel of the world, the rounded stone of the *omphalos* at Delphi, under a glass dome:

> I had the feeling that parts of the rattle collected in my cerebellum. I had to let it seep into my spinal cord, then it wanted to escape through the tail bone, but I couldn't let it out. I saw two surfaces, a white one on the right and a black one on the left; they were moving from left to right, and each one had tall doors, which I entered simultaneously. On the other side everything was covered by fog. For a long time, nothing happened. Then a triangle appeared; it turned into an obelisk, then into a rock representing the omphalos. It was covered by a glass sphere. I wanted to enter it, then once more there was nothing.

To be sure, in the end the men, although terribly tired, were glad they had given of their energy. For listening to the women, they too understood that this exercise in psychological archeology had afforded us a glimpse of a lost world, full of wonder and mystery, like a scintillating jigsaw puzzle. But it was clear that there had been too much of a strain on the men. So I decided to do this exercise only if the number of men and women was more or less evenly balanced.

Considering the individual reports of the women now, we find that riding on the power of the men, a shamaness may make daring voyages into the world of legend:

> DOROTHEA: I was in a small boat, and something was pulling me toward the left. I struggled against it, and finally, I was able to stop. I felt something approaching from the right. A strong wind came up, and I struggled to keep from capsizing. Suddenly the wind abated, and I saw a sea serpent approaching; she was green

and very long, a real sea monster. As I watched, her eyes turned green and her tongue red, then her tongue split into three tongues and she had three heads. She kept threatening me, and I needed a lot of power.

The shamaness of old is also a midwife and healer. Her rattles put a young woman into trance to ease the pains of labor, and then she summons the birds to take her through to delivery:

> REGINA: I heard many rattles, and had the feeling that I could breathe deeply and well. I saw a black bird coming from the right, and a white one from the left. They flew over the valley. Then they came back, and one of them carried a small child in its beak, like a stork. He asked me, "Do you want it?" And the white bird said, "If you want it, you can have it." And I said, "All right, I will take it." So the birds left the bundle, and as they flew away, they winked at me.

Sometimes a pregnant woman is seriously ill, and it takes all the skill of the shamaness to save her, taking recourse not only to the succor of the rattles but also to decoctions that can work miracles and ease suffering. In the case that unfolds before our eyes in Kathrin's story, the old shamaness has been summoned to a woman who is ill and pregnant with twins. The shamaness raises her arms to invoke the helping spirits and, as in very ancient traditions, transmits spiritual power to the patient through her tongue. She administers a healing potion. It transports the patient into a soothing dream; the shamaness appears to her as a praying mantis and a horned beetle. As her strength comes back, she sees the dancing moons, and completely restored, she wakes up in the familiar cave and sees the rock walls outside.

> KATHRIN: I saw a mouth. It stuck out its tongue, and a ribbon came out of it and flowed into me. Then there were some disjointed sequences. I saw a praying mantis, then a horned beetle, which turned into a rhinoceros. I was in a waterfall; there were two moon sickles, and they danced with each other. I saw a drake. I ran after it and came to some water, with a child in it. The drake passed right through me. I became a gold ring, and there were two embryos in the ring. A large tube appeared, and from its opening milk flowed into me. Then I was in a cave lit by burning candles, and I lay down and reddish-brown drops fell on me. Suddenly I was outside the cave, and I had the feeling that I was a part of the rock wall.

One of the most important tasks of the shamaness is taking the soul of the deceased in the shape of a cocoon in a boat to the lower world, to the abode of the Spirits of the Dead. Immediately after death, the soul is still heavy with earthly concerns, and so Pij as the shamaness finds that rowing the boat is tremendously strenuous. After a while of rowing upstream, the shamaness loses her strength. The soul, which has not become reconciled yet to being forever parted from the living, takes advantage of the shamaness's waning strength, turns into fish bones, and tries to escape. This must not happen, for the ghosts of the recently dead will bring disease and misfortune to the living. To renew her strength, the shamaness sinks into the depths, the canyon of her childhood. The restful sojourn takes a long time, but finally she rises from the canyon and begins to dance in the street. The magic strategy works, the street turns into the river once more, and the task is completed: the people who had gone along in the boat return without the cocoon. Everyone celebrates, because the deceased has been successfully taken to the home of the departed. But the shamaness has been to the realm of the dead, and she must now undergo a ritual of death and rebirth before she can return to the world of the living:

> PIJ: The rattle immediately split into many sounds, which moved around me wildly in the form of colored waves or snakes. Then the rattle sound became a waterfall, and the water, coming from the left, hit me hard like hail. I was in a canoe rowing but couldn't look behind me. I had the feeling that somebody was sitting behind me, or that I was carrying a load, and that I had to go on rowing. I knew that behind me, someone was lying in the canoe, enveloped like a cocoon, and there were six or eight people with him. I asked, "Where am I supposed to go?" And the answer came, "Upriver." I found it very strenuous; my muscles hurt as I was rowing against the current. I was proud, but also nearly at the end of my strength.
>
> Suddenly the person in the canoe turned into the skeleton of a fish and wanted to get out. Inexplicably, I had some brief images of childhood memories at this point. It seems that I fell off a high wall into a canyon, and was waiting for something, and the rattle sounded very slow. Then I was standing in a street; I had many legs, six, or maybe eight, and had to dance wildly, over and over again. Suddenly the street turned into the river, and the people of the canoe were coming back. The cocoon was no longer with them. I saw people dancing happily in the streets of Luzern. They laid me down on top of a wall. I had the feeling that it was all right, but then again, I had my doubts. I had to lie there for a long time. Many Indians started emerging from my vagina, ants, then also horses. I became very old; the flesh fell off my bones, which were fish bones, or maybe they were a human skeleton. I had the feeling that all was well, and that it had been worth the trouble.

The second time we did the posture of the Couple of Cernavodă was at a workshop in Vienna in the spring of 1987. This time there were almost as many men in the group as there were women, so I hoped that it would not be as strenuous for the men as it had been in Switzerland the year before. We were in a large, rectangular hall, so I had the men and women sitting facing each other. As a result, some of the women afterward commented spontaneously that they had been aware of the men "radiating" toward them.

Once more, the men's experiences were very meager, although their reports did not reflect the extreme exhaustion suffered by the Swiss men. "The trance seemed very short," said one. "There was the snout of a monkey, but all was very unclear." According to another one, "I saw an eye, and I rushed toward it. It had an enormous pupil. I fell into it and dissolved into my elements."

In Othmar's vision there is an indication of the role assigned to the women in this posture when he sees, as Kathrin had in Switzerland, the shamaness ready herself to transmit energy to her patient through her tongue: "I saw very little. I felt sleepy. I saw images that were unclear and disjointed. There was a witch; a red ribbon came out of her mouth, and then I saw a bird." And both Wittigo and Wolfgang distributed power, the latter characteristically perceiving himself as a leaky vessel:

WITTIGO: I dissolved, then became a hallucinogenic mushroom. I rose as if in a balloon. I was in control of rain and let raindrops fall on the earth. I had small mushrooms, which I cut into pieces and spread on the ground.

WOLFGANG: I saw purple, blue, and green colors; they seemed to weave back and forth, and I was sending out rings of light that were bright and warm. I was a vessel with a hole in it.

Although by this time I had forgotten the details of the Swiss reports, and no one of the Swiss group had any contact with the rather large one in Vienna, the experiences of the women precisely followed the same general outline. There was the trip to the mythological world beyond:

ROSMARIE: I came to an iron fence and went through the gate. Behind it there were many dwarfs peeking out from behind the trees. I came to a round lake. There were dwarfs rowing in small boats toward a canal. There they got out; they were now white spirits, moving like marionettes. They began playing with balls on the seashore. Then some whales arrived. They picked up the balls, swallowed them, and took them away. The sea was light blue; it looked like silk, with white seagulls rising from it. I sat on the bank by a hut and I was an old man. I collected the droppings of the seagulls and fed them to the whales.

In the next experience, there is the topic of delivery, although the shamaness is present only by implication. In addition, except for the perception of the constriction in the abdomen, the birth event is experienced from the point of view of the fetus:

CHARLOTTE: I felt a constriction in my belly. Most images were very unclear. The landscape I saw was pale, but I distinctly heard water rushing by. A black spot appeared, then I saw the sun and in the background a small bird. I was in a pea pod and saw it very clearly from the inside, and then I disappeared.

Or during this second delivery, we are given the impression that the mother died, while the child lived to run and play:

CLAUDIA: I saw the blood running out of me, and I heard someone say, "Lie down." I refused; it was a woman who said that. I again said, "No," and really hated her. But she prevailed; she slit open my abdomen and examined my uterus. I could no longer hear the rattle. I saw a small being running around, and there was dancing and swinging.

And once more, the shamaness appears as the healer, who is called upon to cure many ailments, as related by Irmgard:

> IRMGARD: I had pains in my upper jaw and in my groin; my arms felt heavy and trembled, and my head kept bothering me. A man appeared, made of shadow; his hair glowed as if with electricity. Out of the shadows, the heads of animals began emerging, of a steer first; that turned into a deer, and then into an owl. Suddenly, I felt water splashing on my head, and it turned light. I was given raw mushrooms to eat. I can still taste them now.

The shamaness may even be able to make the old and sick young again, as in Isi's concluding story. The connection of the shamaness to the power animal becomes evident when, after she brings about a cure, pointed ears start growing from her pelt:

> There was so much energy around, but I still felt that this posture was very strenuous. I was in a snowy landscape. A woman came to me on a sleigh; she wore a white fur coat and a white cap. She made me get into the sleigh and off we went, very fast, because we had to save a woman's life. We arrived at a house and went in. There was an old couple in the house, and the woman was dying. As I watched, the woman started getting younger and younger, and pointed ears started growing from the fur cap of the white woman. Suddenly, I was outside, it was light, and the snow had melted. When the rattle stopped, I noticed that I had a backache.

In the summer of 1987, Thomas, a psychology student and friend of Isi's who had also taken part in the above workshop, came to her for help. On a hike through the Austrian forests, he had picked up some ticks, which may spread meningitis, and he had neglected to get inoculated. Understandably, he was thoroughly frightened and depressed. So he asked her to rattle for him. As she wrote,

> I figured that perhaps a rattle session would give him back some feeling of joy and confidence in himself, and that is exactly what happened. The rattling was so intense, I was completely overcome. What happened was that as I rattled I saw the woman in the white fur coat returning, whom I had come to know in the Cernavodă posture. Except this time she came with bells on her sleigh. She was definitely in the room, and with the tips of her fur, she gave Thomas something like an aura massage, and she pointed out to me exactly where the energy was blocked in his body, especially around his heart. The fascinating thing was that afterward Thomas told that he had felt something like feathers fanning him, and that then those feathers settled protectively on his heart. At first, I used a very bright-sounding Huichol rattle, while I had him stand in the Bear posture. Then I had him lie down for a trip to the lower world and used our [New Mexican gourd] rattle and then a drum. Suddenly I knew that he was not in any danger at all, and I suggested to him that he get in touch with his power animal. It was a wonderful present that afterward he felt so well. He was completely relaxed and full of hope. I could feel your presence too all that time, and you kept saying, "Go on. It's all right." (July 1, 1987)

CHAPTER TEN

Changing Shape—
The Shimmering Game

In a tale of Rabelaisian abandon related by Indian fishermen of the Northwest Coast,[1] their culture hero, the Raven, changes himself into a fisherman in order to make merry with the latter's wife. When the fisherman unexpectedly returns and begins beating the intruder into a pulp, the Raven is constrained to revert to his original shape. The incensed husband ties him up and throws him into the pit of the outhouse. But the Raven, being immortal, eventually frees himself of his bonds and lives to see another day and more adventures of a similar nature.

Traces of such "softness," as one anthropologist calls it,[2] of the boundaries between humans and animals, when matters were in a state of flux between the species, are all about. Egyptian and Celtic and Hindu gods have animal heads or shapes. Echoes of the same tradition abound in the myths of every society of the world. They are known among the Australian aborigines and on the other end of the spectrum among the nineteenth-century Germans who were the consultants of the Grimm Brothers. And they are, of course, equally familiar to the Indian societies of our continent. There is a story current among the same Indian fishermen of the Northwest Coast, according to which a hunter once heard laughter coming from a cave. When he sneaked up to the entrance and peeked in, there were the animals hilariously playing at turning into people. In fact, the Haida Indians of the region recount that in those early times animals used to have both human and animal forms. As the Navajo singers put it, "In those times all the animals were like people. The four-footed beasts, the flying birds, the coiling snakes, and the crawling insects behaved the way that earth-surface people who occupy the world today behave" (Zolbrod 1984:98).

It stands to reason that humans should equally have the capability of crossing the boundaries of their species. In fact, various hunter societies that still exist today have sacred dances in which humans turn into those animals to which they have a special relationship. Modern observers of Australian religious life[3] describe dances where the movements of the respective animal are expertly imitated, until in trance the dancer turns into the being depicted. Similar dances are also known among African hunter-gatherer societies. To the rhythm of the clapping of the women, as we see in an old cave drawing (pl. 35), the Bushman dancers are imitating, we might conjecture, the movements of an antelope, and one of them has changed shape and has metamorphosed down to the waist into that animal.

During our trance sessions, we frequently perform such dances, preferably to the sound of a drum. The ritual has also become an integral part of our masked dance, to be described in Chapter 11. During a workshop the participants do a preliminary breathing exercise, the same as for the posture sessions, and are then asked to move rhythmically and to imitate as much as possible the behavior and motions of the

Plate 35

animal whose spirit likeness they encountered in their visions. When I participated in this dance for the first time and danced the movements of the buffalo while doubling over, I felt very clearly that I had horns and large brown eyes and the head of a buffalo. But I was amazed to find that my metamorphosis involved only the upper half of my body, in the same way as I saw it four years later in that Bushman drawing.

The experience produces a surprising empathy with the respective species. One trancer, who danced a snake, told of becoming conscious not only of the feel of the earth but also of the difference in body structure and of being afraid about not having any limbs. Yet she felt strong and supple, and strikingly, "I realized how totally silent I was." At the same dance exercise, another participant perceived how his friend the Bear entered into him, "and my muscles became very strong, but not physically." One participant in a German workshop, a professor of Jungian psychology, recalled with delight his turning into an elephant, and the sensitivity of the protuberances of his trunk that he became aware of as he tore leaves off a tree. And an elderly woman in Amsterdam remarked that she had never known how fresh and green a turtle felt "inside."

While such identification could possibly be explained on psychological grounds, another experience that quite frequently follows a metamorphosis dance cannot. It seems that when a dancer becomes a particular animal, a powerful bond is created between that dancer and the species represented, which breaches the separation between realities. Or perhaps by experiencing another species in trance, we enter a field common to all animate beings, where the barriers of communication erected during our evolutionary history do not exist. When Kristina, after becoming a dolphin during a recent dance in Cuyamungue, went to a marina in California, the dolphins atypically all crowded around the spot where she had stopped to watch. And Walter, a participant in several workshops in the Netherlands, wrote in a letter in 1984,

> [During the metamorphosis dance] I concentrated intensely on being a heron, flying, circling up and down, stopping in shallow water for fishing, landing on a nest, etc.
>
> The next morning my wife and I were sitting in our small garden in the city area of Amsterdam. Within a minute, the crashing sound of a heron filled the air, and the heron for several minutes made low-flying circles above our heads. We have lived about fifteen years here in the city area, and this or something like that never happened before. (September)

The tradition of animal dances continued into the era of the horticulturalists, and their memory is still alive in the deer, eagle, buffalo, and butterfly dances of our own Pueblo Indians. However, while among the hunters the animal dances express the kinship of humans with other species, the complex shifts into a different direction among horticulturalists, i.e., that of postures. Their women were the first to put seeds into the ground, and thus became conscious of the miracle of seeds' turning into plants and yielding seeds once more. Consequently, the central cultural idea in horticulture is that of change, of metamorphosis. Given the propensity of horticulturalist shamans for developing postures to facilitate certain important experiences, it is understandable that they would come up also with the requisite postures for metamorphosis. Or who can tell? Perhaps the experience of metamorphosis and the postures to go with it originated in the alternate reality.

At any rate, postures of this nature do exist, because eventually we rediscovered a few that apparently were designed specifically to facilitate metamorphosis, that is, the change from human to nonhuman form. Such discoveries were made easier by the fact that the softness, the instability of the human shape had become part of our expectation early on, as soon as we started working with the trance postures. The adventures told by the trancers on the preceding pages illustrate this fact over and over again. The shapes assumed without the slightest inhibition covered much of our animate and even inanimate environment, everything from birds, mammals, and insects to clouds, mountains, and sand. In the metamorphosis postures, the same process also occurs, except in more predictable form. What was truly amazing to us, however, was that Ego, the observing person, remained immutable throughout; there was never any of the disturbance in self-concept that psychiatry always expects to see when changes of the state of consciousness of this sort take place.

To date, we have found four metamorphosis postures in prehistoric art. The oldest one, that of a European masked woman of great antiquity and truly magical power, will be discussed in Section III. The other three are all part of the classical Indian cultures of Central America. The postures of the *Prince* and of the *Tattooed Jaguar* come to us from the Olmecs, the most ancient of the classical societies of the region. The latter was known in precontact time all over Central America and as far north as Tennessee. That of the *Corn Goddess* is part of the Aztec heritage.

The Olmec Prince.   The figurine is called the Prince by archeologists, because the young man wears an unusual, rather ornate headdress (pl. 36). It is dated from a time between 1100 and 600 B.C. and was found in Mexico, in the

Plate 36

present state of Tabasco. The figure sits cross-legged and bends forward slightly, leaning on stiff arms bent at the wrist. The man's hands form fists, which are placed on the floor in front of him rather close together. His tongue is between his lips, and his eyes are rolled up, the sure sign of a very deep trance.

The Olmec Prince came to my attention in 1984, and we tried it for the first time in Cuyamungue that summer. As intimated by Belinda, the iconic content of the posture in this case helps set the stage for the transformation, for one readily feels like a four-footed animal when placing his arms before his crossed legs in the fashion described. This was intentional in Olmec culture, of course, for the jaguar was their most important power animal, a spirit being represented innumerable times in their art. By the way, there is also another male figurine, with a somewhat different head ornament but in the same posture. Belinda was not familiar with it at the time, but it is also part of the Olmec record and comes from the same region and time period. The man represented is shown with his head thrown back, and the human face is replaced by that of an impressively exaggerated jaguar mask (pl. 37). Not being part of that culture, however, Belinda was worried about obeying an external suggestion and rejected the jaguar experience offered to her:

A leopard or jaguar face appeared in front of me, reminding me of one of the gold masks in the King Tut collection. But I recalled feeling so much like a cat in this posture that I dismissed the jaguar as simply suggested by the posture.

Plate 37

Even at this early stage of our experimentation, a few features became apparent that continued to characterize this posture. For instance, achieving metamorphosis, we learn from Belinda, requires the investment of tremendous energy, experienced by her as having her molecules scattered like stars. But the great effort notwithstanding, the transformation is difficult to keep going. In Belinda's experience, no sooner had she become a buffalo than she appeared as an owl, and she could hold on to neither, alternating back and forth until she appeared as a giant bee. The theme of the experience becomes evident in her last impressive image: In metamorphosis, humans come face to face with the life-giving power of the eternal sun; they approach a place between the two worlds, where in infinity the ordinary and the alternate reality meet:

> The image of a galaxy appeared, billions of stars, which I realized were my molecules being pulled apart in order to be reorganized. There was a series of images, going back and forth. First there was a buffalo, standing on the plains in the daylight. It was important that he was part of a herd. The second image was that of an owl, flying in the night, singular and alone. It was back and forth between night and day, upper and lower, flying in the sky and standing on the ground, being singular and being one with the herd. I recall that this went on for a long time. Then there was a final image, which was that of a giant bee. It was golden, and it was flying between two mountains toward an enormous rising sun. My feeling was that the bee was flying toward a place between two worlds.

Others in Belinda's group, and in a subsequent one that summer, reported similar impressions. There was the perception of transformation, as in "I saw layers being pushed into each other," or of its attendant turbulence, as in "I saw lots of images half in and half out of the earth." As Christian St. recounted it:

> A jaguar sat facing me, and then there were many animals in vivid colors, changing into each other; a snake became a bird, the bird turned into a turtle, that became a lynx, and then a puma.

In a more complete sequence, Morgan reacts to the iconic content of the posture. She experienced the heat of the relentless generation of energy, and after turning into a mountain lion, she could not retain it, becoming a stone figure instead:

> The posture reminded me of a cat, and I became a mountain lion. I felt extremely hot, and the sun was painfully bright. I kept climbing and running. Then I saw a snake, and our movements became a dance. I was up on a high plain and saw Indians riding by and buffalos running. Suddenly I was a shrine, like that of the Stone Lions in Bandelier National Park, but I don't know whether I was a stone or not. Then I started running again, and turned into a shrine again, and began chasing things. I became aware of the pain in my legs and I began feeling anxious. I wanted to scream, but at that point I was the mountain lion. The feeling of discomfort was gone, and I started catching fish in a stream.

In Scheibbs, Austria, the following year, there were reports along the same line. We heard the reaction to the suggestive posture:

> MARGIT: I felt thoroughly animallike. I found myself in a shadowy dense forest, and encountered a fox; it had a snout with pointed teeth.

or to the sudden transformation and its instability:

> SARI: I was in the earth and felt like I was part of it, and that was wonderful. It was as if I had been hibernating. Suddenly a ladder appeared in my hole, and I climbed up. There were masked people; I was also wearing a mask, first that of a frog, then of a carnivore. My tongue dripped, and my entire body was covered by armor, or maybe by fur. In that disguise, I danced a fertility dance.

and equally in Cuyamungue in the summer of 1987, when Hanna was able to hang on to being a frog, and experienced the instability instead in the changes of locale, until she lost the struggle and was torn apart by an eagle:

> I was a cat, then couldn't decide whether I wanted to be a lion or a frog. So I decided to become a frog. I had a private pool. I was surrounded by flowers. I caught flies and had a good time. Then I decided to go on a trip. It took me over some flat country, where I met an elephant. We had a nice conversation, and he took me for a ride, back to my pond. Then I was in a small river, and I swam to the ocean and had a great time there, too, only it started drying up, and I became scared. But a wave took me back to my pond, although it was hard going against the current, and things were good again for a while. Suddenly an eagle appeared; it tore me to pieces and fed me to its eaglets. I experienced a sudden shift in perception, and that took me back to being a frog in my pond again and the good times.

The Tattooed Jaguar. The two figurines shown in plate 38 were also found in the old Olmec settlement area, in the state of Tabasco, and are of the same period. In contrast to the posture of the Olmec Prince, the one of the Tattooed Jaguar has no iconic content; that is, the trancer is not subject

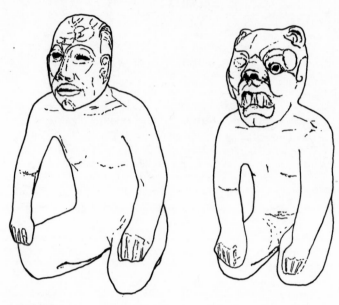

Plate 38

to any suggestion of animalness. Instead, the man depicted kneels with his knees apart and sits on his heels. His hands are on his knees, with the right one somewhat raised, so that his arm is a bit arched, and his left hand is slightly farther back on his thigh and flattened. The two figurines are exhibited in different museums, and in the book on Indian art in which one of my participants discovered them,[4] they were on two different pages. To my mind, however, they clearly belong together. They obviously were created by the same artist using the same model. Both the man's head and the jaguar mask are tattooed, and both are shown in the same posture. But most important, the two figurines taken together are also, as was the case with the two different Princes, a statement about the same experience: "If you go into trance in this posture, you will participate in the power of the Jaguar by turning into him." Interestingly, by the way, the artist was so familiar with what happens in trance that he made a distinction in the way his model holds his right hand, something I too have observed many times. After metamorphosis has been achieved, both the right hand and the arm are relaxed.

Despite the fact that nothing in this posture suggests any metamorphosis, it reliably leads to a change of shape. Without the sponsorship of the Jaguar Spirit, as would be the case in an Olmec ritual, the transformation is not always into its likeness, although it does occur occasionally, especially if the trancer has seen the two figures together, as in the following example:

GERHARD (Vienna, April 1986): The sound of the rattle made me shudder. It penetrated me from the front and pulled me up, then slammed me down with lightning speed. In the distance, the jaguar appeared but then was gone again. I passed under an arc, and in the process something was rubbed off of me and I turned into a jaguar. Behind me I saw a huge figure wearing a jaguar mask as in the figure. He grabbed me by the nape of the neck like a pup and ran away with me and then set me down. Then he fell asleep, and I ran away. At the end I was here in our courtyard, still in the shape of a jaguar. I passed under the arc in the direction of the garden, and then all was gone, as if in a fog.

Here is an example of a clear metamorphosis into a wolf, the mighty power animal of European antiquity:

URSULA ST. (Sommerau, Switzerland, 1985): I felt a strong pulsing around me and inside of me, and I forgot about my legs. I found myself sitting on red earth and became very long, and I saw a hole in the earth with water in it. I heard something dropping into the water. That made rings in the water that turned into a whirlpool, sucking me in. It kept whirling me around until I myself became the whirlpool. Suddenly my feet, thighs, and belly became hot, and somebody handed me a wolf skin. My face acquired the snout of a dog. I slipped my arms into the wolf skin and put it on that way, and it felt wonderful. I was squatting in this posture, I was fat and had thick haunches, and next to me I saw a being looking just like me, except it was much larger and I called it mother. She lay down and I slipped into her belly. The eddy was like a path; I dissolved and the water was warm. Inside my mother's belly, I was all belly and haunches. I saw other little wolves next to me. Then I was in a passageway; it felt like being born. I was trembling, and I was supposed to help. I had just slipped out of the passage when the rattle stopped, with the feeling, now all was well.

My own transformation was also into a large predator, although it never became clear to me exactly what I was:

(Cuyamungue, July 1985): As soon as the rattle started, my fingertips got hot and changed into claws; my face protruded, and I had round ears. This was a clear physical feeling. I could feel my thighs turning into muscular haunches, and from the end of my spine, a tail began to grow. It caused me some momentary anxiety, for what was I going to do with a tail later? What I saw was pictures appearing and disappearing, all in orange light, for example, of a jaguar catching and chomping a bird. I saw an orange sky and a green forest below, and some white shapes that I couldn't identify at first. Then I understood that they were pyramids because I smelled the masonry smell typical of Maya ruins. There was a Maya priest who was like a cutout, and as I watched, he turned like a weathercock. I was still thinking how strange that was when I felt my face flattening out, the most extraordinary experience of the posture. My face just became flat, and it was over, while the rattle was still going on.

There is a vague suggestion in the above report that I had momentarily changed into a bird, and that was the reason I saw the pyramids from above. For Pij, becoming a bird was the core of the transformation:

(Sommerau, 1985): A ray came from below immediately as the rattle started and penetrated me, causing circles and eddies in me and around me. I was dancing; I felt so light, I was enveloped in a white light. There was a wind coming from the right, from above and from below, and I felt a presence; I had no idea what it was, but it was bigger than me. I wanted to become something and was vibrating in my shoulders. I wanted to change, and my head started getting narrow. I was being carried along; I was sailing, then I was flying. I wanted to glance upward, but I couldn't do that, I could only look down. Then I flew over the Salzburg castle.

Plate 39

As mentioned earlier, we occasionally come across surprising confirmations of our experiences in tales connected with a certain posture. Such instances are the journey to the sky experienced in the posture and angle of incline of the Lascaux Cave drawing, and its confirmation by the tradition that Osiris rises to the gods in the sky at the same angle, or the many examples of the healing power of the Bear in the posture we know as that of the Bear Spirit. Something of the same order happened also in connection with a metamorphosis posture. According to Aztec tradition, Chalchihuitlicue, "she of the skirt of green jewels," the goddess of water and the consort of the rain god, is represented in the posture of the Tattooed Jaguar, except that she has her legs crossed (pl. 39). This variant is known from seventh-century figures from Tennessee (pls. 40 and 41), and the experiences it mediates are the same as those of the Tattooed Jaguar. Now, it is told of this goddess that she sent a flood to earth and changed humans into fish, so they would be able to move in the water. It is therefore fascinating how often participants report having turned into fish in this posture. The following are two examples:

KATHRIN (Sommerau, 1985): I was surrounded by red, warm light, which issued from two semicircles. They divided, and their center became the sun. I passed through a point in the middle of the sun. It was made of fire. Then I myself also became fire and started burning; the points of the flames danced around me. Then there was a change; I could feel a rainbow, and a man and a woman held out their hands to me. I sank into a white whirlpool and became a fish. I swam through a tube, and encountered some branches and wondered where I had come from.

VRENIE (Sommerau, 1985): My head opened up and something came out of it.

Plate 40   **Plate 41**

I had the feeling that I was being turned inside out like a glove. A wind came up and started whirling me around, which made me close up, and I became a bird. I flew into the light blue, which then turned light green. As I was gliding along, I saw the sun; it was light yellow. I flew into it and then could not escape; its rays kept holding on to me. I kept struggling, and suddenly they let go of me, and I fell down turning like a top, and still whirling around. I found myself at the bottom of the ocean, and I was a fish. Around me there were figures in green scarves; it seems that the sea was part of the lower world.

The Corn Goddess (pl. 42). The Aztecs represented the Corn Goddess as a young woman, and she is always shown in the same graceful pose, sitting on her heels as a Japanese lady would, and resting her outstretched hands on her thighs close to her body, pointing toward her knees. The cat effigy of Key Marco, Florida (pl. 43), has its hands somewhat closer together. Of the three postures discussed here, it seems the most recent, deriving from a time when the Aztecs were in the process of converting to full-scale intensive agriculture. This may be why it is also the weakest of the three postures. It does mediate metamorphosis, but the transformation is characterized by an inherent uncertainty. "Every time I saw something," one participant said, "it disappeared." Some trancers experience nothing but the whirling agitation that leads into the metamorphosis, as in the following example, in which Anne B. is even proffered help by the Bear Spirit, who often undertakes this task, but except for a brief interlude, she is still unsuccessful. So he and his companions disappear; she sees the fire again, with only humans dancing around it:

Plate 42   **Plate 43**

(Cuyamungue, August 1985): I was in a clearing in the forest, and I was dancing around a fire, a wild, frenetic dance. I went around in circles and kept jumping over the fire with others. Then I danced backward, and there were lots of owls watching us, also a circle of animals. The animals joined us, especially many friendly bears. I became one of the bears. A huge bear, I thought of him as a chief or a god, took hold of me and and whirled me around. The bear replaced the fire, or the fire became the bear; we once more danced backward, I became a human, and we humans danced with the animals. Suddenly the fire reappeared, the animals and the owls were gone, and only we humans were dancing.

Some trancers succeed better, but a certain inconsistency remains. We hear of transformations into elephants, wolves, panthers, jaguars, birds, or even snakes:

ELIZABETH M. (Cuyamungue, August 1986): I was a very large cat, chasing animals, and I felt my power, and the dust blowing over my face. Then I was a wolf chasing a rabbit. I encountered a large snake and became that snake, and could feel how different my snake spine was. Then my spirit guide appeared and offered to teach me how one flies as a snake. And he showed me where my feathers were on my body.

CINDY (Cuyamungue, August 1986): I was a grey wolf; my body was sinking down, and the smell was intense. I felt sharp hunger pains and decided that I needed to go and hunt. I made my chest expand, and I started loping over the ground. It felt wonderful to run like a wolf, but then I got tired of it. I saw Elizabeth and asked her, "Are you a wolf?" She left. And I was told, "You need to survive as a wolf to be human."

NYDIA (Cuyamungue, August 1986): I was in a blue tunnel, which was green further down. I saw a jaguar in front of me; we went on together, with me holding on to its tail. We came to a winding river; the water smelled fresh. The jaguar turned into a lizard, or maybe it was a salamander, then back into a jaguar. Then the jaguar became a wolf. It had golden eyes, and its fur felt soft. I was a puppy. The wolf picked me up, and we walked through the snow. The wolf killed an antelope. We licked its blood and ate it.

GABI (Cuyamungue, August 1986): Something pulled me back, and at that instant my mouth turned into the snout of a black panther. I felt very hungry, and I could find nothing to kill. Besides, my feet began to hurt. So I fell asleep. A black tiger came by. He put his paws on my shoulder; that was nice, but quite uncomfortable.

The only feature that appears with more consistency than the above animal shapes during the Corn Goddess posture is plant and insect life, as could be expected with a pose attributed to such a spirit being. Thus I was told during a workshop in Utrecht (the Netherlands), in the spring of 1986, "I am in the dark, we are roots together." Instead of the roots, the cotyledons appear in another instance during the same workshop:

PETI: I could feel how the energy was building up. I could not see anything, but I felt the colors; they were red and brown and swirling. I had two halves, and they were pumping up energy. The cells and patterns were splitting, then there were more colors. I was growing out of my shape.

Breaking through the earth and growing is yet another theme of this type of experience:

ISI (Cuyamungue, August 1986): I was surrounded by earth and sand. I was feeling comfortable, but I tried to make a hole and didn't know why. Then I heard a voice saying, "You're a seed, you are looking for light, for the sun." So I started growing roots, and I felt that I really was a seed. I broke through to the surface and saw the sun, and it was wonderful. I kept growing, and I was a field of grain. I didn't stop growing until I grew up into the sky, and it was a nice difference. At first I had felt the earth; now I was in the sky, and there was nothing but wind. Then I found myself sitting on a branch. I was a big bird, but the branch was small, and I was afraid. I started playing with the wind, and I lost my fear and began flying around in circles with the wind.

Although as always unaware of the origin and name of the posture, Belinda turned into corn when she tried it for the first time. Toward the middle of the trance session, however, as happens so frequently in metamorphosis postures, she ran out of energy and could no longer hold on to being a plant:

(Cuyamungue, August 1985): In the beginning, I felt nothing at all. I was in the earth, not seeing anything. I began moving out, and I realized that I was a corn plant, and I was growing as tall as a mountain. A brown bear came along, tore off my right breast, but it was corn also, and he ate it. So I was in the bear's stomach, and there was a truly foul smell around. The bear was nursing a cub, and I came out of her breast as milk. Suddenly, I felt great pain, and I was flying. I landed in a circular nest, and I looked around to see what was in it. A black statue emerged from the hole; it was in this posture, and as I watched, it turned into white marble. I could feel my legs hurting, and so I was happy that at this point my Lioness turned up. We had a joyful reunion; she let me become a part of her body, and we went back and forth like that until the rattle stopped.

The following August, although Belinda had been a corn plant the year before, she turned into a caterpillar instead:

> Immediately, there was the sensation of twirling. I was inside a flower. I saw the stamen; it was like a thick rope. I grabbed hold of it and started climbing out of the flower, and then down toward the ground. I sat at the base of the plant, thinking, what do I do now? I went to another blossom; it was an iris. I could see it, and it was beautiful. Then there was the sensation of whirring and breathing fast. I saw a snake next to the plant, so I got excited and got back into the plant. I started breathing hard, and suddenly I broke open and I was a big yellow butterfly on a field of flowers. I started sucking honey, then flew up into the mountains. I huddled into the branches and saw the landscape, and felt protected by the branches. I saw a strong light, and as I turned toward it, I changed into a cobra.

Belinda's experience is quite similar to one related the following year in Switzerland. During that session, the men did the Tattooed Jaguar and the women the Corn Goddess. Yet in a strange crossover, Urs's experience is more that of the Corn Goddess, although with some masculine features:

> Something took me by my hands and whirled me around, then let me go, so that I catapulted away and turned around my own axes. Suddenly I landed on a giant anemone. My feet felt cold, but the sun was shining and felt warm. A bumblebee landed next to me and asked, "Are you also collecting honey?" I said no, but that I wanted to try. The anemone turned into a daisy, and a giant butterfly appeared; it had a red body and white wings with yellow dots. It said, "I like you, would you like to come along?" But I was too slow. I did get out of the flower, but then landed in a cornucopia with transparent golden yellow and orange walls, and I felt compelled to go further and further down into it. Suddenly, there was a blinding light, and the white figure of a woman appeared with outstretched arms, and there was a voice saying, "You will have to pass through the woman to get to your goal." So I passed through her, and did not fall into a precipice. Instead, I was in a Greek temple. In it, there were nine statues arranged in a semicircle, and in the middle of it there was a huge black steer with enormous horns. The statues kept changing their faces, appearing as foxes, dragonflies, and other shapes. I asked what I was suppowed to do in that temple, but then the rattle stopped.

CHAPTER ELEVEN

Celebrations

For the 1985 spring workshop at the Buddhist Center in Scheibbs, our friend Franz announced that we were going to have a masked dance. "Dear Friends," he wrote in his flyer,

> you have all taken part in an introductory course on trance and the religious altered state of consciousness with Felicitas Goodman. For this year, we are planning a more intensive project with Felicitas, to deepen our knowledge about trance and ecstasy and to practice integrating it into our daily lives. This project is not to be as serious as it sounds, however. We want to make it a celebration as it used to be in ancient cultures, a celebration of joy. It is to be a game between the dimensions of the world, a sacred event demonstrating our connectedness with everything that surrounds us.

I arrived late on the first day from another assignment. I had not seen the flyer; we had discussed the matter only in the most general terms, but in no detail, and I knew only that Franz had engaged Rudl, a trained Viennese maskmaker, as an instructor for our project. So I was understandably startled when after greeting the fourteen participants in the upstairs meditation room of the center, Franz turned to me with a confident smile, saying, "All right, Felicitas, so why don't you just describe some native ritual to us, and we'll proceed from there."

What in the world was I supposed to pull from my hat? To gain time to think, I agreed that such rituals could indeed serve as models, but that they were embedded in a social context that we could never replicate, and therefore we had to do something different, something that would be our very own. The question was, what? As I continued talking, born of desperation, an idea was beginning to take shape. This was to be a masked dance, so logically, I suggested, we should first of all discover what kind of mask to make. "Instead of starting with the ritual," I said, "why don't we begin at the other end and think about the masks first?" Remembering that my Friends "on the other side" were always standing ready to help, I added, "So how about going to the lower world? Maybe there we can discover some spirit form to serve as model for the masks."

In other words, instead of choosing a rational path, always the first choice of Westerners in a pinch, my intuition told me that I needed to direct the group to the alternate reality. This novel approach made good sense to people already familiar with ecstatic experience. After all, the masked dance was to be a religious celebration, and so quite correctly we had to entrust the shaping of it to the forces to whom this task properly belonged. Going to the lower world, where every one of us had been before, was a plausible first step. I could see the enthusiasm in the faces of my participants.

And indeed, they were not to be disappointed. Judging from Yolanda's report, who was the first one to recount her experience at the conclusion of the trance, our Friends equally approved. This happens quite often when I am in doubt about a new venture: The first person I call on turns out to be the messenger. The choice seems arbitrary, but in actuality it is guided by a sort of prompting that is as gentle as a puff of wind. In this case, the message transmitted could not have been clearer. For in the cave to which Yolanda was taken, an Indian placed his own mask on her face:

> About me it was night. I flew up to the stars and danced with them. I was among rocks, and water came spouting from them. Then I sank into the earth and I was badly frightened; everything was so dark. I searched for a way out, and the rattle sounded like many shells knocking together. I turned into a bird and flew away together with a raven, who took me to the entrance of a cave. I wanted to rest there, but I was ushered into the cave, and there saw an Indian wearing the mask of a black mountain lion. He placed his mask on my face. Then I was surrounded by smoke, and the Indian disappeared far in the distance.

The other members of the group reported mainly experiences of transformation. That is, encountering the masked spirit being apparently brought about a metamorphosis of the visitors. I was surprised, because, as will be recalled, a visit to the lower world is usually a journey, with changing shape only an occasional secondary feature. I was also delighted, for obviously we were on the right track. This process of transformation was frequently reported from among those societies where masks were used ritually, namely, that the bearer turned into the being represented. My trancers told of changing into a bear, or maybe an owl; into a crow or a cat with black spots; into a tiger, a lion, a snake, and a deer; into a snake or a goat. Gerhard became a panther:

> I took a backward somersault, and as if on roller skates, I slipped down into some sort of room, landing on my back. Something or somebody was dancing

around me. A panther appeared; it slipped into me, and I could feel exactly how that transformed me. I ran up a mountainside, and a man wearing a hat, but without a face, and a bird came with me. Behind the mountain, there was nothing, only indistinct forms, and the three of us jumped into that emptiness. I felt that I was floating, or I was being carried, and placed into a golden liquid, which turned me into a gold-colored panther. I became a horse, then emerged from it, and as a panther I sat on the back of the horse. Then we dissolved completely. The man with the hat carried me over the mountain on his shoulder, then put me down. I slipped through him and found myself back here.

Ewald encountered a dragon:

> I melted into the earth, and there was no air between me and the ground. Then I was at a campfire, and there were people around it. I looked around but could see nothing else. Suddenly he was there, to the right of me, a mere shadow at first, then assuming the shape of a dragon and getting bigger and bigger. The right side of me began tensing painfully. I asked him for help, and I felt it physically how he scraped all that section of my body off, even my eye. It felt great. Then I assumed his shape. I fell into some water, and the rattle stopped.

Fritz found a snowy owl:

> I saw the white head of an owl, like a shadow, and it beckoned to me. Everything else was dark. I was in a black chasm; a river of fire flowed through it, and I became the owl.

We had used a tape for the session instead of my rattling, so that I would also be able to participate, but I was disappointed with my trip. For quite a while nothing happened; then I began to feel a cool and gentle wind brush over me. I saw a few small cometlike streaks of light, then bright green willow branches appeared with dots of yellow sunlight and blowing in the wind. Half hidden by the branches, there were patches of light-brown fur, but I could not make out what that was; the rattling seemed too short, and in the end I merely felt the gentle wind continuing to surround me. Instead of exhilaration, the experience left me with a pervasive fear which I could not place. What was I being told?

The answer did not come to me until the following day. For the first time, it seemed to me, we had not been simply sojourners but had stirred up forces in the lower world when we appealed to them for response, forces that we knew nothing about. Thus, perhaps, my fear. I concluded that we had to turn to ritual now and learn how to deal with those forces, to shape them in some way. In Pueblo tradition, the beings beyond the border of ordinary reality are thought of as "raw." In order to consort with them, we had to translate them into something more akin to our humanness. This, quite possibly, was what ritual had always been about in human history. However, here was the rub: Where were we to find the proper ritual? This time, the answer was readily available. Our trip to the lower world had been richly rewarding, so once again, we should turn to that inexhaustible source of inspiration, ecstatic experience. Because of the nature of our problem, I suggested that this time we appeal to our wise old counselor, the Tennessee diviner.

On this occasion, I chose to be not a participant but simply the recorder. And as I now read once more my cursory notes of that session, I remember again the thrill of seeing the dance ritual unfold before me. With my eyes sharpened by the trance, which had come to me while I rattled, I saw spread out before me an ecstatic, scintillating celebration of spring. "I live a fairytale," I wrote dumbfounded later that day, as I started working out the dance. Simply for the asking, all the details of the ceremony had been revealed. Later on, when we repeated that session several times in order to record it, there were details of the sets, and even such minor instructions as that there should be a fast before the dance. At least this is how we interpreted one of Ewald's experiences with his Dragon. Ewald had seen a table laid with a sumptuous feast, but the Dragon told him that he was not allowed to eat of it. Ewald became obstreperous, whereupon the Dragon took hold of one end of the table and turned it over, spilling all the delicacies. And we were advised to use the soundtrack of the Singing Shaman as music for our celebration. As we see in plates 44–47, this festive posture was a favorite in many parts of the world. It was known in Melanesia and on New Guinea, on the Cyclades Islands five thousand years ago, and surely since that time also in the Americas, from the Arctic Eskimos all the way down to Central America.

Plate 44   **Plate 45**   **Plate 46**

Plate 47

With faces still marked by the black line of the diviner's posture, everyone trooped down into the large hall on the first floor where the supplies for the masks had been laid out. The fever of creation was upon them. They hardly took time to break for lunch and barely realized that they had stood at the work tables for close to nine hours, shaping the clay, spreading plastic foil on the form, gluing layers of paper and cloth on it, impatiently waiting for the time when they could apply the paint to make their vision plain.

I had initially intended to excuse myself and spend all my time writing the dance. After all, I had not been favored by a vision except for those elusive patches of brown fur that I had seen behind the willow branches. I had no idea what was hiding inside that. But then I could not stand being away from all the exciting activities and the companionship in the work hall, and I decided to give maskmaking a try, too. Since I wanted to save my right arm for rattling,

I started to work on the clay with my left hand. As soon as I did that, my indecision dissolved, and to my amazement and entirely without any conscious effort, a presence emerged from the inert substance. The more I worked, the clearer it became: It was the face of a buffalo dancer, half human, half animal mask, simple and powerful. "Look," I kept saying to those working near me, "this is the mystery, here it is!" No one was interested. They were all busy with their own mysteries.

Rudl, our maskmaker, kept walking around the room and shaking his head. Beyond simple technical instruction, he had given no help whatsoever, for none was asked for. Most of us had never made a mask, and yet under our untutored fingers, such beauty blossomed forth as he had never seen in any of the classes he had conducted before. "What I usually get in my courses are twisted, tortuous faces scarred by conflict and decay," he said.

The following days were occupied with finishing the masks, sewing costumes, and creating the sets. I spent happy hours painting the willow branches that ended up as decoration for my skirt. We also did trance sessions, which kept the excitement high and the miraculous energy flowing. To our surprise they also helped those who were still unclear about details of their masks, providing further instructions. Franz was shown to paint his bear mask half white and half black. Rudl saw his red-and-black tiger clearly for the first time. Instead of a healing experience, which everyone else had undergone when we did the Bear posture, Christian St., who had been absent during our trip to the lower world, unexpectedly was given a terse version of what the Spirits expected of him during the dance:

> I was in a landscape that was teeming with wild boars. There was one, I only saw his head, and he stared at me, and I had the feeling of tremendous power radiating from him. A gaunt figure with a boar's mask stood at my left, or maybe at my right, I can't remember, and placed a bristly skin robe on my shoulders. I began dancing, wearing the boar's mask. When I looked down at my feet, they had turned into boars' hoofs. A herd of seven or eight wild pigs thundered by. An enormous wild boar knocked me down, a sow began suckling me, and then the entire herd started devouring me, and my guts spilled on the black earth. I saw all of us dancing, and the man wearing the boar's mask danced with us.

On the morning before the dance, we took the completed masks upstairs in a festive procession and carefully placed them around the walls. As yet, I felt, they were mere forms, bodies without souls. The question was, in what way could I invite the Spirits to take up their abode in these shells we had created for them? There was a posture named the Calling of the Spirits, the story of which I will relate in Section III. It involves the basic leg posture with knees slightly bent; the head is back and the mouth open, and the hands with fingers spread wide are placed on the line between abdomen and thigh (pl. 48). However, as I remembered, it mediated an experience where the caller turned into the Tree of Life, and the Spirits gathered around it. I was not sure whether it could also be employed for the present purpose. But I had no other choice.

So that was the posture I asked the participants to assume. I closed my eyes as I began to rattle and sent a wordless plea. In response, like shadows blowing in the wind, I saw a procession of Spirits entering and soundlessly slipping into the masks. And indeed, on this occasion, no one turned into a tree, and as we see in the examples cited below, all instead had very clear encounters with their mask and its spirit.

Plate 48

CHRISTIAN ST. (wild boar): I stood next to a tree at the edge of a precipice. I wore the mask, and the mask sucked me out. We all danced with our masks on, they united into one; and like an octopus, its many arms touched us all. My body became the mask.

GERHARD (panther): The rattle entered into me, and I slipped into a hole. We were all in that hole. The Spirits came to greet us and guided us out in a snake dance. I was wearing my mask and felt a great force from behind, which entered into me and overpowered me. This turned me into a panther. I started running and got to a clear stream of water. After drinking from it, I slipped into a tree and rested. After a while, I sat up high in the tree together with the man wearing a hat and a bird, and we started dancing together.

EWALD (dragon): The Spirits gathered in this room, and the Dragon put on his mask. I also turned into a dragon, and we started wrestling together, which gave me a lot of energy. Then the two of us passed through a fog bank, and behind it we encountered another masked figure. But when I asked the Dragon what that was, he gave no answer. Instead, he guided me across a meadow, and it was getting very dark. We met a black cat, which was quite aggressive, and a masked figure accompanied by a snake. They were about to attack me, but with my fiery breath, I chased them away.

FRITZ (snowy owl): There was a wild circle of shamans dancing, and we in our masks formed an outer circle around them. I saw myself and a dark figure coming toward me, together with some light ones. They slipped into me and I became the owl. I was completely white. I stood still and waited stiffly, uttering not a sound, the female hunter of the night. I was time; I was the passing of the seasons.

ILSE (goat and snake): My goat came jumping from the left, sat down next to me with her front legs crossed in a human pose, and started conversing with me, complaining that I had made her ears too small. We had an animated conversation until I turned into the snake. Five kids appeared, then condensed into the goat. Behind them there were many figures wearing masks and enveloped in smoke, which curled upward. In the end, I changed into the tongue of the goat, which was also the snake.

SUSIE (bird of paradise): An eagle appeared before me and put on its mask. I heard music, and the eagle invited me to come along. We got to a tree trunk, which had a golden door, and we entered, sat down, and ate. All the animals were there, even the goat with her legs crossed. Then they started dancing, and the eagle and I flew away.

YOLANDA (mountain lion): The Mountain Lion stood behind me and put its paws on my shoulders until I lay down. He put some soil and dry leaves on me, dug small holes around me, and placed a light in each. Then he went up the mountain, and a number of lion cubs gathered around me. Then I found myself standing in front of him. He hit me on the head, then scratched my right breast, skinned me, and boiled me in a kettle. The small lions dumped me out of the kettle. Grabbing my hands, the Mountain Lion then lifted me and took me to a cave. He dug a hole and placed fire in it, and the cool wind played around me, and fireflies started gathering about.

Because according to the divination the dance was to be a celebration of spring, I chose a posture of death and rebirth, called the posture of the Feathered Serpent, for the concluding trance session of the workshop on the evening before the dance. This posture will be discussed in Chapter 13. It provided such a satisfactory closure that we have continued to use it in subsequent trance-dance workshops.

So much had happened during the workshop that it seemed as if we had been together forever when the day of the dance finally dawned. We had walked through the entire ceremony only once. The individual scenes were easy to remember, because the principal role in each one was played by the person who had originally experienced it. Franz was in charge of the sound-track, and my task was merely to provide the cues for the sequence. Obeying the instructions of the Dragon, we had no breakfast, and at an early hour and fully costumed, we assembled in the upper meditation room to take the masks downstairs. We had invited only a few guests, among them Eva D., who was so taken by the beauty of it all that she sacrificed her entire savings and took part in a masked dance in Cuyamungue the following year. I will try to describe the ritual not as I experienced it as a participant but as it might have looked to our spectators.

Imagine a starkly white, rather low room with small windows set into walls of medieval thickness. The first light of the morning is barely sifting through the curtains. All you can see is a small table over to one side with a bowl on it and a large yellow disk hanging from the ceiling in the center, circled along its perimeter by a snake, which appears as a thick dark line in the muted light of dawn.

A door opens behind the columns in the back, and in perfect silence, a line of gowned figures on stockinged feet enter in stately defile, each carrying a mask visible only in outline, and they form an open circle around the table. Each person in turn steps up to the bowl, takes some of the meal, breathes on it for a blessing, scatters it on the mask to feed it, and then puts it on.

Suddenly there is magic in the room, as in rapid succession in the faintly blossoming light tiger and panther, bird, owl, and buffalo, boar and dragon and bear join red and golden beings of fantasy in the line around the goat, whose horns are circled by an orange snake.

Hardly audible at first and sectioned only by the muted beat of the rattle, a chorus of voices starts up, a mere hum at first as if coming from the chasms of the earth, then gathering volume and spreading into a rainbow of harmony like the distant chorale of a Gregorian chant. Now and then bright cadences born of the trance flicker above the somber lines of the base. The masks begin to fall in with the shaking of the rattle, and the unswerving thud of their feet is the thread that to the end will hold together the beaded necklace of the dance.

At the table, the Goat, ancient generative power, hands each mask a small glass bowl, and like the first stirring of life in spring, tiny flames burst under its hand as it lights the candles floating in the water. The masks turn and, following the Goat, dance with the light held high until there is a spiral of flickering flames rotating faster and faster under the disk of the sun. Suddenly, the hands of unseen helpers lift the curtains, and the tiny sparks of the young season melt into the bright daylight of the first day of spring. Then the candles are gone, and with the brilliant colors of the masks awakened, their spiral continues to rotate under the sun disk.

As yet, though, spring has not triumphed over the forces of winter. In the middle of the spiral, the Bird of Paradise appears, its mask a riot of brilliant yellows, blues, and greens. At its signal, the masks dance into the shadows and return, heads bent low, each with a staff on its back, the bond of ice still holding hostage the stirrings of new life. As their circle converges on the Bird of Paradise and becomes ever tighter, its grip seems to choke the blossoming season in the center.

But the new beginning will not be denied. The Mountain Lion takes up the struggle. It breaks out of the line of the dancers, a sleek black streak with bright-blue eyes and the red circle of the sun painted on its palms. The Mountain Lion carries the disk of the new sun in its upstretched hands and, holding it high above its head, dances toward the circle. The new sun's power parts its grip; the line opens and lets the Lion pass. Upon reaching the old sun, it hangs the rejuvenated image over the old tired one, and the snake of renewed life circling its rim now unites both. With the ice on their bent backs, the masks are still tied to the powers of winter, but the Mountain Lion now approaches each one and lifts the staffs. When this happens, each mask straightens up, turns around its own axis, and continues dancing in the circle. A colored scarf appears in their hands; they dance toward the Lion and hand it over as their offering. The Lion gives them staffs in return, which, transformed, will now serve to celebrate the conquering power of life, as each mask, dancing on the spot, marks the rhythm of the rattle by stomping the floor with it. In the meanwhile, the victorious Mountain Lion continues to dance and wave the scarves until, upon a signal, all masks run to one corner and put down the staffs, and the Mountain Lion places the scarves on top, a gift to the earth.

Spring, now fully installed, is the time for initiation. In youthful exuberance, the Black Panther dances to the rim of the circle, where the masks are holding hands. Under their upstretched arms, it dances in and out of the circle, pursued by the Mountain Lion. After slipping through all the openings, the panther runs into the circle, still followed by the Lion. Exhausted, it collapses, and on its chest and back it suffers the initiatory scratches of the Lion.[1] The young Panther is now a full-fledged member of the circle. Guided by the Mountain Lion, it takes over and, breaking the circle of the dancers, leads the masks in a snake dance.

But initiation is not only a triumph of life, it is also descending into death. A golden mask, half man, half beast, wrapped in a black shawl, dances to the front of the masks, which now form a straight line. The dark shawl is heavy; the mask tries in vain to shake its oppressive weight and finally collapses under it as under a shroud. Two Birds of Paradise arrive, carrying a totem pole. One of them holds the pole upright, the other one pulls the shawl off the prostrate figure. The golden mask pulls itself up, holding on to the pole, and finally supports it alone. The Birds return to the line while the sorrowing mask dances holding the pole. It begins knocking it on the floor on the first beat of a four-quarter rhythm. Each time that happens, one of the masks leaves the line, turns on its own axis in the struggle against death, and joins the circle of twirling masks.

In the end life, now complete, emerges triumphant. In the circle, the masks have stopped twirling and have moved on to a pendulum pattern of two steps to the right, then two to the left. Two masks leave the circle, then come back carrying a skeleton. The tall Bear, striking in its yellow-and-sepia gown, goes to meet them, takes over the skeleton, and, while they rejoin the circle, begins dancing by hugging its ghostly partner. The circle of dancers begins to dance to the right, while the Bear with its skeleton dances outside the circle in the opposite direction. After twice repeating the round, the Bear suddenly jumps into the middle of the circle, lifts the skeleton high, and, turning it around, reveals the blooming Tree of Life on its reverse side. Small bells are attached to its blossoms, and they ring out as he shakes it and knocks it on the floor. The Birds of Paradise come fluttering by and pick at the seeds scattered on the ground at the base of the tree.

Night, the time of magic, descends on the scene. The Snowy Owl shoos the Birds of Paradise away and dances around the Tree, ushering in the miracle of transformation. The masks are now what they had seemed, birds and animals of the forest and beings of story, and they stomp, slither, slink, and flutter around the Tree of Life.

Finally the music ends, and the world of fancy subsides with it. The dancers return to the bowl of meal, take some, bless it with their breath, and scatter it as a final offering to the Spirits. The last thing I remember seeing as I sat on the floor exhausted, still half buffalo and half woman, and with the sound of many rattles ringing in my head, is two toddlers over in one corner, a little boy and a girl, children of couples living at the center, crawling over to the Tree of Life lying on the floor and playing entranced with the shiny bells. Spring had truly come.

As I am describing the dance now, several years later, it seems to me that for Sigrid, the golden mask that reminded me of the picture on a tarot card, death under the dark shawl of the dance, had had an additional meaning, something she had no way of understanding at the time. I checked once more what she had told after the divination, and indeed, after describing the scene with the shawl which she later danced, she told how she saw men squatting in a circle in the diviner's posture, and she was told that they would decide and that she should not be afraid.

> Then I turned into a small girl, climbed up an incline, and became a woman. I found myself in a dark passageway and asked where it was leading. Someone handed me a glowing staff. A large bird came, and once more I asked, where does all this lead to? With my staff, I started drawing glowing circles in the air, and then I died.

Soon after the dance, she met a man, her golden figure of the tarot card. They fell in love and got married. A month after the wedding, on a distant California seashore, the young husband climbed up on a rock ledge and exuberantly started to dance. The rock shelf broke off and buried him under the rubble, killing him instantly. Sigrid remained behind, and in the future-past of the masked ritual, she danced her sorrowful dirge with the totem pole.

The format and the approaches developed during the 1985 masked dance in Scheibbs served as a basis for other dances to follow. Altogether, I think, the most important outcome of the masked dances was the realization that here was an opportunity to apply the postures to one particular purpose. It was as if one reason we had been introduced to them was so that we would learn a new way to be joyous, to celebrate in ecstasy, something sadly lacking in our own culture.

Nurtured by the inexhaustible source of the alternate reality, each dance was different, both in theme and in detail, for every time we asked, we received new instructions. We also have a sweatlodge now on the institute grounds in New Mexico, and a sweat has become an integral part of our yearly masked-dance celebration. We continued to experiment with other postures that could meaningfully be integrated into the dance. For instance, while in 1985 in Cuyamungue we used the Chiltan posture to gain extra energy, we later discovered still another posture that produced a similar effect. We call it the *Maya Empowerment posture*. I saw it first in photographs accompanying an article about a Maya sculpture in wood,[2] the only example of such a wood carving in the round from the tropical lowlands of Middle America. A standing variant of the posture was known in classical antiquity in Europe, both in the

Minoan culture at about 2000 to 1700 B.C. and in Mycenae, and in Persia two thousand years later, as well as with bent knees as far in time and place as modern Polynesia (more about this in the Conclusion).

As seen in plate 49, for this posture the male figure is kneeling with legs apart and sitting on its heels. The head is slightly inclined toward the back. As the most salient feature of the pose, the arms are raised to shoulder height and the hands touch. It is not clear how the hands are held. We assumed that the figure has its fingers curled, so that was what we did. We also pressed our index fingers together along the lower joint, which seemed to come close to what the carving shows. In this posture participants report the accumulation of a radiant, "peaceful" energy, experiences such as falling through smoke and heat but then ending up in a refreshing bath, of having access to learning and wisdom, of being "able to do anything," and quite generally, of joy and empowerment.

Plate 49

Since that first masked dance in 1985, we do several every year, and special memories are associated with each and every one. In Switzerland, for instance, we danced the play of chaos and order around the Tree of the World, and we will not forget our tall trickster, who had never seen or heard of his prototype in our own Indian Northwest, and yet shaped his mask in the trickster's image with deer antlers and represented, as Paul Radin put it, "god, animal, human being, hero, buffoon, he who was before good and evil, denier, affirmer, destroyer and creator" (1972:169).

In Cuyamungue during the first dance there, our procession sanctified the land, and our animals came to watch. After the completion of the dance and emerging for the first time that summer, our own big garter snake wound her way down the hill behind the Student Building, wended her way to the garden, and then slithered back up again to her home. Hawks circled overhead, and the shy hummingbirds swooped at us wildly as we sat in the arbor next to their feeder. Another time, as I told before, as we got ready to dance around the sweatlodge on the eve of the ritual, a thunderhead rolled up only above that small spot in the vast land. As we started to drum and dance, rain began to fall, splashing cold and invigorating drops on our shoulders. When our dance stopped, so did the rain; the cloud turned pink in the evening light, and on that rosy cloud, a rainbow formed.

In Cuyamungue in 1987 we were instructed to invite the Spirits of the region to our celebration, and we did so, scattering the sacred meal in the four directions. We had carried out a sweatlodge ritual on the eve of the dance, and afterward some of the participants lingered behind and continued drumming. I thought that was what I heard when I awoke from a deep sleep of exhaustion sometime close to three in the morning. But the drumming was curious; it sounded far away at first and then came closer. Others on the porch where we slept heard it too, and one got up and went to the Student Building to check things out. But no one was using the drum; it was safely on the table, drumstick neatly beside it. Others about the same time smelled tortillas being warmed and bacon frying. No one on the land eats bacon, and so I think the Spirits did arrive, and to make sure that we would know, they brought along a cooking smell we knew could not be ours.

Then there was the last dance we did in Scheibbs, in 1986, before program changes there closed the center to us.[3] In lieu of dancing to the soundtrack of the Singing Shaman, we asked two men of the center staff to drum for us. The weather was pleasant, and instead of performing inside, we danced around a fire under the tall fir trees behind the building. I had been worried about this dance; the center was in a period of transition, and although the core group of experienced trancers worked with great dedication, the attendant tensions inevitably made themselves felt in the quality of the preparations. "Are you with us anyway?" I asked, as I passed into the metamorphosis part of the dance. As if in response, three things happened simultaneously. There was a sudden gust of wind, which caused the fire to crackle and made the sparks fly like tiny stars into the dark branches of the conifers, and one of the two drummers momentarily stumbled in his rhythm. I felt that I had been answered, and I was grateful.

Most of the participants left soon after the dance, but a friend who was going to give me a ride to Vienna in her car had gone for a walk, and I used the time to rest in my room. I was awakened by a knock on my door, and upon opening, there was Guschtl, one of our two drummers, leaning on his broom. "Excuse me for bothering you," he said, with obvious embarrassment, "but I just have to ask you this. Are there any Indians four meters tall?"

I became confused. "I have never seen any," I said, "but why do you want to know?"

He clutched the broomstick. "I don't know whether you noticed it, but at one point I lost the beat when I drummed for you. That was when the fire suddenly crackled. I got confused because I looked up, and standing next to me there was this extremely tall Indian. He wore white pants and a white shirt, and he had long, straight black hair. I couldn't see his face, it was in the shade. He just stood there, and then he disappeared. I can't figure it out; I haven't done any drugs for years. Do you think it was something evil?"

It took a moment before I could answer. "Oh, no, Guschtl, don't worry, he is a friend of mine," I said, and wondered why the young man looked at me rather confused and left in such a hurry. But it was really true. During the very first workshop I did in Cuyamungue, Joseph, an Indian friend from a pueblo to the north of us, had seen him too, looking just like Guschtl had described him, white garment, black hair, towering over the kiva. In his vision, Joseph heard him call to him, and when he went outside, he saw him coming from the direction of the shrine. The tall Spirit then handed him a ritual as a present that he needed in his work with young people. I asked what the apparition's face looked like, and Joseph said, rather perplexed, "Why . . . dark, of course."

CHAPTER TWELVE

The Pit of Death
and the Psychopomp

$\mathbf{T}$he postures we have explored up till now have all dealt with life in its manifold aspects. They taught us new insights about spirit journeys and divining, about healing and metamorphosis, and about celebration. But they had nothing to show us about death. For that, we need to turn to two other postures that instruct us about the final journey awaiting all of us at the end of all the "sound and fury."

The trip to the Realm of the Spirits of the Dead. It will be recalled (see Chapter 9) that there is a posture where the arms are placed on the chest in such a way that the right arm is up. We called it the Chiltan posture, because the healing spirits that Uzbeki shamanesses call on for help bear this name. In scanning the archeological record, however, I found that there was a parallel series, where instead of the right arm being up, it was the left one. It was known in Central America and in the thirteenth century in New Mexico (pls. 50 and 51), where it appears in two painted tablets, one a man, the other a woman, found hidden in a cave. Traces of it occur in sub-Saharan Africa and Polynesia, and early representations were found in prehistoric Central Europe and Eastern Anatolia (Turkey) (pls. 52a and b).

There is an especially touching figure of a young warrior from the fifth century B.C. (pl. 53) shown in this posture, his arms folded on his chest as though he were cold and apprehensive of his way. It was discovered at Hirschlanden in the present state of Baden-Wuerttemberg (West Germany). As archeologists reconstructed the site (see inset, pl. 53), this sandstone figure, about five feet tall, had been placed on a hill, which was a central grave, ringed by stone slabs. The youth is naked, and his thighs and erect penis are shaped in naturalistic detail. However, his chest and arms seem more like a bas-relief.

Plate 50   **Plate 51**

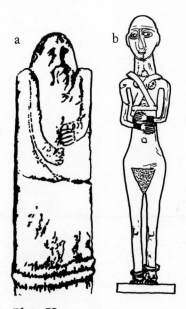

Plate 52

Apparently, the writer of the catalog text remarks, the Hallstatt tradition, of which the statue is a part, allowed the artist some latitude in shaping the lower part of the body, but the representation of the position of the arms was circumscribed by rigid convention. Remnants of sculptures from the same century of young men holding their arms in an identical pose were found also in Istria (northeastern Italy).

No speculation is offered as to the reasons for this curious arm position. Its significance becomes clear, however, if instead of looking at it as a peculiar artistic affectation of the age, we treat it as a trance posture. The following is what Bernie, a sculptor by profession, experienced at a session in Cincinnati in the fall of 1987, when we tried the posture for the first time:

I had a very good experience, very powerful, I felt. From the time I got into the pose and heard the rattle, it just flowed very, very naturally, without too much trouble on my part. I had not been too happy with my performance this weekend. Today I thought I'd take a little more initiative than I had taken in the past, get a little more directness in approaching the postures and without prodding and questioning. And I'll tell you what happened to me.

At first I became alarmed; there was a sudden cold, sweaty kind of a feeling. I was feeling ill, sick, maybe even dead, and being transformed into a corpse. Then I was traveling along a long, cold, horizontal landscape, with the leaves off of the trees, a snowy, breezy roadway, and moving and moving and moving, it seemed like forever along that particular path. Until finally I came to a rack, I guess you might call it, with bones and skin, things of that nature, all piled up as if they had been discarded. And what struck me then was that the entire landscape was being transformed from being a landscape into this rack with bones and skins. And immediately next

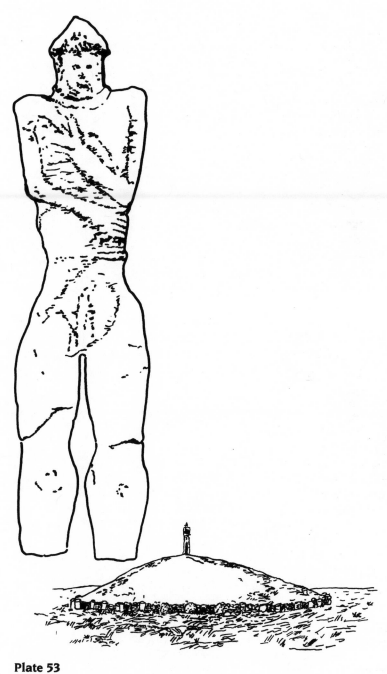

Plate 53

to that rack was a huge pit, with darkness and individual flickering lights in the darkness, which seemed to be spirits. I recognized it from some past trance experience, and I was very eager to enter that space. And what surprised me was that in order to enter it, I didn't just have to take off my clothes, but all my skin, my flesh, my bones, and everything else to enter this place of the spirits. And it was a very curious thing. But I guess I was very willing to do that.

Once on the inside of the pit—from the beginning of the trance experience I had asked the Bear once more to come back and help me through this—I felt that once I was inside, I was being reconstituted and clothed in the warmth of the Bear, the quality of the Bear, and the image of the Bear; there was this fur and the skeletal structure. And I was given a great sense of power. I guess that was what impressed me the most, this sense of strength, really strength, I guess, of physical strength that I had through this experience. Out of that, then, it seems that we began moving away from that pit back through the cold, and with this big sense of warmth and power and light, different kinds of lights—I can't describe them— and with an overall feeling of well-being. And that was my experience.

In other words, Bernie experienced dying, then traveling to the entrance of the Realm of the Spirits of the Dead in the lower world. There he discarded his human physical attributes and, aided by the Bear, his spirit friend to whom he had appealed for help at the beginning of the session, he experienced a resurrection. With a tremendous surge of power, he was reinvested with a different body and arose to new life in the shape of the bear.

No one else in the group had thought to invoke any spirit help, and curiously, not a single one experienced any return to a new life. The women—and, as we see in plate 52b, the posture is also assumed by women—reported mainly details of the passage. One saw a black statue standing next to the road, with red lips that moved soundlessly. A man's face appeared in a hole and turned into a skull—"he had eyes, but the eyes were the first to go"—and eagles perched on bare tree branches. One of the birds unzipped the earth so Terry, one of the participants, could look inside.

The experiences of the other men in the group were similar in texture. Bob saw an Indian chief wearing a headdress from which colors kept flying off like sparks into the darkness. Michael, whose spirit guide was an Indian girl, was taken away by her over snowy land on a horse that turned into a bald eagle. They encountered a threatening owl, the spirit bird of the night, then ended up at a lake, which is where one arrives upon dying, according to Pueblo Indian tradition. Bill's experience was the most instructive. He found himself in the same black spirit pit that Bernie had described, that is, at the entrance to the Realm of the Dead. However, he had appealed to no spirit helper, and so the animal spirits that he encountered there could not help him. They had no energy to give to him: there was "no breeze, no wind at all." He tried to raise the energy on his own, but he floundered, achieving only a helpless rocking motion, not enough to award him a return to new life:

As soon as the rattle started, I felt a powerful forward movement around my shoulders. It was like flying, and I was a bird. Suddenly a bear, a wolf, and a bison appeared, and many eyes and muzzles. It was dark. There was a hole above me through which I was able to look up into the sky. Around me, there were some earthworks, with a series of holes. The moon was shining, and I saw the grass growing above, but there was no breeze, no wind at all; it was a calm night. I had a strong desire to get out but couldn't. An eye appeared and was going to act as my guide. Almost immediately, I began rocking in rhythm with my breathing. I wanted to stop it but couldn't.

With the Hallstatt youth we are taken back to a time centuries before our era when the horticulturalist tribes, we may surmise, struggling against encroaching agriculturalists, sent their young men, members of the warrior age grade, out against them on the warpath. The shamans, we might imagine, would teach them this posture of the passage to the Realm of the Spirits of the Dead, which then became their hallmark.

Actually, the Hallstatt youth and his contemporaries are not the earliest ones to show this posture. Almost three thousand years earlier, at the time when the waning Neolithic began blending into the new Bronze Age, this posture experienced an intense local flowering on the Cyclades, a group of islands north of Crete. Subsistence was still clearly horticulturalist. People grew some barley, they had a few olive trees, goats, and sheep, but mainly they were fishermen. With the appearance of Minoan culture traits a thousand years later, the art of the Cyclades collapsed.

Every grave, it seems, of that particular period, whether of a man or of a woman, contains a characteristic figurine exhibiting this posture (pl. 54). Prehistorians have speculated that we are seeing a good-luck charm, or perhaps a local deity, but recalling the above experiences, a different conclusion suggests itself. I think that what is involved instead is the representation of a psychopomp and a power object. Psychopomps are shamans who have the office of accompanying the soul of the person who just died on its way to the beyond. Although the posture shown by these Cycladic

Plate 54

figurines is always the same, usually with the left arm close to the right arm or in a few instances with the left arm higher up in the manner of the Hallstatt youth, they exhibit individual characteristics. Some are slender and graceful, others are squat like peasant women; one even has a goiter, and two have their infants on their heads. Those figurines, then, are most likely the local shamanesses, women one of whose tasks it was to guide the spirits of the dead over that perilous path to the Realm of the Dead. It was clearly a woman's office; men took it over only under exceptional circumstances. Of the 121 figurines shown at an exhibit in West Germany in 1976,[1] only two are male.

But more important, I think, the small figurines acted as power objects, so that once the soul arrived at the black pit leading to the abode of the dead, it had the strength to return to the living, albeit in a different shape.

Confirmation of this view comes from a totally unexpected source—"London Bridge Is Falling Down" (Hopscotch), a traditional, highly popular children's song game,[2] well known in Hungary and in the German-speaking regions of Europe, and in a somewhat abbreviated form among English-speaking children as well. Manhardt Wilhelm (1859) summarizes the plot of the German variant, called *Brueckenspiel* ("game of the bridge"), as follows:

It seems that there is a bridge that leads to the sun and the moon, to heaven and hell, or to the angels and devils. A golden gate is substituted for the golden bridge in some variants. A group of people desire to cross the bridge. However, the bridge is *broken*, perhaps by the actions of the king, or the goldsmith and his youngest daughter. It can be repaired only with stones or bones. In order to cross the bridge, a toll must be paid, in the form of the last one of the group, or perhaps a golden horse (in Hungary, the toll is a beautiful maiden). This player becomes a prisoner in the *black kettle*, and on the basis of certain rules, it is decided whether he/she is to be apportioned to the sun or the moon, to heaven or hell, etc. In the end, the two groups struggle with each other by trying to pull each other over. Wilhelm notes that the game refers to the passage of the soul over the bridge of death.

The agreement of the game with our experiences is truly remarkable. As we saw in Bernie's case, he had to divest himself of all human attributes; that is, the bridge of life was broken. He ended up in a black pit, the "black kettle" of the game. According to the game, a contest ensues concerning the fate of the soul. Is it to end up with the sun or the moon, in heaven or hell; that is, is it to be forever consigned to the abode of the dead, or is it to enjoy a resurrection? A toll must be paid at this point. We may interpret that as meaning that the soul needs some extraneous power in order to gain resurrection. Bernie had the help of the mighty Bear Spirit, and he reentered life. Without such help Bill had to remain confined in the black pit. This additional power, I think, was what the small marble figurines in the graves of the Cyclades were intended to provide for the dead.

While the role of the psychópomp seems secondary for the shamanesses of the Cyclades during the above posture, it is the focal issue for the next one. We originally called it the mourning posture, although in view of the fact that it made it possible for the shaman to act as a guide to the lower world, this designation was not a particularly good choice. Instead, this is in fact the posture of the *Psychopomp*.

I saw the posture for the first time in a clay figurine created at Cochiti Pueblo about 1890 (pl. 55). The man has his arms lifted and with his fingers touches the upper edge of his earlobe, and his mouth is wide open. The posture is duplicated in sub-Saharan Africa (pl. 56), in a polychrome rattle fragment from the Northwest Coast (pl. 57a), as well as on a totem pole from the same

Plate 55   **Plate 56**

region (pl. 57b). The latter was carved a hundred years ago by a Tsimshian artist. It has a hole in its lower part, and the central figure above the hole is clearly tugging at the upper edge of his earlap, in the same way as the Cochiti figurine, and his mouth is equally as open as is that of the face on the rattle fragment. The hole is called a "place of opening," or a "hole through the sky." "Ladders," we are told, "led to this hole on the inside and the outside of the house, so that it could be used during ceremonies; on these occasions the normal entrance to the house was covered over."[3] According to local Indian tradition, those entering the house recreated the ancestral cosmic passage between this world and the other world. I had not seen this totem pole at the time we tried the posture, but the tradition, as we shall see, is once more a telling external confirmation of our experiences.

The first time we tried the posture was with three friends in the spring of 1986 in Vienna. I did not have the Cochiti slide with me, and all I remembered was the position of the arms. Gerhard spoke of a tall figure of light he had seen during the last few minutes of the trance. Christian St. saw a tiny man slipping in and out of his gullet. And Eva D. experienced suffering, "but not the way we understand the word," and a long, stout pole being driven through her as part of a burial rite. The use of the pole was in itself remarkable, for early observers of Pueblo Indian funeral rites speak of a pole being driven

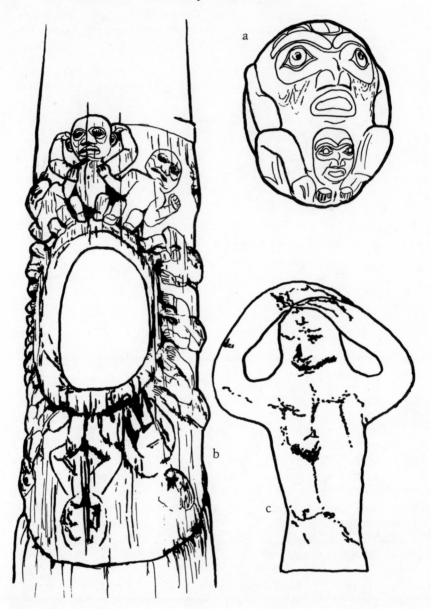

Plate 57

through the chest of the corpse after burial. Besides, we were clearly dealing with a trance posture, so I resolved to explore it further. The opportunity presented itself when nearly a year later we scheduled a research meeting in Columbus. Then, on the day before our meeting, I had the following vision:

(January 20, 1987): I heard the lines of the old song, only the last three words, "[And we won't come back 'til it's] *over, over there* . . . repeated several times, then very loud church bells, which lasted for a while. After a pause white flowers appeared, as if on a grave, and people huddling around it together with a young man on his knees in profile, in a posture that made him look like a rabbit. His hair looked slicked down like that of a movie hero of the twenties; I was surprised to see his face, but it was more like a mask, white and motionless like a cardboard cutout.

Once more, there were intimations of a burial, but other than that, I could see no connection between the posture we wanted to try and what I had recorded about it in Austria. Since my three friends were all experienced coworkers, I mentioned that this might have something to do with a funeral rite, but I did not tell them of my vision. It was not until we actually looked at the slide that I realized that I had made a mistake in Vienna: In addition to the special position of the arms, the figure also had its mouth wide open. That we had not done during the first trial.

Belinda was the first one to talk, and her experience to some degree fitted in with my—much briefer—vision:

When we started the breathing, there was an image of a brightly colored toucan with a big beak, sitting on a branch, profiled against the night sky in brilliant turquoise, purple, and magenta colors. It was very clear and very bright. When the rattle set in, the branches of a tree appeared with umbrellalike leaves with colors so intense, it was notable for that. I looked beyond to see a beach of white sand curving and waves coming in, and there was no one there. I could see the waves clearly, and on the waves were many little spirits "body surfing," coming in; there was the sense of the spirits coming in on the waves.

Then I was very aware that the posture, with my arms and the way my legs were, and my mouth open, made huge holes in me—and there was the wind blowing through, drying me out like a weathering wooden statue. My mouth was very dry, and saliva was collecting in a dark, deep pool in the bottom of my mouth and filling it up. I was sure I was going to start overflowing with this water.

Fairly quickly then there was a shift, and my arms seemed connected in a straight line, with a circle of light circling right to left and back, again and again. The slow, gradual effect was one of loosening connections until I realized that it was pulling my body apart, and there was a jagged crack right down my body, splitting me in two. The physical pain in my shoulders was terrible, and it intensified the feeling that I was coming apart. Eventually I felt as though my left arm was crumbling, not exactly to dust, but my arms were crumbling apart.

Then there was a decided shift again, and I saw the image of a white plate with a piece of nut pie on it. Then I noticed that the pieces of nuts in the pie looked like teeth. Then it became like a dog's head, with the teeth, and as I focused some more, it became the pointed head of a dog with its teeth gnashing. I, too, became dog-wolflike and interacted with the dog, who I thought must be Cerberus. And I thought that I must try to get past that dog. And then there was a dark hooded figure with the big staff by a river, and I thought, naw, this is too intellectual, but it wouldn't go away. I did not want to be taken by the boatman; I didn't see a boat or a raft or anything. So I jumped into the inky, oily water and swam the short distance to the other side. It didn't take very long, and when I got to the other side, there was this same hooded figure, but it was much more pleasant on the other side. It was much easier to be there. The figure tossed back its hood, and he had on a white mask, and I could see the back of his head with very short cropped hair. So then he started to walk this path along the river back into a tunnellike cave, and I followed, and then quickly he was no longer leading me and the rattle took over. There was a dancing figure rattling, but I couldn't see the figure. What I could see were these little sparkling diamonds, shimmering starlike things that were shook along the path. My impression was they were souls, they were spirits, the essences of the people. And I followed the figure as it danced along, and it almost brought them to life, there was almost a sound. And as we went into the cave then, there was another change.

All along, the pain in my shoulders was so intense that I thought I could not stand it anymore. And I kept saying to myself to remember the pain of those who had gone before me, and sometimes it helped, and sometimes it didn't. But it was very important to acknowledge those others' pain and to not [reject it]—I could choose to not feel the pain, and it was my choice to keep with this. And I saw a skull with crossed legs, and as it started to crumble, I thought, how can I bear the pain? And then I started convulsing, and as the rattle stopped I was still convulsing a little. I had heard you two making noise, and there was the feeling that I wanted to make noise, to moan and wail. I started to make a little noise toward the end. If I would do it again, I would want to do it from the beginning consciously, as with the Singing Shaman, to allow the sound to come out.

Taking Belinda's experience as a guide to interpreting my own vision, those little spirits arriving on the seashore "body-surfing" seemed qualitatively the same as my people around the grave, souls arriving to be guided to the Realm of the Dead. That this was the reading to be given to my own vision was then further emphasized by Belinda's drying out and beginning to crumble, that is, dying, and by the appearance of a doglike being, something like Cerberus, the dog at the entrance to Hades. Although she had seen a psychopomp at the outset in the guise of a bird, which I had not, we agreed on the details of the external appearance of her second psychopomp: We had both seen his short-cropped hair and his white mask. His posture had reminded me of a rabbit precisely because he was getting ready to descend into the earth, like a rabbit into its burrow. But there were two features of her account that puzzled me: her pain, which she had rationalized as something she shared with the dying, and her intuition that there should be sound, "moaning and wailing," as she said.

Elizabeth's experience, which followed next, can be viewed as having a frame: At the outset, she is in a teepee, created by our composite energies, and is attending a person who has just died. And that is where she once more encounters herself at the end, piling stones on the corpse. This frame holds together what the dying that had just happened was like, the progressive dissolution that is really only a change in the expression of states of energy, as well as the kindly presence of the animal spirits. No psychopomp appears, but once more we hear of the pain:

During the breathing I was aware of our breathing together, and that intensified the feeling of being together. During the breathing, the Bear came into the room, and my spirit guides and the Lion came in, and the Buffalo came in, and a huge white owl, it was very feathery. I felt very protected during the whole posture. I felt the presence of the Spirits very strongly, and their protection. They even tried to hold my arms up for me. [She laughs.] Our breaths met in the center and swirled together; it was a lot of red energy that just swirled around and then formed a teepee.

Inside, I was leaning over a dead person, and I was with somebody else. And then my shoulder started to hurt really bad. During this whole session I was in excruciating pain, and I couldn't maintain the posture the entire time. I would have to break it and then get back to it again. When we began the posture, the whole thing was really physical for me. Besides the pain, I first noticed that the left side of my head—I would want to say disappeared, but it didn't. It was more like it filled up what it had displaced before it was there; I felt it filling up the room, the energy in the room, so that it wasn't there anymore [in my head]. It was different from disappearing; I don't know how to explain that any better than that. It was a filling-up feeling. But the left side of my head was gone. And then slowly the right side of my head was gone, it was just gone, and I was real aware of the rattle, and of myself, going down a ladder very fast in time to the rattle, down into myself.

I was a little small person inside me, a big person with no head, and climbing down inside myself as fast as I could, in time to the rattle, while parts of me were slowly disappearing above me. And I got down to a level above my solar plexus, and there was a slime, the little green monster that I sometimes have to deal with. This creature that was in my solar plexus wouldn't let me go any further. I felt for minutes very stuck and in a lot of pain and couldn't keep the posture. I would get back in the posture, and finally I called for the Bear to come and help me.

The Bear crawled down inside and asked what was the matter. And this little green monster said, "Well, nobody asked me if this was all right." So the Bear said, "You can ride on my back." That definitely appeased the little green monster. He got on his back, and we went on further down and came to a place where it was very dark blue and pretty uncomfortable. It felt like— you know, when the guides shake me out and the stuff crumbles off—that crumbly stuff was stored in this dark-blue place. It seemed like what we were going to do was clean it out and dust it. We all had little rattle dusters, and we were inside of me, rattling and dusting, and rattling and dusting in time to the rattle.

Then again I was back with the pain and breaking the posture, and then back again in the posture, and I became aware of that same filling and disappearing and going down probably to my lowest part. But then the energy changed, so that I was back into my head, and it was still not there, but it was there in a different form. But I felt at a molecular level that I had changed form, and I was still invisible or not there; there was a lot of light and colors. Then it shifted again, and I was back in that teepee where the dead person had been, and we were piling stones on top. I thought, this isn't right, this was a teepee and we should be burning him, but it was definitely stones; the person was being buried under lots and lots of stones.

Jan, finally, picked up on the problem of producing sound, and transmitted a stern lecture on our failure to provide it:

There was a lot of energy ahead of time and with the breathing for me. And when the rattle began and we assumed the posture, it was like I knew from the minute we started that something was wrong, that something was missing, and it was the sound we were talking about. It was like I was being torn apart in the posture because we weren't sounding. It felt like a light trance to me, off and on, although there was a lot of energy building up. Some of the messages that were there were like—this is about guiding, with sound, the energy of the dying, of the spirit, so it can get where it needs to go. When we assume the posture, it's like we are agreeing to be those guides.

And so we were standing here in this posture agreeing to be those guides and listening to the sounds of the spirits which were like wind, that need to get where they needed to go and we weren't doing anything; we weren't doing what we were supposed to do. I was in that conflict the whole time, and it was really difficult. On the intellectual level the conflict was, go ahead and sound, because I knew that was what I needed to do, versus disrupting the trance of the other people. So for the most part I just tried to deal with it myself, and I noticed what I was doing was a lot of movement; I was doing things like tapping my feet to create a rhythm, or using my breath to create the rhythm of a sound that would do the job. Because there were spirits here that needed to go. The times when I was forgetting to open my mouth, and my mouth was closed, there was tremendous energy in my heart center, and it was like taking in all that dying energy and not releasing it. I would open my mouth, and it would be like I could hear myself singing, and it was the Singing Shaman. It needs to be like the Singing Shaman.

There was one point where I remember shifting my arms, and it felt like blood running down my leg. When that happened, the energy shifted, and it felt like you, Felicitas, were on a ladder and you were using the rattle to lift the energy up through my body. The energy at that point became very different; it was a heightened kind of energy. The conflict was still there, and toward the end I did then make a sound. It was like I didn't want to be responsible for being in this posture and not doing some of what we knew we were supposed to be doing; some of it was like I couldn't help it anymore. That was my job.

And it was like the posture and the mourning sound were a signal to the other reality. It was the guide that was making the connection with the guides of the other reality requesting them to come and do their part. When I heard Belinda breathing loudly, my thought was, well, we are all doing something trying to cope with the problem. Right at the end it felt like we got it a little bit, and it was like the spirits understood that we didn't know what we were doing and it was allowed this time, but don't do it this way again.

In our discussion afterward, the lesson finally sank in. I must confess that I was not particularly proud of myself, especially in view of the fact that, as

Jan was given to understand, the sound acted as a signal to alert the guides "on the other side." With that remark, a considerable volume of customs about the "bewailing" of the dead all of a sudden fell into place, as well as highlighting our own total lack of any such mourning behavior. No wonder that the Spirits had been so anxious to make clear that they wanted us to add the sound, first alluding to the song with its suggestive "over, over there" in my vision and then practically hitting me over the head with those bells that I had heard. At one point they had been so loud, I was afraid I would lose the vision and come to. Yet I did not propose singing in trance to my group. We also concluded that had we given voice and thereby acted as proper psychopomps within the confines of this particular posture, there would not have been any pain, either.

The assumption was confirmed when we repeated the posture with a larger group at Camp Agape, Ohio, in October 1987. This time I included the instruction to use the voice the way we do it with the Singing Shaman, that is, starting with an open *a* vowel and letting the tone ride on the trance. This time, there was no pain, and both Belinda and Jan were clearly psychopomps. As Belinda reported, "I was with a group of miners; we were on an expedition and we had to climb up a mountainside, and the sound provided the energy. The sound knew where to go." It is easy to see that the "miners" were the souls traveling to the abode of the spirits of the dead, and it was the sound that made the passage possible.

> JAN: Even before the rattle started I had the clear impression that I did not have any body. Then I was surrounded by white fireworks. The rattle seemed to provide access to unfamiliar ranges. I was a magnet, gathering up energy. I called out to the energies and they took on form, and I started separating them by color. I was directing their traffic by using the tones. The tones and the colors had personality.

Even relatively inexperienced participants not familiar with the posture saw the psychopomp in action, for instance in the shape of a bird—"I looked up and saw the sun rising, and a bird was wrapping its wings around Norma [a participant who had been audibly crying during the session] and lifted her up"—or experienced the burden of the task: "I had to fly over a terrible crevasse, and it was frightfully hard for me. Then I remembered my feather; I screamed and became a hawk, and I flew up and felt strong."

I later became aware also of what I think is another variant of the psychopomp posture, which I saw in a television documentary some time ago. In that report the camera focused on a group of Sudanese women mourning a relative whom the men had gone to bury. The women had their hands on their heads, in a posture identical to one seen in a figure several thousand years old from Azor near Jaffa (in modern Israel) (pl. 57c). In our experiments, however, we have explored only the Indian variant to date.

CHAPTER THIRTEEN

Life Everlasting

In the first of the postures treated in Chapter 12, there was a clear indication that life's story did not end after the vestments of the body were surrendered at the entrance to the Realm of the Dead in the lower world. After arriving there, Bernie received a new form, that of the bear, full of power and joy. This metamorphosis is rather restricted, however. There is another posture, which allows this theme to be played out much more fully. For reasons to be explained further on, we have come to call it the Feathered Serpent posture. It is one of the few postures the origin of which can actually be traced back reliably to our ancient hunter roots.

Plate 58

According to traditions still encountered among hunter-gatherers and some horticulturalists to this day, it was the task of shamans to descend into a cave, the womb of the earth. There they created likenesses of the animals surrounding them, and by no means only of those that provided food. They then lifted the soul essences from the drawings and took them up into the world of the sun, thereby helping the Earth Mother in the task of increase, of propagation.

This tradition offers a satisfying explanation for the innumerable pictures of animals our ancestors pecked out, incised, or painted in caves and also on exposed rock surfaces in many parts of the world. Humans are also often represented, dancing and engaging in many other activities, and naturally also in the role of hunter. However, human figures appear in some extremely old representations (pl. 58) which are not engaged in any of these activities. They were created during the fifth to the fourth millennia B.C. and were discovered by Russian archeologists on rock faces all across Siberia.[1] As the authors of that work point out, these human figures, which they tentatively identify as shamans, are usually placed above the animals, exerting, as it were, their power over them.

Of these figures, the one shown in pl. 58a is quite naturalistic. It clearly indicates what to me looks like a specific body posture: This person has slightly bent knees, his hands rest on his hips, and artfully, there is even a minimal indication of the bent wrist shown on the right side. To my eyes, this is an astoundingly articulate "instruction" about a trance posture that we are quite familiar with. It is a deceptively simple posture: We stand straight without locking our knees, as nearly always, and cup our hands, as illustrated best by the African figures (pl. 59), resting them palm up on the waist. The core of the experience is the eternal renewal of life.

How ancient the knowledge about this posture must be is attested by the fact that plate 58a is the only representation that is this naturalistic. Others, although easily recognizable as treating the same posture, are quite abstract, which means that people drew the figure so many times and it was

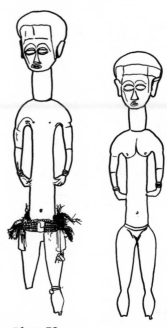

Plate 59

so well known that eventually, a few sparing lines were sufficient to make the meaning clear. During times of great cultural stability, such as the era of the hunters in fact was, a development of that nature takes a very long time. Thus plate 58b abstractly represents a shamaness according to the Russian researchers, the round hole being her womb, while plates 58c and 58d are so highly abstracted that they seem like an ideograph, communicating in ultimate abbreviation the message that the animals shown will return to life once more because of the action of the shaman.

In this context it is revealing to note that nearly three thousand years later, in the Ganges River valley, people cherished copper objects (pl. 58e) on which the practiced eye of the archeologist was unable to detect any trace of use.[2] This motif is so similar in shape to the Siberian petroglyphs that it may have been brought to India by cultural diffusion. Quite possibly people carried these copper plates because they reminded them of the promise of resurrection.

Plate 60

For the same reason, surely, in the city of Ur, in the fourth millennium, one of the most frequently encountered effigies is a clay figurine of a deity standing in this posture.

However, I saw this durable posture for the first time in a drawing by a modern American Indian shaman. In the 1970s, Gerhard Baer, a Swiss anthropologist, did fieldwork among the Matsigenka Indians of eastern Peru. One of their shamans, Benjamin Sanchez, made him a drawing of the places and beings he habitually encountered on his spirit journeys (pl. 60). Of the three spirits drawn large, whose power is indicated by their facial hair, which is not a moustache but jaguar whiskers, the one on the right was standing in the posture of the Bear Spirit, the middle one in that of the Singing Shaman, and the one on the left in a posture that I was totally unfamiliar with. But soon after I came across the photograph of a clay figurine from a pre-Columbian grave site in eastern Peru,[3] of a man being

Plate 61

carried aloft by a plumed serpent that grabs him by the head (see pl. 61). His posture was the same as that of the Matsigenka spirit, and in addition provided details not discernible in the above drawing on how to do the posture, which has become one of our favorites over the years. Quite often the trancers in fact do experience the presence of this mighty, ancient being of fertility. For Westerners it is hard to recognize a Feathered Serpent, and it was an occasional source of merriment when participants confessed that they had taken it for "a seal with feathers stuck in" or "an eagle, but maybe more like a caterpillar."

With Judy Ch. and Jan, we are introduced to varying impressions of the actions of the Feathered Serpent. For Judy this is principally the motion of a curving serpentine body, which sometimes is a woman and then again a serpent, while Jan assumes the role of the Feathered Serpent as a giver of fertility, and in fact becomes her.

> JUDY CH. (Columbus, 1985): I felt much movement; I was like taffy being stretched. Somebody behind me put his hands into the holes in me and stretched me and bent me over. I felt tremendous heat pouring out of my chest and rising up, and my eyes began to itch. Then I was pulled again, and I was moving in figure eights. The loops moved into vertical flip-flops; they circled, and started spinning, and were illuminated in a vivid purple color.

> JAN (Columbus, 1985): I was flying over the earth and was cross-pollinating. I was taking seeds and planting them, and that felt like Mother Nature doing it. Then I was shown how life patterns were woven into one and saw all realms dancing. I was moving in a figure-eight pattern, and was asked to be the movement. "You are the dance," I heard, "you are the dance."

In Vienna, Christian St. was really confused about what exactly he had tangled with:

> Something or somebody got hold of me from the back. It was a powerful being, but I couldn't figure out if it was an eagle or a caterpillar. Then I saw the seashore, and at that point I was confused again: Was I a caterpillar? And who was doing the flying? Was I doing it or not? There were strange fish in the sea, and a white dot. There was a lake, and a thick worm was reflected in it, and what seemed to be a butterfly. Then I was standing on a rock ledge. I was supposed to fly, and over my back there was a huge hand, and its fingers reached down on my chest as far as the nipple.

Eva D., in the same session, recognized the powerful feline head of the serpent. She went through dying, when it suddenly turned dark, and also the repose when she watched a spider digging itself into the sand. Finally she is reborn in a number of different shapes:

> I saw the face of a big cat above me, looking at me, then it was gone. It was dark. I started running up toward the bright light. There was a house on the side of the mountain. I was a panther and went into the house, which was very bright inside. A black spider or maybe a scorpion was crawling over the yellow sand and then dug itself in. I became the spider, then a woman, then a ball of light raining golden drops, and then I was inside a bird's body that had a long beak.

Except for the above motifs, there are also a number of other elements that appear during this posture. Thus Jane, a beginner, told at a workshop in Columbus, Ohio, in the spring of 1985:

> I felt my body splitting in half. Then I was being rolled up to a mountain peak. I fell into a foggy, grey, soft light, and instead of stopping when I reached the bottom, I kept right on falling through the earth, through many different layers and

through crevasses right into the center of the earth. After I got there, I rested. Finally I emerged, and that was very comforting.

Jane clearly experienced a sum of the outstanding features of what the posture mediates, being carried aloft, falling into what might be a hollow mountain, resting, and then rising once more. The report also throws sudden light on a symbol carved into the chest of a female figurine shown in this posture and wearing a bird mask, unearthed in central Yugoslavia and dated about 6000 B.C. The marking (see pl. 62) consists of a V, with a line penetrating into it from above. Amazingly, the symbol is an exact representation of the salient experience in this posture.

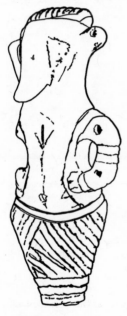

Plate 62

For Elizabeth R., at the same workshop, falling into the mountain passes rapidly before her eyes, and the transformation is touched on only briefly, when, after receiving the crystals, colored rays issue from her head. The important experience for her is the repose under the cozy Eskimo skins on a slab of ice:

I felt tired; flashes of flowers and animals passed before my eyes, and I did not seem to be able to stop. Suddenly I saw the face of an Eskimo, clothed in a fur outfit. He took me into an igloo. I had to take a step deep down into the ice, and everything was bathed in this bluish-white light. "Do you have any questions?" he asked. But I couldn't think of anything, so he left. In the igloo, it was pretty big; there were other Eskimos, all working on bones and stretching hides. My Eskimo gave me a hat. It was made of the skull of a polar bear. Then he had me lie down on a platform of ice. I should rest, he said, and do nothing. That felt so comfortable, and so restful. A woman was sewing beads on a skin. She came and implanted crystals in my head. After she did that, I could see rays of color coming out of my head.

With Gerhard (Vienna, 1985), we are introduced to some other features of the experience in this posture, namely, the dance that follows the repose of death, and the fire of regeneration in the depth of the mountain, which for him takes on the shape of a glowing circle:

I felt the rattle in my body. I ran up into the air at an angle and found myself in a dense, swirling fog. I started walking; it was pitch-dark. I saw a circle of black people dancing in a glowing white circle. I slipped into an egg and was alone in a dark landscape. A bird and a shadowy figure took me along up to the crest of a mountain. Then I came to the sea, which was as yellow as gold, and I lay down in it.

We may assume that Gerhard was a bird after emerging from the egg. Eva D., too, had been of a different shape at the conclusion of the experience. In fact, the risen shape is hardly ever human. This aspect of the posture of the Feathered Serpent illustrates a view about animate life that is quite different from our own. It is all a game, it seems to say; you have one shape today, another one tomorrow, and over it all arches the miracle of everlasting life. As the Eskimos held,

> Animals sometimes chose to die because they had grown tired of their present existence and wished to come back as some other form of life. In one Eskimo tale, the soul of a dead human fetus is successively dog, fjord seal, wolf, caribou, dog again, and finally, by slipping into the body of a woman as she bends over a seal, once more a human fetus, eventually to grow into a dutiful son and successful hunter.... This is more than transformation, however; each being contains many forms simultaneously, sometimes manifesting itself as one, sometimes as another. (Furst and Furst 1982:141)

In Scheibbs in 1986, Franz was not carried by the Feathered Serpent but was guided by a psychopomp, which assumed, as it had for Belinda (see Chapter 12), the shape of a bird, a motif frequently encountered in folklore. There was no dance at the bottom of the hollow mountain; it was a soccer game instead—also intense motion, in other words.

> A bird appeared before me. It had a black body, a many-colored neck, and wore a little crown. The bird began dancing around me for a long time. I was at a curious mountain; it was hollow inside like a volcano, relatively high. The bird and I started climbing up that mountain, then the bird carried me the rest of the way. Inside the mountain everything was reddish-brown, but in the middle there was a vivid emerald-green spot. Very far below me people were playing soccer. I wanted to see more, but a red layer began to cover the scene, and I was at a loss what to do next.

The basic features—the hollow mountain, in this case a wall formed by slanting pillars, the movement, the fire, and the transformation—are easily identifiable also in this 1986 account from Switzerland:

> VRENIE: We were in a circle, surrounded by slanting pillars. Inside the circle there was a lot of movement by small beings. Above there were many colored ribbons swirling around, and below a fire was burning brightly. Then the rain started falling, and water came rushing in from all sides. The fire dissolved, and I with it. I turned my head upward and saw many orange-red suns. Then I changed into a vessel, which was open toward the top, and in it there was a golden ball. A fragrant liquid kept dropping on my right side. Suddenly, a white feather came floating down, and the fragrant liquid began to spread. I left the vessel and did not know where to go. But a black cloud came and carried me up in a whirl to the brown earth above that was full of life.

Pij's experience during a workshop near Salzburg (1987) has a similar idyllic cast. She mentioned that shortly before the session, she had been to a cemetery and had admired the crocuses growing on a grave. She took their image with her into her trance:

> The light around me was pale green, and the rattle seemed far away. Some soft gold-colored good-luck feathers stroked and tickled me and gave me a feeling of happiness, of harmony. I became a cross on a grave and had to bend down in order to be able to see the crocuses that were growing there. I bent down so low, I began to see their roots. I sank into the earth; it was cool and lovely to be down there. I sat down next to the crocus bulbs and turned into a bulb myself. It was a quiet feeling. I had many layers, I had become a real firm bulb, and I was in the earth for a long time.
>
> Then the light began to dawn, and I figured it was a matter of logic, I would definitely turn into a crocus, and I was looking forward to that. Instead, however, I became an ancient, thick, gnarled tree with spreading branches. This condition lasted a long time. Under the tree, there were tiny snakes wiggling around. The branches had meadows on them with red and yellow flowers, and when Felicitas had to sneeze, all the blossoms closed up. The scene was bathed in a soft green light. My roots sucked water out of the ground; it spread all over and fructified everything. It was beautiful. I saw a Mexican female figurine from a distance. It turned into my mother, and I became a very small child and crawled around through the roots. My mother placed me into a nest with tiny green snakes that had feathers on them. I was in an eggshell, and I had to chew my way out, and it was fun the way the eggshell crunched between my teeth. I was a very tiny child, but then I became a snake, and enormously big, and from high up, I could see the entire earth.

Finally, there was Edeltraut. She had never done any trance before, and unaccountably, the fire of regeneration took on a very special meaning for her during a workshop in Utrecht (the Netherlands) in 1986. She saw herself wearing an ugly mask and being burned at the stake as a witch, and then flying away free with a swarm of white birds.

> I heard insects flying in and out, and it seemed that I couldn't stop the insects from buzzing in my ear. I had a distorted face, and I thought that I was very ugly in this mask, which was like an animal mask, like a caricature. I became an insect, which had big ears; actually I was two insects flying around. I was an insect in the rattle, being battered in between the stones and the seeds in the rattle. Then I had human shape again, and I was hanging forward and was rolling down headfirst into a valley. I straightened up and started dancing. There was light above me. I was naked and felt very hot. There was a fire. I was burning in the fire; I was standing in one place, me, but not me, I was a witch being burned at the stake. I felt my face burning, but there was no pain. Suddenly everything went black. Then I saw a light. It was like an eye, and I wanted to go through that light, up into the sky, up into the air and into freedom. Above me, there were white birds circling, swans, or maybe geese, and I was flying with them. I thought I was a white bird, too, but when I looked at myself, I had no body. I was invisible.

Edeltraut seemed to have gone through a curious, special application of the experience of the Feathered Serpent, and I recall puzzling over it. But other impressions intruded, two years went by, and I more or less forgot about it. It was not until I started working on this chapter and looked through my notes that it occurred to me that possibly there had been a special dimension to Edeltraut's experience which I needed to explore. The more I thought about it, the clearer it became to me that her account actually represented an invitation to the mystic ranges of human myth.

Section III

MYTHS OF THE
ETERNAL PRESENT

Introduction

My first reaction at rereading my notes about Edeltraut's account of her experiences during the posture of the Feathered Serpent was amazement. Through the magic of the posture, the burning of a witch, the obscene crime perpetrated against uncounted women in centuries past, had here undergone a miraculous, a redeeming transformation. But at closer scrutiny, there seemed to be even more to it. As though witnessed from the inside, the event assumed an eerie reality. Joan of Arc might have experienced her trial this way, the Inquisitors tormenting her like the bothersome insects whose buzzing she could not stop; the distorted mask of the heretic that had been forced on her, and which hid the gentle girl who used to dance around the trees at her father's homestead; the battering of the endless hearings that bruised her day after day. Finally there she is, standing naked at the stake, burning and yet not in pain, and flying through the blackness toward the light, a free spirit at last, an invisible companion of white birds.

It was all so specific, much more than simply a recreation informed by whatever Edeltraut might have read. The question was, had we been listening to Edeltraut, or had it been Joan who told her story? On the one hand, it is Joan's life, obvious to anyone familiar with the tragic fate of the peasant girl who in the fifteenth century raised the siege of Orléans, thus helping to free France from English domination. On the other hand, it is also myth, for we are told how her life triumphs beyond the flames of the pyre.

If we accept this interpretation of what Edeltraut experienced, we will have to rethink what myth is. It may be a fanciful tale about imaginary beings, or a repository for nearly forgotten historical events, or a story invented to give meaning to some ritual. But principally, a myth is a report about events that took place in the other reality and that involved people or beings who straddled the two dimensions. Joan heard and saw and was guided not by a military high command but by spirits whom she did not disguise as saints until she came in conflict with the Inquisition.

The question is, how did Edeltraut come to experience this vision in its vivid immediacy? After all, Joan died in 1431. The extraordinary incident may have something to do with the fact that the alternate reality does not have a dimension of time. Gernot Winkler, the director of the Timekeeping Service of the U.S. Naval Observatory, defines time as "the abstract measure of change, an abstraction of an abstract notion." In order for a flow of time to exist, in other words, there must be constant change. And the more we experience the alternate dimension of reality, the more proficient we become in our travels through those misty ranges, the more we are struck by the fact that such a flow of change does not make its presence felt there. Its absence becomes obvious in such minimal observations as not being able to locate a certain experience in sequence. Was it at the outset of a vision or possibly later on? While in trance, that does not seem to matter, but a correction is quickly made when the trancer tries to recollect the details in the ordinary state of consciousness.

This does not mean that the alternate reality does not change. But the change is not a linear one, not a continuing process, where one event is added to another one like beads on a necklace. Instead, once in a very great while, a shift occurs, in the way the earth occasionally lurches on its elliptical path. The religious philosophy of the Yąnomamö Indians makes this matter beautifully clear.[1] They hold that the cosmos is layered, and humans live on the third layer from the top. The topmost layer is simply there. It has no present function; whatever originated there sifted down to the other two layers a long time ago. The next one is the sky layer. Again ages ago, in a cataclysmic event, a piece of this sky layer broke off and formed the jungle where the Yąnomamö and many other people live today. Then another such event occurred, another piece broke off the sky layer; it crashed through the earth-surface layer and came to rest below it, forming the village of hungry spirits who go after souls because they have no territory to hunt in. The point is that there were really only two such lurches of the world. Essentially, the cosmos is forever suspended in the eternal present of the alternate reality.

An event such as the trial and death of Joan of Arc is a fragment of reality that penetrated into the other dimension not as a part of an "orderly" history, but by virtue of who she was and the spirit company she kept. Once there, it remained, ephemeral yet lasting forever, floating in that mystic space like a rainbow-colored cobweb. That was why Edeltraut could reexperience it in such untrammeled freshness. In order for these fragments to become visible, however, conditions must be just right.

The first of these conditions concerns the behavior of the crack between the earth and the sky on the horizon. According to a tradition known around the world since ancient times, that is the hole, a kind of slit, that leads from our ordinary reality into the alternate one. This gateway is not always open, so the time for attempting a passage must be chosen correctly, obviously when it happens to be ajar. For us, who are so ignorant in these matters, there is no choice; we enter by chance, or perhaps by invitation.

The second condition refers to the intruders. It seems that their bodies, to use a technical simile, must be tuned to the frequency of a particular event for it to become visible. This tuning is accomplished by the posture. Yet paradoxically, most of time the experience seems curiously at odds with what is usually experienced in the respective posture. Edeltraut's was not an experience typical for the posture of the Feathered Serpent. Such incongruity has occasionally been the red flag for me that something out of the ordinary was going on.

The third condition is the most illusive. We might think of it as the angle of vision. There are occasions when only a single person in a group accidentally finds that correct angle. And for that to happen, it does not really matter whether that person is experienced or not. Edeltraut was a complete novice. At other times, as we shall see, several participants may hit it just right, or even an entire group. When all these conditions are met, the perceiver usually turns into the actor, as Edeltraut did in our example. Finally, the event, which is always sketched out in the most gossamery of details, must be recognized. The stock of myths of humankind is infinite, and my knowledge, regrettably, is quite limited. I am sure that many precious tales were alluded to in our workshops that I did not recognize and that therefore escaped me.

The experiences I am going to recount in this section, then, are myths that a favored few among us participated in as present events. They are present in the sense that once they happened, they did not vanish, but became forever suspended in a dimension that has neither past nor future, the true treasure house of our species.[2]

The Emergence Story

Two Indian friends, Rosemary from Taos and Joseph from Picuris, were participants in the first workshop I ever did in Cuyamungue, in the summer of 1982. We had done the postures together that I had worked through for the German television program, and then the question came up whether there were also others that I had not tried yet. So I got out the few examples that I had collected at the time, and we decided on the posture of a man squatting on a carved red sandstone pipe, an exquisite piece of art created about A.D. 1300 and discovered during excavations in Hale County, Alabama (pl. 63). The man is naked except for a cap, perhaps made from strips of hide. He has his tongue between his lips. His left hand grabs his lower left leg at an angle, his right hand is on his right knee, but stretching upward on the side of the leg, and his buttocks rest on the ground, a posture extremely demanding physically.

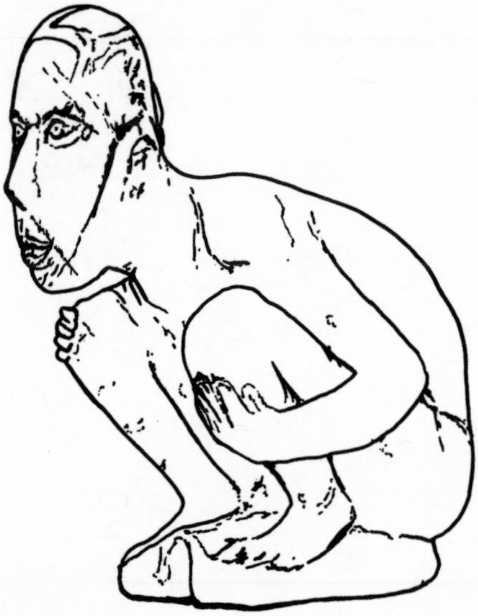

Plate 63

Both Joseph and Rosemary were shaken by what they had seen in the trance using that posture. It was dark, said Joseph, and the earth had burst open, as if an enormous volcanic eruption was about to take place, and the sky was lit up by exploding stars. Rosemary had heard people screaming, sighing, and moaning as if they were about to die. They both said that they would not try that posture again.

Listening to them, I thought that perhaps they were describing the emergence of humans from the third world to the fourth world, which, as I told before, is said to have taken place across the valley from Cuyamungue in the sacred Jemez Mountains. But the modern Pueblo tradition[3] is much gentler than what my two friends had seen. It tells about the third world being dark and crowded, and so the Corn Mothers decided to send out one of the men to examine the earth above if it was solid enough, and after some difficulties were overcome, humans did emerge and started their southward migration.

But there is also another, more harrowing tradition, part of the Navajo emergence story,[4] according to which humans escaped from the fourth to the fifth world. They were moaning and groaning and in fear for their lives because of the threatening floodwaters that were churning below them, which had arisen because of a foolish deed of Coyote. That may have been what Joseph and Rosemary had witnessed, but an event even more grandiose than either tradition describes, with the earth itself moaning and the stars exploding as humans came forth to start their earthly journey. In some brown kiva under the southern sky, we might imagine, men knowledgeable in the art of trancing would sometimes get together for a sacred ritual, light the pipe, and, seeing the crouched figure in the swirling smoke of the tobacco, experience over and over again that marvelous event, the way it truly happened when humans set foot on the dark new world that was to become their home.

Coyote Comes Calling

As told by the Navajo singers, the religious specialists who are the guardians of Navajo oral literature, Coyote is the child of the sky but was born from the embrace of the sky with the earth. It seems that one day, the people saw the sky swooping down:

> It seemed to want to embrace the earth. And they saw the earth likewise looming up as if to meet the sky.
> For a moment they came in contact. The sky touched the earth and the earth touched the sky. And just then, at exactly the spot where the sky and the earth had met, Ma'ii the Coyote sprang out of the ground. (Zolbrod 1984:56)

Thus in his parentage, Coyote bridges the earth and the sky, the ordinary and the alternate reality. But something else also entered into his makeup, for his birth happened at the same time the elders were involved in an important ritual. They were giving a penis to a boy who had come of age, and a vagina to a girl who had come of age, which they had not had before. Coyote went to where the people were, and meddler that he was and fascinated by sex obviously from the time he sprang from the ground, he decided to make the young people even more beautiful than having a penis and a vagina made them. And so he blew some of his own facial hair in such a way that it landed between their legs. However, First Woman, in charge of uncontrolled impulses, was worried that now the young people had become too attractive to each other, and so she ordered that they cover themselves.

Here we have Coyote's problems in a nutshell. As the child of the sky, he wants beauty, but as the child of the earth, he has an unbridled interest in procreation. And not being accountable to anyone, having no neighbor glancing over his shoulder, no mother to be ashamed of his shenanigans, he is able to give free rein to his wildest impulses. Yet while he can cause havoc and even disaster, he has in common with his northern cousin the Trickster (Chapter 11) that he also brings forth much that is new and useful. He is credited, for instance, with bringing fire to humankind. Other innovations he is responsible for are frequently blessings in disguise, such as death, which came about because Coyote disobeyed the shadow people and touched his wife after bringing her back from the Realm of the Dead, a Nez Perce Orpheus tale.[5] No wonder that, as Zolbrod says, "To this day, Navajos of all ages take great delight in heaping scorn upon Coyote for his misadventures, yet they maintain a sturdy reverence for him" (1984:355, fn. 22).

Coyotes are much in evidence at Cuyamungue, and enchanted, we listen to their song in our sleeping bags on moonlit nights. One time, we did the posture of the Singing Shaman on the ridge rather than inside the kiva, and to our delight, we heard their answering call from across the Cañada Ancha. But Coyote rarely appears in our trances. The reason may be that in the culture complex to which the trances take us, sexual behavior, although much freer than in the agriculturalist societies to which we are heirs, is still under tight social control, very much a concern of ordinary reality, and that may keep him in check. But he cannot be suppressed forever, and in the summer of 1986 in Cuyamungue there was one girl whom Coyote obviously could not resist, and with conditions being just right, he took advantage of the situation. So this is what happened to one of our participants in the posture of the Feathered Serpent:

> ANN B.: I saw a yellow path to the left, and I started following it. It kept turning and twisting, and finally went spiraling through the clouds. I looked down, and below me there was a lake, and I was startled. Suddenly, a coyote appeared beside me and started leading me along the path, and I was grateful for the company. I finally got on the coyote and started riding it, which went on for quite a while. I was feeling extremely hot and began shaking. We were in the desert; there was a medicine man who was rattling all around me. Then the coyote made love to me, and when it was over, I found myself in some cool mud, and the coyote was gone. But when I turned, there were now two coyotes dancing around me. A rope ladder appeared, and I climbed up toward the sun, getting hotter and hotter.

Ann's encounter with Coyote is admirably in character. He appears, knowing full well that she will be a willing partner. Slyly he offers to help her on the perilous path in the clouds, even letting her ride on his back. To take away what resistance she might still muster, he has a medicine man dance around her and with his rattle benumb her senses. Or was that a shape he himself assumed? It could well be. At any rate, he makes love to her and then disappears.

How right Coyote had been about Ann became clear in a letter I received from her during the following winter. After some personal news, she continued as follows:

> If you remember, my dying/rebirth trance was very special for me. I met a coyote who accompanied me through my journey, and with whom at one point in the sky, I made love. It was most beautiful, and I felt very lucky to have been chosen by the coyote spirit. I told the man I am in love with about this, and he started reading up on coyote. He took out from the library a bunch of coyote tales. They were about coyote man, this trickster, who is constantly on the move, in search of young female spirits. He convinces them to meet him in a remote place, and then he makes love to them. He is supposed to have love-making down to a fine

art and always causes the young female spirits great pleasure. Anyway, I thought that was funny and it makes sense to me. I'm very trusting and always think the best of people. I guess it's naiveté. The coyote knew how to appear to me to charm me. I trust guiding spirits. (Letter, January 3, 1987)

The Man of Cuautla

For years Ursula S., a Swiss painter, had been telling me about a figurine she had inherited from her grandmother. Her uncle had immigrated to Mexico and settled in Cuautla, not too far from Mexico City, and when his new house was being built, the workers came across a perfect little clay sculpture and brought it to him. During a visit to Mexico, Ursula's grandmother saw it in her son's house and liked it so much, her son gave it to her. Ursula was familiar with it from early childhood, and when her grandmother died, she inherited it. She finally brought a photograph of it to our workshop in Switzerland in the spring of 1987 (pl. 64).

The man is sitting flat on the ground, his legs apart and bent at the knees. His right hand is on his knee, the left arm is stretched a bit more than the right, and his left hand is placed somewhat to the side of his knee. He wears a feather crown, and his head is slightly tilted back. His tongue is between his lips.

What the Swiss participants told after we did the posture did not suggest any particular experiential type to me, healing, for instance, or divination. If anything, it seemed to be a spirit journey of sorts, but not a very productive one. Urs R. repeatedly saw three "pointed mountains." Kathrin told about a wall and hearing rocks falling down a stone stairway. Monica had to look down, very deep down, past legs of stone. There were shadows of lions, according to Romana, but they had no manes. She came to a cleft in the earth; it was like a cave, and a shaft of light illuminated two or three more caves. Vrenie turned into a spectator:

> I came to a rock wall. In it there was a circular staircase which I was supposed to climb up, but that was difficult in this posture. So finally I grew wings and was able to fly. The wind current carried me up, and as a bird I came to perch on the banister.

Krischta had been pulled backward into a cave, and in a hall lit from above had seen a woman in white and an altar with sheaves of grain, grapes, and fruit, and when she asked what that was for, she was told that these things should be distributed over the earth as gifts:

Plate 64

Then beings appeared, a tiger, a deer, a man who came from the forest, looking untidy and clothed in leaves and tendrils of plants—I could not see his face—and a large bird, whose wings were hanging down, but they were really arms, and it turned into a woman with the head of a bird, who had snakes curling around her arms.

Ursula, on whom I had called first, had the longest tale:

It was dark. To the left of me there were stones forming a wall next to a ditch. The wall was quite high straight in front of me and to the left. I saw an opening in the floor. But I didn't want to go down into that hole, and I asked, "What does this mean?" As if in answer a black shadow lifted itself out of the opening, slipped back down, then reappeared. The shadow repeated this action several times. I thought it was showing me what to do, so I slipped down after it, past lots of cut stones and down many steps, down and down, sometimes with the shadow before me. We arrived at a stone toad, which suddenly sprang to life. There were also eyes of stone, and they too became alive. Then there were more steps and more stones. The shadow that guided me now had a red spot in the middle of its chest, which glowed and rotated. I finally arrived in a large hall with a domed ceiling, and at that point, the rattle became quite audible. The stone frogs and also some stone snakes, all wanted to get out, but they had to use the stairs, and they went as fast as the rattle. The air became warm; I saw the sky and the light of the sun, and once more there was the wall and the shadows standing beside it.

The majority, including Ursula, had apparently been someplace underground, among walls, in a cave, in a number of caves perhaps. But it was all quite opaque, and poor Ursula, I think, was disappointed that I could not make more sense out of the experiences mediated by her small treasure.

In the summer of 1987 I had a minor accident in Cuyamungue, which forced me to cut down on physical activity, and so I did some reading instead. One of the books I spent time with was Dennis Tedlock's new translation of the Popol Vuh.[6] This "Book of Counsel" is a remarkable work, an epic collection of Maya myths, written by Quiché Maya priests shortly after the Conquest. And there sudddenly, to my utter delight, and I must confess with a bit of a shiver, I saw spread out before me the context for the experiences of my Swiss friends, connected with the Man of Cuautla.

In one of the Quiché Maya myths, we learn that the four heads of the Quiché patrilineages decided to acquire patron deities to whom they could bring offerings. To this end they went to a great eastern city called Tulan Zuyua, Seven Caves, Seven Canyons. It is a famous incident, and I had read about it in one of the earlier translations of the Popol Vuh. What I did not know was that this place could actually be located geographically. As Tedlock points out,

> [But] in giving Tulan Zuyua the further name Seven Caves, the Popol Vuh preserves the memory of a metropolis much older and far grander than any Toltec town. The ultimate Tulan was at the site now known as Teotihuacan, northeast of Mexico City. It was the greatest city in Mesoamerican history, dating from the same period as the classic Maya. Only recently has it been discovered that beneath the Pyramid of the Sun at Teotihuacan lies a natural cave, whose main shaft and side chambers add up to seven. (1985:48–49)

So that was where the man of Cuautla had taken his charges! The "three pointed mountains" that kept reappearing to Urs were pyramids, having walls faced with cut stone, reliefs of people with "stone legs," effigies of sacred toads and snakes, and the great power spirit, the jaguar, a "lion without a mane," hovering nearby. Entirely within the classical Maya scheme of things, Vrenie turned into a bird that sat on a banister watching. In Maya myth the Celestial Bird has the task of witnessing events for the gods. And Krischta saw offerings of grain and fruit, relating to an account in the Popol Vuh where the Quiché turn against human sacrifice and offer resin and produce instead.

However, the adventure got even more specific. Krischta had actually seen the Quiché lineage elders arriving at the Pyramid of the Sun to pick up their deities. They were not city people, such as the white-clad woman who was expecting them, but men from the forest, dressed in leaves and tendrils. And some of them wore animal masks, because they were hunters and gardeners, people who in their dances turned into animal beings. On a wall painting in Teotihuacan, a priestess bringing sacrifices is shown in a long garment, and some others, also bringing offerings and identified as "tribesmen," wear animal-mask headgear.[7]

Ursula, finally, in return for her love for the ancient figurine, was singled out for the most wonderful gift of all. The guide who took her into the depths of the caves was not an ordinary spirit. He had, as she clearly saw, a glowing red spot on his chest, which kept rotating. In the world where she was taken, that shadow could only be Tohil, the patron deity of several Maya lineages. In the classical Maya period, as we know from inscriptions at Palenque, he bore the name of Tahil, a Cholan word meaning "Obsidian Mirror," and he was always shown with a mirror on his forehead, from which a burning torch protruded. That Ursula saw him with a rotating red disk on his chest may well be the manifestation of a more ancient form, for as Tedlock (1985:365) explains, Tohil was the giver of fire, pivoting in his own sandal like a fire-drill.

A Maya Whistle

In tomb 23 on the Rio Azul in Guatemala, archeologists came across a figurine representing a young man (pl. 65). He is sitting cross-legged and has his arms folded over his chest. The posture is also seen in a warrior from a classical Maya site at Jaina, on the western coast of the peninsula of Yucatán. Two features, however, distinguish the Rio Azul figurine from the Jaina one. The man from the Rio Azul has his tongue between his lips, and the figurine is a whistle.

When we did the posture for the first time in Cuyamungue in the summer of 1986, one participant was advised to heal a split in her body, another one was to guard something, and Isi was told, rather severely, "If you don't have any questions now, come back when you do." Although there were also other kinds of visions, of a hammock, of finely decorated pots, "as if from Mimbres," of potsherds scattered about, we still decided mainly because of Isi's report that the posture was intended for divining. However, when we did the posture once more in Columbus in November 1986 with a rather large group, Belinda was informed emphatically that divination was not what the Spirits had in mind: "No—that won't happen here."

The question was, what was it we were going to be shown? Listening to the subsequent reports took me back on the wings

Plate 65

of magic to my own many fieldwork trips to Yucatán, to the warm nights of the rainy season, to the modest pyramids that are still standing choked in weeds outside the village at the end of a road as straight as the flight of an arrow. For a moment or two that basement room of the university building was filled with the intoxicating fragrance of the blossoms of a jasminelike bush the villagers call "Juan de noche." I had the feeling that we had been witness to an ancient funeral, with the soul like a will-o'-the-wisp flitting about among the corn plants and the lanky papaya stalks, looking for a home.

Accounting for my intuition afterward, though, became a frustrating exercise, somewhat like attempting to reconstruct a pot from a thousand sherds scattered over a rough terrain, while being ignorant of what the finished piece was supposed to look like. It was not until a year later that Linda Schele's book *The Blood of Kings* helped me find the basic design.

So here it is. The cracks still show, of course, and the doubters may look in the drawer and weigh the evidence for themselves.[8] Here and there, a piece needed to be created born of intuition and not of fact, but all in all, I have the feeling that the Spirits are satisfied.

A Ghost Says Good-Bye

This is it, this is the official story. It happened, they say, a long time ago, when the Precious Red Stone had barely completed the spiderweb of the order of the world. It was then that Hunahpu and Xbalanque, the Hero Twins, were playing ball. The noise disturbed the Lords of Death in the Underworld, Xibalba, the Land of Terror.

Then the Lords of Death ordered the Twins to appear before them, it is said, and they put them through many frightful trials. Those trials had killed their father and their uncle before them, but the Twins were young and strong and cunning, and they survived. And they decided that they would trick the Lords of Death in turn. So they pretended defeat, allowing themselves to be burned to death and their ashes strewn on the waters. It is said that on the fifth day they rose to new life and traveled the land as entertainers. They showed the people their mastery over death, how they could sacrifice a dog, and even a man, and yet they lived. The Lords of Death were curious. They summoned the entertainers to their court in Xibalba, and thinking they would live again, they let themselves be killed. This is how the Hero Twins gained over the Lords of Death—they did not resuscitate them. Since then, it is said, life is triumphant, and after the soul passes through Xibalba, it will dance to the North Star and join the ancestors and the gods.

Much time went by, and many souls took that road. And then it happened that the crack between the worlds was open, and the story of a young warrior who had gone that way came whispering on the wind:

—We were in among the trees on an errand for our prince, looking for captives that would increase his renown. It was hot, the afternoon rains had not come yet, and the perspiration was burning in my eyes. Suddenly, there was a rustling behind the bushes. I thought it was the army ants and turned to jump across their stream of a thousand vicious stings. But I did not get to vault. Somebody had grabbed my long hair and yanked back my head as the priests do during a sacrifice. I thought—no, not my heart! But it was not to be my heart. I felt the blade slice into my belly; it twisted and turned. My abdomen became transparent, it was on fire; my head opened, and flowers sprouted out. Then I was cool and wet, and the world turned dark.

When I opened my eyes again, I saw my companions, who were carrying my body away. It was night by then, warm and soft, and the fragrance was overpowering. I followed them for a while then slipped away, up a mountainside, in among the tall trees, whose every twist of bark has its own thorn. I laughed, for now I had no skin to bleed and burn. I was among reptiles, I was one of them, and as they crawled up my spine, a fierce pain shot through me. Then they were gone, and up and up I went. I was like a feather, and in my head there was a light, and I flickered among the bushes, a giant lightning bug. Suddenly something tugged at me from the left, and I shrank back. No, not yet, not yet to Xibalba. The terror must wait. I have a right to tarry, four days, the priests used to say, and that I will demand.

Up, up, higher up on the mountainside. A flute sings far away; the forest is moist and warm, and I want to stay. Somewhere in the distance, people are dancing to the drum. The moon has risen, and there is a whisper among the trees. They say it is the memory of the souls that succumbed to the trials and remained in Xibalba, buried forever in the stinking rot of the flesh and the blood. I will go on, I will make it through like the Hero Twins, Hunahpu and Xbalanque. They are in me, facing each other, then they are a chalice. They have the sun on their tongues. But I am not going, not yet.

Over there, to the right, is a man. He is tall, but old and toothless. He sits cross-legged, and as I watch, he pulls out an eye and motions for me to take it. I freeze in terror. A messenger from Xibalba—the jewelry of the Lords is eyes, torn from their sockets. His belly is distended; he is going to fart, and the stench will be about like stinking mist. I turn and flee.

Am I drooling? No, I will not drool, I will not be like the Lords of Xibalba. But perhaps I strayed over by mistake and did not see the passage? No, it couldn't be—there was no water. There must be water; one sinks below it to reach Xibalba. God of my Day, watch over me, let there be no water yet. I stumble and fall backward, and am held as if in my mother's womb. But the womb expands; it is the forest once more.

I see a fire through the trees and men dancing around it. The man over there, he is the one whose knife slipped into my belly. Without that knife in my bowels, we would be the ones dancing now. I could dance with them, but this is not my time. First through Xibalba, through the knives and the cold, and the murderous bats, and the fire. After that, I will dance, dance to the north, all the way to the North Star.

I slink around the dancers to the hut. A hammock is slung from crossbeam to crossbeam. For a moment I rest in it and let the breeze cool my chest. Or maybe I am the breeze now, I don't know. The men bring in a deer. They have cut out its heart. We are the people of the deer, it is said. Outside, the fire has gone out. Uy, uy, I am the breeze. I blow into the embers and the flames leap up. Then I melt back into the trees. I am tired and want to rest. But I need to stay alert. How long has it been since the knife?

I turn and am with my companions. The priest is working with clay; he is making my likeness. He is powerful, that priest. He sees me and there I am, in his clay. It is a cage, and he is rolling me around, crossing my legs, folding my arms, pulling out my tongue. I struggle, but I cannot escape. Then he shapes my back; it is hollow, a whistle, and I am in it, I, the breeze. I expand and expand. Soon I will shoot out, the Twins and I; we will create the sun, and the moon. My body will break into droplets; I will be a newborn star.

And then I saw the water. It was huge and dark, and stagnant, and it had not moved in eons.

The Story of Kats and His Bear Wife

During our exploration in 1985 of the Chiltan posture, the one about the forty-one girl knights whom the Uzbeki shamanesses call on to help them in curing (see Chapter 9), there were two reports that did not seem to fit the picture. One of them was Belinda's:

> Even during the breathing exercise I began seeing bark figures dancing. When the rattle started, I realized that I was flying very high; the ground was very far away. Then I approached a scene that was brown and green. There was a little pool of water that was like a mirror, and in it I did not see my own reflection, but a stick figure in the shape of a Y. There was a tree, and through it flew a little bird. In place of the pool, there was now a nest with three eggs. The little bird invited me to sit on the nest and intimated that to do that was very important. I stayed on the eggs for a long time, feeling intensified. Then I saw a totem pole, and was embraced by it, by the spirit in the wood. On the other side, there was snow, and pine trees. A hand moving a feather was making marks in the snow. An enormous she-bear appeared; she stood upright and we danced together. I grinned because she made me feel so light. She sat down and embraced me from behind, giving herself to me and penetrating me, and I felt greatly moved. My Lioness came and brought some twigs for the fire and then left. There were the horns of a mountain goat; everything felt high and cold.

The other anomalous one came from Elizabeth R., a close friend of Belinda's:

> When the rattle started, I saw all of us with our masks on, and we danced. We had on long flowing robes, and our hair was blowing in the wind. Belinda became a statue, and a bird built a nest in her hand. The colors became very vivid; twigs and leaves grew out of her all over, the life force was in her, she was a magnificent tree. She started dancing on her roots, and then we danced together. As I put my arms around her, I felt her wetness; I knew she was crying, but she was happy. I faced the tree, the sun came up, and I felt so powerful.

I filed them, as I always do, but I had no idea what to make of them. Then for Christmas 1986 I received a book about totem poles in Alaska.[9] Looking for postures on those poles, to my surprise there was a Tlingit pole housed at Saxman Totem Park near Ketchikan, on which one of the carved figures, embraced from the back by a huge bear, stood in the Chiltan posture (pl. 66).

When these poles were assembled and restored, the Forest Service asked the Indian craftsmen about legends they might know about the various poles. And for the pole in question, called the Loon Tree because of the bird perched on top, one of the artists recalled the legend about the man and the bear.

It seems that a young man called Kats, who lived a very long time ago, when humans and animals were still as one, was caught by a grizzly bear. He was supposed to be eaten, but he was saved by the she-bear, who fell in love with him and became his wife. He later returned to his village together with his bear wife and his cub children. His bear wife warned him never to look at his former human wife, but quite by accident, it happened anyway. Upset, his bear wife gave him a shove, meant to be gentle, but the cubs misunderstood and tore him apart.

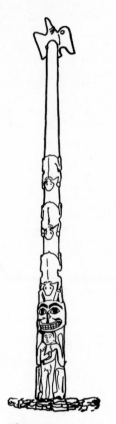

Generations later, one of Kats's descendants became a powerful shaman. The boy's initiation started when he killed a mountain goat, and after skinning it, he began dancing while wearing its skin over his shoulders, and then he fainted. Over and over again he danced, fell into a dead faint, then danced again, until the multiple spirit powers which his ancestor had acquired from his wife during his sojourn with the bears had passed into him. After becoming a shaman, the young man decided to take revenge on the bears for killing his ancestor. While his grandmother beat the drum, he danced, and in that way he lured the grizzly bears into the large communal house.

Soon the people heard a noise far back in the woods coming closer and closer. They recognized the grunts and growls of grizzly bears, and they all ran out and hid as the bears crowded into the house. Soon there were so

Plate 66

many that the old woman was not able to beat the drum. She nodded her head toward it, and the drum continued to beat while the shaman danced. Soon the spirit powers began to leave the boy, and the grizzly bears began to drop over dead. When all his powers had left him, every bear was dead.

It is said that the grizzly bears were the descendants of the cubs born to Kats and his bear wife and that they were killed by the shaman's powers.[10]

Now finally Belinda's experience took on meaning. Perhaps it was the shaman grandson of Kats who was the stage manager, arranging the play so his forebear might once more encounter his beloved bear wife. After all, he signed his creation: Belinda saw the horns of the mountain goat of his initiation. With a few delicate strokes of the hand, marking the snow with a feather, the ancient Indian legend awakens to new life. Like the first roll of the drum calling to a dance, the sign of fate appears reflected in the clear pool, the forked emblem of the Tree of the World. A bird, messenger of the Spirits, invites the stranger to sit brooding on a nest of eggs. Behold, the saga will be of love and procreation. The totem pole appears; its spirit embraces the guest, and she is changed and she is Kats, lending for a fleeting moment her human strength to the sorrowing spirit man. Now the huge she-bear may step on the stage; she embraces her husband, and they laugh as in the old days, when she found him so light, and they melt into each other in loving embrace. Then the play is over, the shadows dissolve, but the cheeks of the human woman are still wet with tears when in her vision, Elizabeth puts her arms around her. In a jubilant finale, she steps across the threshold of magic once more. She turns into a totem pole, and twigs and branches sprout from her in celebration of the power of love.

The Spirits and the Wounded Tree of Life

MYSTERY IN THE MUSEUM
In addition to books on native art, museums often yield tantalizing representations of postures. This presupposes, of course, that what you think you see
on that rack or shelf is actually there. In this business, you cannot always be
sure.

The story I should like to tell next started in a museum. The School of
American Research in Santa Fe had asked me for a luncheon lecture. Afterward
one of the associates of the institution took some of the guests and me on a
guided tour of its private museum, which possesses an outstanding collection
of Amerindian art. The first spacious hall contained a great number of the
most magnificent ollas, large clay vessels no longer made today. This hall had
a door that opened to the right. The other members of the party had already
walked through, when my attention was caught by still another shelf to the
left of the exit. Instead of ollas, this one contained an exhibit of figured pieces,
the likes of which I had never seen on the Indian markets. Always on the
lookout for new postures, I immediately noticed a male statuette in an unfamiliar stance. It was only about five inches high, made of yellowish clay with
red-brick markings, and it stood on a small pedestal which carried the inscription "Calling the Spirits." I carefully noted the posture, how the hands
were positioned on the groin with fingers spread, and how the head was tilted
back slightly and the mouth was open. I wanted to sketch it, but the young
woman who acted as our guide came to close the door, so I quickly jotted
down a brief description and did not even check if the figurine had a number
or some other identifying code.

As soon as I got home, I showed the posture to the group working with
me at Cuyamungue at the time. We made a comical mistake at the first try
because on the basis of the inscription and because the figure had its mouth
open, I thought that one actually had to "call" the Spirits. We assembled on
the ridge, and I had someone else do the rattling. Meanwhile I took up position
outside the circle and started yelling, "Heya, heya. . . ." If there were any
Spirits present watching us that day, they must have had a hilarious time. For
the only thing that happened was that I went into trance and started singing
in glossolalia. Everyone thought it was lovely, so they listened to that instead
of doing what they were supposed to do, namely, go into trance. After that

fiasco, I remembered that Siberian shamans opened their mouth and "yawned," as the ethnographers describe it, when they called their spirit helpers. As soon as we tried the posture without giving off any sound and just keeping our mouths open, things began to make sense. Being helped by the fact that we knew from the inscription what to expect, we soon saw the Spirits approach in manifold shapes, as rolling fog or colored veils, as geometric shapes or eyes, or wearing a mind-boggling variety of masks, everything from Mickey Mouse to all the birds and beasts of the forest and the plains. We also either noted or became some sort of upright form, usually a tree.

The following summer it occurred to me that it would be useful to own a slide of that small statue. So I called the School of American Research and described to the staff member exactly where it was exhibited and what it looked like. She went to search for it but could not find it. So we drove down to Santa Fe. I showed the lady the spot where I had seen it, but the statuette was gone. In its place there was another one, in a similar but not exactly the same posture, and much larger, so it was exhibited lying on its back. It was not yellowish with red markings but grey, and its design was black. Nowhere was there a single figurine standing on a pedestal with an inscription on it. Since I kept insisting that indeed that was what I had seen, I was shown all the slides of the collection, but my small friend had vanished into thin air. He was simply not there. And nowhere in the records was there any hint of the information about calling the Spirits.

It is possible, of course, that the Spirits were making sport of me. They have a very earthy sense of humor. I have vivid memories of being made their plaything and ending up in particularly undignified situations, as the time when they knocked out my sense of place and had me wander around lost in a village that I had known for twenty years. But in this case, that may not have been their intention. I like to think that they really wanted to give me a present.

There are only faint traces of the posture worldwide. It seems to have been known in Europe from the Neolithic on, for instance in the Ukraine, and in more recent times in sub-Saharan Africa, in Melanesia, and especially in New Guinea. Most representations I have seen are from our hemisphere, however, starting from the Eskimos and going south all the way to Central America. Plate 48 is a fine Olmec example. But to me, the most impressive artwork showing the posture is a Salish *tamanus* board from the late 1800s (pl. 67). Little is known about such boards; they were usually deposited at the shaman's grave and left there to disintegrate. The intensity of the face has no peer. That shaman must have seen some pretty mighty Spirits.

As we began working with the posture, we discovered that the Spirits could be asked to come for a number of different purposes. We used it, for example, to invite them to possess the masks during the masked dance ritual, as I told in Chapter 11. Or, as I also mentioned, we can summon them to help with a cure. Not always do they appear invested with power, or in the best of health.

They may, in fact, occasionally need our help, as will become clear from the following little incident, which illustrates what an unholy mess we humans have made of things, in this reality and also in the other one.

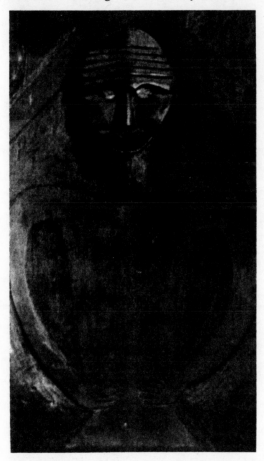

Plate 67

A housing development in Austria where I occasionally go visiting is built into an old factory, which used to obtain its power from a turbine, driven by a narrow and very fast river. In the course of modern "development," this river became severely polluted. In a letter, Johanna, one of the members of the settlement, told the following story about it:

> On the 25th of December we held a rattling session and did the Calling of the Spirits. We could not find a tape, so we asked one of the men to rattle for us, and it was very intense but also lovely. We did it by the side of our small river, and we also lit a fire. During the trance Walter saw a bedraggled, down-on-his-luck, and clearly suffering river spirit who was barely alive anymore. If you remember the sad straits our river is in, the condition of the river spirit should not surprise you. So after the trance, each one of us cast an offering into the water. Then we drank a bottle of champagne to the river, and the river got some of it, too.

ENTER THE TREE OF LIFE

For quite a while, my attention was taken up by the Spirits in this posture, and I paid little attention to the tree around which they assembled. But one summer, as we continued exploring its experiences, Joanne Mc. experienced something extraordinary:

> I saw a tree; it rose high into the sky. Its roots went very deep. I became an ant and went about exploring the roots that penetrated into a cave. There were tunnels,

which were dark, confining, endless. The roots went even further down, and finally, there was an opening into an airy world of light and spaciousness, with whitish, light fog. I ceased being an ant and drifted in the fog. There was a fire glowing, so I turned back into an ant and saw that it was a dragon that was spewing the fire and making amusing noises. The dragon's eyes were green. I began exploring its tongues and crawled around on its underbelly. It was enormous, miles and miles of it, and the dragon was connected to the world above.

Even as Joanne talked, I realized what I had been missing, and I wrote in large letters across the page, *THE TREE OF THE WORLD.* Joanne had seen the *axis mundi,* the axis of the world, Yggdrasil, the mighty ash. She had been down to its roots in the lower world, so huge it made her turn into an ant. She had seen the mighty dragon Nidhogg and heard it gnawing at its roots down there in Niflheim. Legends tell of the Tree of the World everywhere tales are told. Its branches harbor the sun and moon and touch the home of the Spirits of the Sky. As we hear in Hungarian myth:

> There is in the world a marvelously tall tree, which has nine spreading branches, each one vying in size with an entire forest. When these branches begin to twist and rustle, the storms start arising. It is such a marvelously tall tree that not only the moon is hidden in its branches, but also the sun. But only that person can find this tree, only he can discover where it is, who is born with teeth, and who for nine years has taken only milk for nourishment. That kind of a person is a *táltos* [Hungarian shaman]. This marvelously tall tree grows in a special place so that only such a man of knowledge can get to it. Other people merely hear of it but can never see it. (Diószegi 1958:270–271)

The Tree of the World, the Tree of Life, grows at the navel or at the vulva of the Earth Mother, at the stillest place on earth, according to the Siberian Yakut, where the moon does not wane and the sun never sets, where the summer is everlasting and the cuckoo calls incessantly. It is the world pole, the Huichol Indians say, which penetrates the layers of the cosmos, connecting the earth with the underworld and the heavens. Cascades of honey, the Teutons told, flowed down Yggdrasil. We are reminded of the pole that the sacred clowns of Picuris Pueblo climb during their yearly feast, to garner the presents attached at its tip. Shamans make their drums of its wood, and the witches' brooms are its branches. On this Tree of Life, the shamans ascended in their magical flight, and the victims of Maya rituals of sacrifice fell down along its trunk to the underworld.

The mighty tree has many stand-ins. It used to be a fig tree for the Greeks or an oak, and a birch in Siberia. Altaic shamans placed a stripped birch tree in their yurt; its top reached through the smoke hole, and its stem bore nine notches on which the shamans climbed to the world beyond. Yggdrasil was an ash, but many traditions contend that the sacred tree is really a yew.

The yew is a curious tree. It looks like a conifer with glistening dark-green needles, but it has a paperlike bark and it bears red berries. All parts of the tree except the outer part of the berries contain taxine, a poisonous alkaloid, which evaporates in sunlight. A friend and I once suffered its strange effect when we visited a grove of yews near Meggen, a small town in Switzerland. Inhaling it made us feel faint. Our throats became dry, and we were nauseated, and since it is hallucinogenic in minute doses, we became giddy and started chattering and giggling as if we were tipsy. The following tale is about the yew.

A Dutchman's Cure for the Tree of the World

At a workshop near Nieuwaal, a town in the Netherlands, we had done the Calling of the Spirits. "I saw a tree with a hole in it," Hennie, the first one to give her report, started out, "and all sorts of things came out of that hole, like presents." Annmarei had heard a breathing, like the rustling of the leaves in a forest. And Tineke noted that she had been a tree: "It had very big branches, and the branches grew into rainbows." Then it was Ton's turn:

> For a while, it seemed I was simply waiting to see what was going to happen. Then I saw something very tall, maybe a mountain, and out of it oozed a brook of old, coagulated blood. There were many loud noises; then I heard a bird singing a little song. My throat became very dry, and I felt sick to my stomach.

During my subsequent remarks about their stories, I mentioned that in this posture people usually turned into something tall, such as a tree, and Ton volunteered the comment that although he had not gone through that trans- formation, his experience still had something to do with a tree. It seems that there was a tree in his yard at home, a yew. It had poisonous needles, and so he and his father were going to cut it down. But its wood was very tough. They managed only to cut off some branches, and the resin continued to ooze from the cuts. He thought that the tall dark mountain he had seen might have been the tree, and the coagulating blood the oozing resin.

No one else had seen an injured tree, but we had all heard the "loud noises" Ton mentioned. The sound had been massive, like many feet jumping up and down on the wooden floor at the vacant end of the rectangular med- itation room. After the session ended, we went to investigate. Some of the men thought that machinery operating in the basement might have been the source, but there was no basement. We jumped up and down, but the boards were heavy and nailed down solidly and so gave off no sound at all.

The next posture we did was that of the Aztec Corn Goddess, which mediates metamorphosis. For Ton, however, an entirely different experience took center stage:

> A dancer appeared and started using Felicitas's rattle. She came over to me and began pushing me, saying, "Go on, go!" I did not want to leave my place. I started fighting with her, but she was a very exotic girl; she put her arms around me and started kissing me, and dragged me over to where Felicitas was standing. There

she turned into a red female Buddha, and many presences rose from her head. Then she changed into an old man in very poor clothes—I didn't think much of that; and then he became an eagle, and he said to me reassuringly, "Don't worry, everything is all right." He grabbed me and carried me to my house, into the garden with the bleeding tree. There was a pile of bandages, and I started bandaging the tree; there were so many bandages, and I put them round and round the tree. After that, everything was very peaceful in my garden. I saw my wife; there was such peace, and I also saw my dog. He had been sick, but he was fine now. I touched him and he licked me. Then the dog was a deer. I sat on its back, and it took me to the seashore and down to the ocean floor littered with discarded oil cans. Then I came up to the surface and I walked on the water. A big whale appeared, but I knew that I had the power to stop it. Finally I came back here and saw the female Buddha again. She had many arms and was glowing in yellow light.

What had happened? In ordinary reality, Ton had tried to cut down a yew. But when Ton put an ax to the tree in his yard, he also injured the Tree of the World in the alternate dimension, and its agony reverberated through the spirit realm. Injuring the Tree of the World can have disastrous consequences. An Iroquois story tells how the celestial Tree of Life was once carelessly uprooted in the sky world, and the daughter of the chief tumbled down through the hole. Luckily, quick-thinking Mud Turtle dove down to the bottom of the sea and brought up some mud for her to stand on, thereby not only saving the girl but also creating the earth and with it a place for a new Tree of Life to be planted.

Of course, yews are being cut down in many places, continually causing damage to the Tree of Life as well. But at least on this particular occasion, the Spirits saw a chance to do something about it. Here was a group of people in a condition to listen to spirit suggestions, and they were not about to let the opportunity slip by. That tremendous noise they caused in the Dutch meditation hall was only a part of their strategy. Another was prompting the participants to describe the nature of the tree, with one woman seeing a hole in it and presents emerging, and another one hearing the rustling of its leaves and watching how the branches turned into rainbows, all properties of the Tree of the World.

But the principal effort of the Spirits was directed at Ton. After all, he was the one who had wielded the ax. As soon as he became accessible to them, they revealed the frightful emergency he had caused by making the Tree of Life bleed. The problem was that Ton, being a novice, had not been fast on the uptake, and the rattle was about to stop. There was just enough time to give him a quick nudge. His mouth became dry and he felt sick to his stomach, the selfsame thing that had happened to him as he began cutting into the yew tree in his yard.

Worried that time was running out for helping the Tree of the World, the Spirits then decided to take extreme measures. They took advantage of the very next trance, the metamorphosis of the Aztec Corn Goddess, and, not having much faith in Ton, decided to do the changing themselves. One of the Spirits turned itself into a voluptuous girl, knowing of course that Ton, a ruddy, lusty Dutchman in his early forties, would not be able to resist her. And she dragged him to me, the ritual center, for extra power. Since lecturing Ton would not have been effective, and besides is not part of Spirit nature anyway, the Spirit then changed again and assumed the aspect of a "female Buddha," something that Ton, according to the Spirits' alternate-reality intelligence reports, was said to be familiar with. Spirits always wear the mask most acceptable to their human, this being a very effective communications device. The "female Buddha" was Kwannon, the deity of mercy and compassion, identified for Ton by the "presences" emerging from her head, the eleven faces of compassion. And compassion is what was expected of him.

But they reasoned that Ton, so he could grasp the seriousness of the situation, should also be made aware of the fact that the event in which he was called upon to play a role had much more ancient roots, going back long before the birth of Buddha to a time when yews were still venerated as the representation of the Tree of the World. So the Spirit in charge now showed itself as an old man, in tattered, timeworn clothing. It seemed a very clever thing to do, but apparently using sign language did not work out, and only confused Ton. So shrugging their shoulders, the Spirits decided on the direct approach. All right, Ton, forget the old man. No more historical allusions. We made a mistake; he is really an eagle, and look what power *he* has. The eagle took Ton to the bleeding Tree of Life. Now it was Ton's turn, for this is what the Spirits had needed him for all along, and the bandages had been readied and were waiting.

To their great relief, Ton's good heart took over. Round and round he twisted the bandages about the wounded tree, until all the bleeding stopped. Then there was peace in the garden, but also power. His touch healed his sick dog; he got to the ocean and walked over the waters and commanded the whales. And in his own terms then, he was praised for having performed an act of kindness. For as the rattle stopped, he was shown the Kwannon once more, the many-armed Goddess of Mercy, bathed in golden light.

In the Land of Centaurs and Mermaids

In scanning a book recently about archeological finds in Europe,[10] I noticed the picture of a figurine dug up in Thessaly (present-day Greece), about eight thousand years old (pl. 68). It represents a nude, rather full-breasted woman, sitting with both her legs turned toward the right side, her hands resting on her knees. Examining the figure shown a bit more closely, I realized that what at first glance seemed merely an oddly shaped face was really a mask, possibly that of a bird. That was exciting, for wearing a mask among hunter-gardeners or horticultural- ists, as we know from their modern coun- terparts, is always a sign of a religious oc- casion, involving a trance experience as a matter of course. But what was even more intriguing was that in this case, the mask was combined with a totally unfamiliar pos- ture. Ordinarily, the postures that come to

Plate 68

light from such early horizons in Europe are those that are encountered in many other areas of the world as well, of birthing, of the Bear Spirit, of metamorphosis, and so forth. But here was one that was completely unknown in the later record. We had planned a workshop anyway for experienced participants only, to be held in a camp in rural Ohio, so this was an opportunity to try and see what the lady from Neolithic Thessaly had to teach us.

As I rattled in the gathering dusk of the autumn afternoon, I was trying to guess what my friends might be experiencing as they sat unmoving in a circle in that awkward position, their faces drawn inward in the familiar trance expression that artists of bygone days loved to sculpt and carve. Would it be something neutral, divorced from time and space, being healed or resurrected, having a divinatory revelation, going on a spirit journey? I could not know not only that this was going to be another one of those times when the crack between the worlds would be ajar, but also that as a special boon, the Spirit of the posture we had assumed would act as our guide to her ancient world:

MAXINE: In the beginning, I couldn't close my eyes and watched the rattle until I could feel its beat in my mind. It felt as though the beating was the coursing of the blood through my brain. Before I closed my eyes, I looked to the right and I saw an old woman, and I thought it was Felicitas sitting on the floor, and then I realized that that couldn't be, she was standing and rattling. And I closed my eyes.

I could sense the presence of the old shamaness filling the room, shaping our experiences as she began to spread her lost world out before our eyes with apparent urgency. "Listen to me," she seemed to be saying, "listen to me, you women of another generation, and I will tell you our tale. It is a mighty tale, the tale about our world and how it was. Listen first to the tale about the beginning of things. I learned it when I was a child and had not been to the pool yet, to the pool where you die and are reborn."

ELIZABETH R.: As soon as the rattle started, I saw lots of light, lots of exploding light, and I was looking at volcanic eruptions. And then all of these scenes played out before me rather rapidly, big chunks of earth falling into the ocean, cliffs, land falling, trees falling, lots of falling earth and clouds.

And the old voice continued, "From the passionate mountains, this was the tale of our mothers, rose Phoenix, the giant bird, soul of the nubile Earth, to search for her mate, the Sun":

ELIZABETH R.: And as I was starting to be aware of the clouds, I noticed that I was flying, that I was a bird, a big, very large bird, and I flew around for a while, watching all kinds of big earth changes, shifts, things sinking, and other things coming up out of the ocean. It wasn't alarming at all. There was really no emotional attachment, I was just watching it. And I flew higher and higher; I seemed to be drawn to this light that eventually became the sun. As I approached the sun, I could feel the feathers burning and falling away, and then the skin melting and falling away, then the bone getting dryer and dryer, until as I passed through the sun, my bones became dust. As that dust passed on through the sun to the other side, I spent a long time in darkness, as dust, and there was nothing else around; it was very peaceful. I thought this was wonderful.

I heard the Ancient One again. "Then the breath of life rose from the ashes, that was what our mothers told, life and its young laughter, and took on flesh in the nest prepared for it in the Mother's womb":

ELIZABETH R.: But at that point my right hip was hurting very badly, and I decided that what I needed to do was to lift my right knee up just a little bit. So I shifted the posture ever so slightly to raise my hip, and the pain went away completely out of my hip. What I experienced then was passing back through the sun and coming back to earth and just seeing a nest being formed by real tiny, fluffy, downy white feathers, and this wonderful soft nest being formed was beginning to twirl around. And eventually I changed into a big white bird that had a woman's legs, and I thought, now this was a really bizarre thing to turn into; it wasn't anything that I had seen on this planet. It had very lovely legs, of course [she laughs], and big white plumes. And I was getting ready to say, well, now what am I up to here? And I became aware that I was really on a different planet, I was not on earth, and I started walking around. And I found this big wall, shiny; I didn't identify it as a gemstone, it was more like marble. It was dark blue, and I slid down it, like on a big sliding board, sliding around on it, having a wonderful time, and the sensation was very good. And then I landed in what I thought was grass. It wasn't; it was these really lush pomegranate seeds, only they were brilliant green. As I walked through them, they would kind of pop under my feet. It was a wonderful sensation.

"Then it was time," the old shamaness continued, "to endow the body of this magical being with the capacity to bear the young, and that was, our mothers told, how women came to have a womb":

ELIZABETH R.: And then I flew back to the sun, and this time I did fly back to the earth, after I flew through the sun, and I landed in a nest, and my spirit guide came. I was in a huge nest, and my spirit guide and I lounged around in the nest, peeking over the edge, feeling very satisfied with ourselves. This was a real special warm feeling that we had. He reached in and made some adjustment in my second chakra area, and said that he had some more things to teach me, and we were feeling all cozy in the nest and having a wonderful time.

Leaving the happy couple behind, our old Spirit Friend then turned to a new topic: "Of the spirit beings, our mothers told, which roamed the earth, some turned into plants":

SUSAN: At the outset of the rattling a voice said, "Lose your fears, Susan, lose your fears." And then I saw new green curlicued vinelets growing and starting. Later those vinelets grew and curlicued all around my body, and I budded.

"Of all these things our mothers spoke," the old voice continued, "and we listened, in the gardens as we weeded and while we spun and wove. And when we were old enough, they also taught us to see, these events of the beginning of all things and much more. For that to happen, though, and also many other miraculous things, we had to die in the pool and change, to come to life again":

BELINDA: Immediately after the beginning, I briefly felt a tingling in my legs. I was swimming with a mask on, and I tried to dismiss that image until I remembered that the woman in the posture was wearing a mask. I was swimming out to a place in the sea, where there were some rocks and a cave. When I got out of the water, there had been a fire built in front of a very black cave entrance. I realized that I felt young, and I knew that while this was a ritual, I was doing it for the first time. I went into the cave. It was completely dark; I knew that I was there to find out about a mystery. The rattle became very loud, and it became skulls on sticks, and there was something in the skulls that made them rattle, and they were being rattled all around me. I knew it was something about birth and death. The older women—I just felt them, but I knew they were older women—took me and dumped me into a pool. It was oddly like a baptism, except that they kept me down in there. There was a funny little reed in my nose, somehow to help me breathe, but I almost drowned. That was part of the ritual, of almost drowning, like to go into the other realm.

Later there was a sinking sensation of going deeper and deeper into the sea. My mind was thinking about the times when the whales first were there. It wasn't like going to when the earth was first being formed, but in young days. Then it was as though the planet was still Gaea, a consciousness, and she was remembering when she was in her youth, and the land was very fresh; it was formed, but still very fresh. It was almost as if there was a connection with a consciousness. As if the earth was remembering those earlier times of herself, and there was a deep sense of us being connected with her as her daughters.

Then there was a shift, and there were images, dazzling images of sitting on a rock by the sea that was really glistening. And I saw Jan sitting in water up to her bare shoulders. I could see through the water, and beneath the water, she was human above, but below she looked like a sea mammal, a manatee maybe. I looked up and down, and I saw Elizabeth sitting beside her, and she was the same way. And then I saw my shoulders, and all of us, above we were women and below we were manatee. It seemed like we shifted and we became even more like mermaids. It was the same quality, but the lower part of the body was different from a mermaid as we usually think of her. I feel a little mischievous about this, like see? The old Greek stories are really mere remnants of what I just experienced—like now I know what the mermaids really are.

And then the tired old voice continued: "All this happened a long, long time ago, and I can see that I must be patient with you women of so late a generation. Listen how your friend wanted to gain it all in a single gulp, the knowledge of precious things that it took us years to acquire when we were young":

BELINDA: And I knew that I was supposed to find out something in that cave, and I kept asking. Finally it was like these voices said, "But you haven't been prepared!" And they were saying, "You can't just come in on a Friday night and expect to understand the mystery of an entire culture, of an entire process, and the history of it!" And I sit here on a Friday night and just expect that it will happen like that. And I asked, though, "Do you want the ritual known? Do you want it to be practiced again?" Kind of like it has to be retrieved in order to be practiced. But the rattle became very loud, very intense, and then it stopped.

Our old guide was getting impatient. "I must hurry on; there is so much to tell and so little time given to me. You should know that we were a seafaring people; the sea was the skirt of the Mother, and if we wanted to be close to her, that was where we went and sank into the waves. She reveals herself in the sea":

NANCY: I felt a tugging at my right leg. I thought it was the cat. There was only blackness, but there was no sense of fear about it. I had no body form, yet I was not out of my body. There was a sense of changing form. I felt the grace of the swan, the beauty of it; it was being pulled, it was without a spine, without a body, but not being out of my body. I was being pulled to the left, then there was a sharp pain in my eyes. This was repeated three times. From there I went to a dark place of nothingness, with no feeling of joy or sadness. The sound of the rattle changed from soft to hard, and when that happened, the blackness changed from soft to hard too. It got deeper, more intense, then there was a sense of sadness, being in touch with this lack of existence, this form. I was in a place of healing, a sense of healing in nothingness. Going to deeper levels, deeper down, deeper, there was eye pain to the point of burning, and then being pushed back.

The shamaness sighed, "My daughters loved the sea, and longingly, I too remember sinking into the waves":

> NORMA: I saw the sea and the sky, both in different blues. The land is way off. I traveled through dark spaces. Then I bathed in seawater; it streamed through my body in a continuous cycle. It was a cleansing, and I felt the bubbles of the water. My left body side relaxed, but the right side was tense. As the left side began to pull away, the right side begged it not to leave, but I kept saying, "Don't worry, I'll be back." The left side of my body was female, the right side male. I became a white female horse, and I shook off my male side. It really wasn't a mean thing to do; I said that later it could come back. There was a white bird. I melted into the earth, oozing, soaking in.

The Old One nodded. "In the sea, there was much to see for those of us who had learned the ways. The Mother's skirt had seams of emerald, and in it hidden memories of still older worlds, of cities that once bloomed and then sank beneath her folds":

> LIBET: I was traveling through this incredibly lush emerald green. It wasn't like a forest, it was just green with plants; not heavy like a forest, but it was very beautiful. I wasn't walking, but I was just moving. It wasn't conscious walking, it was more like gliding. There wasn't a path—when I looked down I didn't see a path—but there was a path in my body; there was not a path before me. And this wonderful black panther came beside me as a guide to me. Part of the time I rode her, part of the time she was ahead of me, and there was a connection like a leash, but not that formal, like a piece of leather that bound us, and sometimes I would be ahead of her.
>
> We moved through this green, lush space for a long time. Then on my left as I looked up, the entire space to my left was a wall, a precious stone, a clear, precious gem, but it was huge; it was green, sometimes it was red, and bright, shiny, incredibly different colors. And as we moved past that, we continued through this green space; the cat became a bird, and we flew off into the sky, and she was one of those very ancient birds, and we flew over every terrain that could be possible—it was green, it was brown, it was desert, it was mountains, it was glacial, as we rose very high.
>
> We then went down into the water, just kept on moving through water; I was very much aware of the difference between the air and the water, the way it

surrounds your body as you move through it. And we came to this city under the water, and I was just enjoying being there; it was an incredibly developed city. And at one point there was this judge; it was a judge person that was there, that was his role. Then my bird took me right out of the water, up into the sky. And at that point I moved away from the bird and into darkness, but I was still flying, and I didn't have anything on; it was just darkness, and moving through this space of darkness for a long time, there were seemingly no guides, no other things around, but just moving in this darkness, for a long, long, long time.

And then there was a light. I moved toward it, and I perceived that it was a sun, but it wasn't a hot sun, it was a cool light. I moved through. I aimed right through it and into darkness again, and the rattle became everything, the darkness and the rattle was everything, and then the rattle ended.

Again there was the voice. "When our mothers left for the beyond and it was our time to serve, we were called on for advice about many things. We were the women of knowledge; we knew how to heal and when to place the seeds in the ground. We turned and turned and sent our spirits out and spoke to the Spirits of the Above":

JAN: I became aware that there was another part of me right on this spot in another time and space that was just walking around. I wasn't doing very much, and I kept wanting to know what I was doing; it was like that part of me was in a circular room and kept pacing and pacing. Not nervous, just kind of walking, and I perceived that perhaps I was getting ready to do something. And I didn't know what it was. It seemed very normal, and she, that other part of me, seemed very comfortable in what she was doing. I felt like being in my other body that was sitting there in trance, and that was different than this one. I could feel both of them at once, and that my other body was in trance also. I've never had that specific feeling that my trance body was also in a trance state over there.

And then I saw everybody in this room, doing the same thing in their own little room, their own little spaces. And I had on some sort of long robe; that was all I could see, it wasn't very distinct. I was a little uncomfortable in this body, so I shifted a little bit to the left, and as soon as I did that, I felt a wind that came from my left side. It was quite strong, and so I leaned into it, and I found myself shooting through darkness, very fast, but not seeming to go anywhere; there wasn't much there.

And I shifted a little again, and I think I leaned back a bit, and as soon as I shifted, I shot up and exploded. As soon as that happened, I found myself sitting in front of a cave that was totally dark behind me, and I was nude. It wasn't exactly like I was sitting in this posture, I couldn't say that, but I was sitting there and I was very aware that I was performing some rite or ritual, that I had come out of the cave and I was sitting there. The moon was out; everything else was very black. And the wind was just blowing past me incredibly, and the cave was black in my back. I was doing something about contacting, and the words that were there were "Sky people." And this part of my consciousness said something like, "Oh, that's just because she's got a bird mask on." And immediately there were these words, "Be still, you know better than to talk." It seemed to have something to do with finding out what needed to be done, to have a good planting was the word, that it was a night of planting. And if the plants were going to grow in the way they needed to, and have a good harvest, then there had to be certain information that was received and acted on.

And the wind at that point really picked up, and it was saying, "Listen, listen, listen" in my left ear, and "be still." It seemed like it was a metaphor for growth in general, it was like, don't be silly to think that this is just about planting seeds. It had to do with the growth of the culture, or the growth of the community, or something. And that there was very specific information. But right at the time that it seemed that I was going to get some needed information, the rattle stopped.

Our ancient guide then changed course: "But where were the men, you might ask me? Our men, they disliked the backbreaking labor of the gardens and tended the horses instead, and if they wanted to see, to divine, they turned into their shape, man-horse, horse-man, and sometimes into the magic one, the one that had wings and flew up to the moon. I see no man among you, my daughters, so one of you will have to tell what it was like. It is not easy for a woman to assume the shape of a horse, but we too have done it. Go, my daughter, go, see the brown earth and the rock faces of my land, and the shimmer of the sea in the distance, and be one of our youths, in the glory of his manhood and of his braided hair."

ANITA: Our whole group began twirling around in a circle, and the colors became blue and red. We all swirled around and became one by circling around, and that happened at the very first. The first thing I then saw was an Indian on a horse, but it didn't seem like an American Indian—he was shorter and muscular, he had very thick braided hair in strands all around, and I had the sense of maybe an Australian aborigine or an African, I wasn't sure. I had the experience that I was the Indian, but I was also the horse. And that experience kept changing throughout the whole trance. Sometimes I was the Indian and sometimes I was the horse; it got to be kind of funny, because just when I would be reacting as the Indian, I would be the horse, so that was kind of fun.

And the scene was what I picture the American Southwest being, somewhat barren, but plateaus, craggy rocks, and reds and oranges and bluish haze in the distance. While I was on the horse, which was black, I also saw some wild horses, and they came nearer, and they started to fly. And there was one that had kind of an electric silvery mane, and it was silvery, but I only saw that for a moment, and there was this sort of longing in seeing that creature. It was a very mystical sort of creature. And then the horse, being definitely the horse, was extremely tired of the bridle, and there was the sense of wanting to run around, of wanting freedom, and the Indian at this point was not on the horse's back. So the horse threw off the bridle and was experimenting with walking around and running around. And then the horse went over and joined some of the other wild horses that were grazing but also moving as one in one direction and then in another. Then what happened was that I became half horse and half woman, and again the interesting thing was that part of the time the head was the horse, and part of the time the bottom part was the part of the horse. The images kept changing that way.

There was also the sense of seeing, in that there was something I needed to see, but again in the wider sense, and I found myself as this horse-woman creature gazing into the distance and trying to see what it was that I needed to see. I didn't see anything, but there was the sense that I needed to do that.

The Old One agreed. "Listen to her, my daughters. She knows with the horses that the rain is coming. Horses are the children of the moon, and it is from the moon that we receive the blessing of the rain":

> At several points there was a very strong sense of breathing like a horse; I actually felt like a horse, and breathing through the nostrils, and I could hear the breath of the horse in my own ears and experience that. At about the same time, the rhythm of the rattle changed for me, and again on my left side there came something that I imagined to be like drops of water, rhythmically dripping into a canyon, and quite separate from what the rattle was doing. I didn't turn to the left, however, so it remained that way.

"I can feel it too now," sighed our old friend, "the presence of the horses. There is a drought; the land is parched and yearning for moisture, and I can sense the anxiety of the horse. It runs, it wants to outrun its fate, but it cannot. It will be sacrificed to the moon in exchange for the gift of rain."

> MAXINE: My heart is beating at a very high rate, and I feel air moving into my lungs. It is real hot and searing, and when I take a breath, it burns and is uncomfortable, and I am running. I am all alone, and I am aware that I have been running a long, long time, from the time it's dusk until it goes into darkness. I can feel the heat of the sand rising and touching me; I can feel it in my feet, the grittiness of the sand, and I can feel the day's heat rising up through my body and touching my face with every breath. I can feel the dust from the sand hitting my legs as I run, and the air is all full of this dust. And I become aware of my body. I am a young boy, and I am all brown and naked. I can feel the dust embedding itself in my face, in my eyebrows, my eyelashes, and I can feel it in the little hairs above my lip.
>
> As I run across the desert, I become aware that I have four legs, not two, and I can feel the wind through my nostrils; I can feel the tiny hairs in my nostrils as they swell and shrink. And I am running all alone, but then I am in a herd of horses and running amongst them. We are running so fast that I think I am going to be overwhelmed by them, that I am not going to be able to escape. We run for a long time together, and I am completely surrounded and enclosed. But then I break away and head to a mountaintop, and in the darkness I try many paths, but none of them go to the top. Then finally after many tries I reach the top. I am aware that I am extremely thirsty. And I look over to the moon, which is full, and I see myself with the moon reflected across my body. My mane is glistening in the moonlight. And then I jump into the moon, and when I jump into it, the darkness is replaced by silence, and even though I know the rattle is rattling, I can't hear it, all I hear is the silence.

"We women too offered sacrifices," our guide explained, "but ours were for the Sun, the consort of our Mother, and we turned into birds and sent our souls to the eternal flame. But having been consumed, we returned, sleek and black and fresh, in a thousand glistening drops, bringing the renewal of spring. It was a fearful journey; I took it many times and never knew if I would return alive. It took us through the furnaces of the volcano, down to our Mother's womb, and then on, purified, to the fires of the Sun, as He was about to turn toward spring on His path":

> JUDY CH.: I felt heat in the solar plexus. I was nude, running up a spiral staircase. I was half woman and half bird, white. I was soaring up in a spiral, higher and higher, feeling that I was calling out a warning. I could see a volcano; I went through the lava, into the earth. My feathers burned off. I felt a dramatic change; there was complete darkness. After a long time, I came up again. I became a slick and black bird; there was a definite feeling of acceleration. The speed was so great that I felt I was a rocket or a comet, breaking through a barrier. And when I broke through, there were thousands of stars, each one a mirror; there were millions of mirrors, and I saw the same image in each one, repeating what I had experienced in the beginning, the whole story. There was vibration and heat on the back of my neck. There was a repetition of the vibrations, hard, then soft. There was calmness and silence, and I felt myself going toward the sun. I plunged headfirst into the sun. I was burning, but I was not afraid; all my flesh and the skin burned off, but there was a hand that pulled me through and popped me right up, and there was a feeling of freedom, of darkness, but there was light around my essence. I broke through the earth's atmosphere and became a bird again.

Our spirit guest was gone. The hills outside lay still in darkness, as if holding their breath before the first glimmer of the new crescent would appear in the sky. And I wondered if our spirit caller would have come at any other time.

Epilogue. I believe that the old shamaness who graced our meeting with her presence gave us a true view of her world. Anthropologists are trained to watch for details that others might overlook; to them such minutiae often clinch an entire argument and validate an observation. That Eva D. smelled the putrefaction of the animal sacrifices in the posture of the Greek maiden, as we shall see in the Conclusion, confirmed to me that she had been to the Eleusinian mysteries more than all the other experiences put together that she brought back from the trance. There is a similar "signature" detail also in these reports. Anita tells of the strange hairdo of the rider she had seen, as though he had twisted his hair into many strands or braids. Archeologists unearthed a beaker (Gimbutas 1982:114, pl. 70) from the mid-sixth millennium B.C., found at Tsangli in Thessaly, that is from the time and the home region of our figurine. It has a black-painted design of eyes associated with hair "portrayed like snakes."

Prehistorians propose that the way of life of the Neolithic Thessalians was continuous with the later classical Greek culture.[11] And indeed in our reports we are witness to the emergence of such beings as Phoenix, the magical bird, and of the mermaid. And then there are the horses. There is no clear evidence about when the horse first appeared on the eastern borders of Europe, but it is not supposed to have been in Thessaly at the outset of the sixth millennium B.C. However, our shamaness tells us that at the time she lived, the horse was already there, magical, Pegasus, endowed with flight, and the shamans of her world possessed an important secret: they could at will turn into this most magical of creatures, and then they had the gift of sight.

What was the life of the ancient Thessalians like, who lived close to eight thousand years before the present? There was no writing as yet, only perhaps some ideographs, such as the one on the chest of the figurine from the same region demonstrating the posture of the Feathered Serpent (see Chapter 13). But written into the earth there are clear traces of a horticulturalist way of life. These Thessalians cultivated wheat, barley, vetch, peas, and other legumes in their gardens. They had pigs, cattle, goats, and sheep; they hunted, and especially they were fishermen. Pictures of their sailing boats are incised on their ceramics. They lived in permanent villages and built shrines. As mentioned before, there are indications that they knew a number of postures, mainly those of Birthing, of the Chiltan spirits, and of the Psychopomp, all shown on female figurines. And they knew this unique and special one, the vehicle for the present myth. Through it our old spirit shamaness gave us access to her world, a mysterious one, enshrined forever with all the other treasures of a similar nature in the Eternal Present of the alternate reality. To her and all the other Spirits who took us to that realm, our profound thanks.

The Twilight
of the Spirits

There is no doubt that the societies that used postures in religious ritual highly valued this knowledge. Shamans must have cherished them; that was probably why in a first-century Eskimo grave, three finely incised statuettes were found as grave offerings, carved out of walrus ivory, and clearly created by the same artist (pl. 69). They are (from

left to right) shown in the Singing Shaman, the Calling of the Spirits, and the Bear Spirit postures respectively. In each instance the hands are placed somewhat lower than we are used to seeing them. Perhaps it was the intention of the artist to indicate that this was the shaman in death. Not only are the postures recreated over and over again in native art, they are also considered attributes of the Spirits, part of their power, as we see in the drawing of the Matsigenka shaman (pl. 60). Going from left to right, the "pure and invisible Ones" are shown in the posture of the Feathered Serpent, of the Singing Shaman, and of the Bear Spirit. And they passed into later traditions as conventionalized characteristics of the gods, as in the Aztec examples (Chap. 10).

The most intricate of these types of inventories comes to us from a temple on Rurutu Island of the Austral Group in Poly-

Plate 69

nesia, carved from ironwood in the eighteenth century and said to represent the god Tangaroa generating gods and men (pls. 70a-d). With beautiful logic, Tangaroa himself is shown in the Birthing posture (pl. 70a). On his right upper arm (side view, pl. 70b), a figure, presumably a human, is in the hunter's Porcupine posture, and the tiny woman under his right elbow uses the Birthing posture. The somewhat larger figure on his upper right thigh is appealing to the Bear Spirit, complete with the ecstatic, inward-directed facial expression, his head slightly tilted back, his eyes closed, and that lightly smiling mouth we know also from the Northwest Coast carving of the same posture (pl. 1).

While these figures are all human, I think we need to consider the four paired figures on the god's back to be spirits (pl. 70c). They use the posture we call Empowerment (compare pl. 49), which makes good sense: Spirits possess, as we know from our experiences, tremendous, highly concentrated energy. They are placed above another human in the Bear posture, supplying the energy for healing. Special care is lavished on the upper torso and head of Tangaroa. The only posture I do not recognize is the one forming his left nipple and his ears. That still needs to be explored. His right nipple is once more a figure in the Bear Spirit posture. The place of his heart is marked by an upside-down figure in the Chiltan posture, right arm up, a reference to the restless, multiple, pulsating energy of the heart. With his eyebrows and the crease between them, the god is the psychopomp (remember Chapter 12, pl. 50, the Chiltan posture with the left arm up), and his cheeks are the seat of power with the paired Empowerment figures on either side. Only his mouth remains a secret. It has a small inset face above the double line of the lips. The Indian carvers of the Northwest Coast used to represent spiritual essence that way, but I would have to know more about the traditional culture of these Polynesian islands before I could come to any conclusion. However, even this way, Tangaroa is certainly a magnificent god.

There are many unanswered questions about the mystery of the postures. Because no observers paid any attention to them, we do not know whether they are still in use anywhere, except in Uzbekistan and possibly among the Matsigenka Indians. Neither do we know what neurophysiological changes might correspond to the differences in experience. These physical shifts are apparently so subtle that to date, at least, we have not been able to pinpoint them in our laboratory research. Still another puzzle is the fact that they were known in many parts of the world, often nearly simultaneously. If we consider in how many different ways we are able to hold our bodies and heads and can place our hands, arms, feet, and legs, it is truly astounding that these roughly thirty specific combinations should appear over and over again world-wide. How could they have spread without any modern communication techniques? We could speculate that they were available in the other reality; we talked about sudden shifts that according to many traditions occur occasionally in that dimension of reality, and religious specialists would have gotten hold of them there. Another mode of propagation is suggested by Rupert Sheldrake.

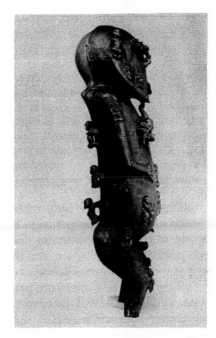

Plate 70a

Plate 70b

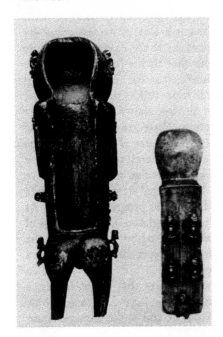

Plate 70c

Plate 70d

He calls his theory the "hypothesis of formative causation." The nature of things, he says, depends on fields he calls "morphic fields." Each kind of natural system has its own field, that is,

> non-material regions of influence extending in space and continuing in time. They are localized within and around the systems they organize. When any particular organized system ceases to exist, as an atom splits, a snowflake melts, an animal dies, then its organizing field disappears from that place. But in another sense, morphic fields do not disappear: They are potential organizing patterns of influence, and can appear again physically in other times and places, wherever or whenever the physical conditions are appropriate. When they do so, they contain within themselves a memory of their previous physical existence. (1987:I-4)

Sheldrake's work awaits further testing, but his hypothesis fits neatly with our observations about the postures. The archeological record, by no means complete, of course, demonstrates that a particular posture will appear at a certain point in time and space, and then unaccountably will spread to other regions as well. This process behaves very much like his morphic fields. When a posture dies, that is, is no longer performed as part of a particular ritual, it does not simply go away. If the conditions are right, as when we began combining the physiological arousal of the trance with a particular way to tune the body in the posture, the entire behavioral and experiential complex reappears.

The greatest mystery of all, however, is the agreement in visionary content. Where we do have evidence in local traditions, it is clear that cross-culturally the postures elicit almost identical experiences, as in the case of the posture of the Bear Spirit or the Chiltan Spirits. This flies in the face of one of the most cherished tenets of anthropology, namely, that the individual cultural system shapes the content of experience. It is supposed to supersede all else, even structuring visual illusions, as Segall et al. have shown in their research on the influence of culture on visual perception. There are those who would argue that the reason for the agreement is that the source of the visions is the body itself: We all have the same nervous system; therefore, everything else being equal, that is, the posture and the religious trance, we of course have the same visions. It seems to me that those holding this view contend, taking a simile from technology, that the source of the radio program is the set. As should be clear by now, I take a contrary position and consider the source of the visions to be the alternate reality. The body is tuned by the posture in the trance in such a manner that we are enabled to experience, to perceive a certain part or aspect of the other dimension.

Others point to the iconic content of the postures that might suggest a certain kind of experience. As I mentioned earlier, we have come across only two postures, those of the Australian Bone Pointing and of the Olmec Prince, where such a process could possibly be construed to take place. So this approach does not lead very far.

In other discussions on this topic, it is sometimes suggested that the visions are merely archetypes which appear because we all have equal access to Jung's collective unconscious. According to this psychoanalyst,

The creative imagination has at its disposal, in addition to obvious personal sources, also the primitive spirit with its peculiar images, which, although long forgotten and obscured, are expressed in the mythologies of all times and peoples. The totality of these images forms the collective unconscious, which as a potential is transmitted by inheritance to every individual. It is the *psychic correlate* of human brain differentiation. This is the reason mythological images arise anew spontaneously and in complete agreement not only in all corners of this wide earth, but also at all times. They are present all the time and everywhere. (Carl G. Jung, 1938:p.iv; emphasis of the author; my translation)

In refutation of this hypothesis, the German anthropologist Adolf Jensen argues,

A myth is not the succession of individual images but an integrated meaningful entity, reflecting a distinct aspect of the real world. . . . The individual elements meaningfully refer to one unit of action. . . . We have stated that fundamentally we consider it to be entirely probable that in the psychic realm agreements can be found with the myths of ancient human history. But there will never be a case where such contents of consciousness will be drawn so clearly that with a larger number of experimental subjects the same integral idea could be found, from which one might be able to read one and only one particular myth. (Jensen 1966:115–116, my translation)

As I have shown over and over again, our visions act very much like integrated myths, and our experiences with the postures amply illustrate Jensen's point. Individual, highly fragmented archetypical images simply will not account for what we have experienced.

The question is, of course, why did the postures vanish from the scene in so many instances? Why would a snowflake melt, to refer back to Sheldrake's image? It turns to water when there is a change in the temperature. The same way, we may assume, postures also disappear as a result of change—in this case, of the cultural ambience. Why that would happen, we cannot tell. Is it a development of the human scene? Or did a piece of the sky world break off once more and crash into the world where humans live, as the Yanomamö might say? All we can observe is that in many areas of the world, the demise of the postures coincides with the intrusion of intensive, open-field agriculture, frequently coupled with animal husbandry.

Such cultural change brings about frightful human misery and pain. Since, for the most part, the societies involved were not literate, we can only intuit what horror the loss of a way of life entailed. In the Nordic myths we hear of Ragnarök, the doom of the gods, of their struggle against enemy forces, and of the eventual destruction of the earth. The Popol Vuh equally tells of murder committed against such men as Seven Makaw, a stand-in for the independent horticulturalists, by the new gods, who then create docile humans entirely of cornmeal, whom they even deprive of the gift of "seeing."

Even when the change takes place in literate societies, we do not often get the entire story. The history of preclassical Greece is a case in point. According to the renowned Greek historian Herodotus, the wise lawgiver Solon of Athens (ca. 638–ca. 558 B.C.) once called on Croesus at Sardis, an important city in Asia Minor at the time. Intent on trying to impress the famous Athenian, Croesus showed him all his magnificent treasures and then asked him, with the proper compliments, whom among all the men he had known did he consider the most fortunate. He expected Solon to name him, of course, but Solon was not only wise but also honest, and so he first nominated Tellus, an Athenian who had seen sons grow up and grandchildren born, and then died with honor on the battlefield. Croesus now hoped that he would at least make second place. But when he pressed his guest further, Solon named a pair of brothers, Cleobis and Bito of Argos.

It seems that these two men, great athletes of their day, wanted their mother to attend a festival in honor of the goddess Hera. But they arrived home late from working in their fields, so instead of spending time going for the oxen, they put the yoke on their own necks and pulled the heavy cart with their mother in it the entire five miles to the temple. Everyone praised the young men for their great strength and for having honored their mother in this fashion. Their mother, overjoyed at the deed and the praise it had won, besought the goddess to bestow on her sons the highest blessing to which mortals can attain. The youths offered sacrifice, took part in the holy meal, and then fell asleep in the temple, never to wake up again. Their countrymen were so impressed by this chain of events, they caused statues of them to be made and given to the shrine at Delphi.

Herodotus interpreted the tale as meaning that death was better than life. But the story of Cleobis and Bito is quite puzzling. Why was everyone so impressed with what on the surface seems an accidental death of two young men brought on by their own carelessness? They had worked in the summer heat in the fields all day, then they had pulled the heavy oxcart with their mother in it over a five-mile stretch of a bumpy dirt road, and in the end they had eaten a greasy meal. The transition from the heat to the cold temple, the tremendous exertion, the heavy meal, and then lying down to sleep could most certainly have caused a sudden physical collapse. Clearly there is something odd about this story.

The fault lies not with Solon, however. In the sixth century before our era, when Greece was still predominantly horticulturalist, we may be sure that he knew what he was talking about. The great boon that Cleobis and Bito had received, their "falling asleep" in the temple and then dying, was their successfully achieving an intense ecstatic experience during initiation. The question is, why would Herodotus misunderstand the tradition in this manner?

The answer lies hidden in the statues that the Argives caused to be made of the youths and given to the shrine at Delphi. Statues of that sort, with both the youth and the girl stereotypically always in the same posture, were made for hundreds of years in Egypt and then were carried to Greece. But as we learn from art historians, a startling transformation occurred in these so-called Kuroi statues by the early fifth century B.C., the time Herodotus was born. The artists began to be concerned with the "visual reproduction of natural forms." Put differently, a fundamental change had taken place in Greek culture; the significance of the posture was forgotten, and interest shifted to the person instead and to "natural" movements. Simultaneously, in the same century, the Greeks also began formulating a theology, something totally alien to the kind of religion characteristic of horticulturalists.

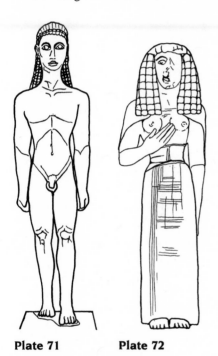

Plate 71   **Plate 72**

When we started exploring the two respective trance postures, a fascinating difference emerged between the male and female experience. As seen in plates 71 and 72, the youth is standing with his knees locked, resting his weight on his right leg. His arms are hanging straight down, and he seems to be carrying a small object in each hand. We used crystals for that purpose. The girl is standing equally straight; her right hand rests between her breasts, the left hangs straight down in the folds of her skirt.

When we attempted the postures for the first time in Vienna with only three participants, the brief experiences seemed to take us back to early, preclassical Greece. U. found herself in a forest and saw the entrance to a cave. It was outlined in red, and looked to her like a vulva. Eva D. also saw the cave, but she managed to enter, and once inside, she tasted blood in her mouth. She also smelled such an intense stench of putrefaction that afterward, she minutely searched her living room, where we had done the session, to make sure that there was no dead rat someplace in a corner. Christian St., on the other hand, was in a town with gleaming white rectangular buildings. He saw a square hole in the ground, outlined in white, but was unable to get in.

During another visit to Greek antiquity two years later, Eva landed on a sunny seashore, not doing anything in particular, but wondering all the time why she was "outside," instead of in the cave once more as before. U. was no longer in Vienna, and her place was taken by Amitaba, who had done seven years' fieldwork with the Paï Indians in Paraguay. In her trance, she was once more in South America, but more to the north, in a village in the rain forest. "You know how those villages always smell," she said, "of cooking fire and ashes." She saw the Indian villagers and had the premonition that soon a number of them would die. Christian returned to his white town but was in something like a basement, part of what seemed to him a labyrinth. There were many exits, but he could not enter any of them. Instead, he saw a flight of stairs leading upward, and he joined a row of figures wearing white robes who were walking up the steps toward a gilded statue, and all of them bowed before the statue. Then everything disappeared, and Christian held a brown envelope in his hand. He was given to understand that it was important, but when he opened it, it contained a sheet of paper bearing marks that he could not read.

What do these experiences tell us? I think the women in this case found themselves back at a time when the Eleusinian mysteries were still in full swing, a celebration of the return of Persephone from abduction, and in honor of Demeter and Bacchus. Participants were sworn to absolute secrecy, but reconstructions based on a number of sources, for instance by Jensen,[1] show an outline of rituals containing many of the elements reported by U., Eva, and Amitaba. The mysteries involved animal sacrifices—thus the feeling of imminent death that Amitaba noted—especially of piglets to the Earth Mother. These were thrown into crevasses and putrefied there, emitting the stench that so startled Eva. Many of the rituals took place in caves, and the conclusion was usually a bath in the ocean.

It is well known that the women held on to the old rituals longer than the men in classical times.[2] While the women in the trance session knew what was going on, Christian was unable to enter the caves, and was constrained instead *with other men* to bow to a gilded statue in the white city. Yes, the message of the envelope he received seems to say that the mystery is still there, but it is no longer accessible to him. The transition is reflected by the story Herodotus tells. At the time of Solon, everyone knew what the boon was that the brothers had received. That is why the Argives commemorated the event by taking statues of the young men to the Delphi oracle. But in the continuing and separate culture of the men, that knowledge had by Herodotus's time, only two hundred years later, effectively dissolved, causing conflict and sorrow for the women.

Agriculturalist societies also utilize the trance, but it is used for possession, an experience where an alien entity penetrates the body and takes over its functions. The poses of agriculturalist religions, the kneeling, the folding of the hands, the bowing, are not designed to tune the nervous system for specific experiences, for participating directly in events in the alternate reality, but are intended rather to express symbolically such contents as surrender and humility.

Agriculture ushered in the unbounded exploitation of our earth. As a result, the "tribal" societies, the living treasures of humankind, who should be protected and cherished because they still possess an easy access to the spiritual

homeland, are vanishing at an accelerated rate. Their habitats are being destroyed and taken over by developers and exploiters, the vultures of the modern age. Retribution was swift and merciless: the development threatens everything, the earth, the sky, the waters, the plants and the animals, our very existence. As the Navajo creation myth warns, if things are no longer held sacred, the monsters arise and will devour the people.

And, we might add, the Spirits will withdraw, with our spiritual base becoming increasingly narrower. This account is an attempt to demonstrate what riches are hidden in those ranges of mystery. But what is accessible to us is but a meager remnant, and with every myth that vanishes because no one is there to tell it anymore, there is less that we can understand of our trance experiences. In the late 1700s, a Haida carver on the Northwest Coast created a most delicate work of a naked young woman being taken away by a dogfish (pl. 73). She is shown in the posture

Plate 73

of Calling the Spirits, but no one living today can remember why she was carried away. We may have seen the story, but without the legend to give us a hint, we did not recognize it. Extinction is forever.

APPENDIX

Some Practical Points

—If you would like to try any of the postures I have described, you will need rhythmic stimulation. With some practice, you can record a tape for yourself, using either a drum or a rattle. The beat should be even and rather fast. Mine is timed at 200–210 beats per minute, and one session should last about fifteen minutes.

—Familiarize yourself with the posture first, then do a breathing exercise. It consists of fifty light, normal, complete breaths, with inhaling, exhaling, and pause constituting one breath unit. At the conclusion of this exercise, assume the posture once more, close your eyes, and start listening to the beat of the instrument. After a while, you may no longer hear the soundtrack. Do not worry about it. Your nervous system registers it anyway, although out of awareness. If you try to get back to the sound, you may interrupt your vision.

—As soon as the soundtrack stops, and provided you are clinically healthy, you will return to ordinary consciousness. Once in a great while a person does not manage this transition well. For this reason, *a beginner should always have a companion*. If the companion notices that the trancer does not come to right away, the first thing to do is to call his/her name. Gently releasing the trancer's posture is also a good strategy, and providing a glass of water will help, too. As the group leader, you will occasionally go into a light trance yourself. One of my participants told that as she was rattling, her Indian spirit friend appeared before her and rattled along with her.

—Ask your participants to take notes immediately after coming out of the trance. Precious details are sometimes forgotten later, as happens also in the ordinary state of consciousness. As mentioned before, I do not tell a group beforehand what the experience is going to be. With the publication of this text, such secrecy will no longer be possible. Quite often, the "ideal" content of the posture, the basic outline of the experience, is immediately obvious; sometimes it is not. The posture is like the tree of story: You may have to shake it repeatedly before the golden apple drops down. Point out the basic outline where it appears; such teaching is always practiced where visions are a part of the religious ritual. However, extraneous material must not be rejected out of hand. It may appear for a number of reasons: a personal matter must be resolved first; a Spirit anxious to make friends may intrude; the fragment of a myth with some tenuous connection with the posture is unaccountably perceived. Even if the "standard" content is experienced, remember that each posture can be likened to a melody, and no matter how often it is done, there is no end to variations on the basic theme. They are not, however, as easy to recognize as in the case of one friend in Switzerland, who attended my workshop several years in succession and saw a crystal castle the first time she went on a spirit journey. She badly wanted to get in but could not enter. The following year, she arrived at the same castle. It was closed once more, and when she insisted on trying to get in, an invisible antagonist dumped a bucket of cold water on her head. It was not until the third try that she was finally admitted and then found it to be empty.

The constancy and accompanying great variability have stimulated a group of my coworkers to plan a phenomenological study, which will be undertaken in the near future. In the meantime, we have come up with some interesting statistics. From 1982 until the end of 1987 and including the one exploratory project in 1977, I have offered a total of eighty workshops. Of the 890 participants, 592 were women, 298 were men. This number includes repeat attendances of 159 women and 68 men. Subtracting those, we had 433 women and 230 men participating in the workshops.

NOTES

SECTION I

2. GETTING IN TOUCH WITH THE SPIRITS

1. Erika Bourguignon, ed., *Religion, Altered States of Consciousness, and Social Change* (Columbus: Ohio State University Press, 1973).

2. Felicitas D. Goodman, *Speaking in Tongues: A Cross-Cultural Study of Glossolalia* (Chicago: University of Chicago Press, 1972).

3. V. F. Emerson, "Can Belief Systems Influence Behavior? Some Implications of Research on Meditation," *Newsletter Review*, the R. M. Bucke Memorial Society, 5:20–32.

4. Unless obvious from context, speakers are identified by first name, or first name plus initial where necessary, the location of the workshop, and the year. In a few cases I changed the name in order to spare the person unnecessary exposure. In later chapters, the descriptions of the physical trance processes are abbreviated or left out entirely because they are tediously repetitious. The quotations concentrate on the visionary, the ecstatic events instead. Other than that, editing has been minimal, concerning mainly the sequence of episodes in Section II. In Section III the nature of the material called for more extensive editing. I used both copious notes, often checked against the notes of the participants, and tape recordings.

5. This research was originally planned as part of a medical doctoral dissertation by Ingrid Mueller, a medical student at the time at the University of Freiburg, West Germany. For personal reasons, she did not complete the thesis, but I was given the data for publication. A report by Professor Kugler is in preparation.

6. Several students working for an advanced degree are at the moment continuing with this research.

3. THE OLD ONES REMEMBER

1. My research on the Anneliese Michel case resulted in a book, *The Exorcism of Anneliese Michel* (Garden City, N.Y.: Doubleday, 1981).

2. Adolf Holl, *Der letzte Christ* (Stuttgart: Deutsche Verlagsanstalt, 1979); English version: *The Last Christian* (Garden City, N.Y.: Doubleday, 1980).

3. In 1683 the Pueblo Indians revolted against the oppression, the greed, and the religious persecution of the Spanish conquerors. They succeeded in forcing the invaders to retreat to the south. Twelve years later, the Spanish returned with armed might and took revenge. Many Indians were killed, and numerous pueblos were deserted.

5. THE WAY OF THE SPIRITS

1. Hans Peter Duerr, "Fragmente eines Tagebuchs (1981)," in *Satyricon* (Berlin: Karin Kramer, 1982), pp. 77–92.

2. I included this incident, as well as the incident in the Santa Fe museum and the story about Kats and his bear wife, in a collection of tales from the alternate reality entitled "Der Hauch im Spiegel" (Breath in the Mirror), written for an anthology edited by Adolf Holl, *Die zweite Wirklichkeit* (Wien: Ueberreuter, 1987), pp. 109–123.

3. Hans Findeisen and Heino Gehrts, *Die Schamanen: Jagdhelfer und Ratgeber, See-lenfuehrer, Kuender und Heiler* (Koeln: Diederichs, 1983).

4. See, e.g., Colin M. Turnbull, *The Forest People: A Study of the Pygmies of the Congo* (Garden City, N.Y.: Anchor/Doubleday, 1961).

SECTION II

6. GOING ON A SPIRIT JOURNEY

1. Mircea Eliade, *Shamanism: Archaic Techniques of Ecstasy*, Bollingen Series 76 (Princeton: Princeton University Press, 1964).

2. In his 1980 book *The Way of the Shaman: A Guide to Power and Healing*, Michael J. Harner is principally interested in teaching his participants how to heal.

3. See ibid., p. 38. Harner's students encounter their spirit guides in the lower world, as we do frequently also. But their task is to fight with these beings in order to gain power, and this is indeed what many experience, which hardly ever happens to my participants. The difference may be due to the fact that in Cuyamungue we are located, both geographically and culturally, among Pueblo Indians, who have a pacific tradition. Harner, on the other hand, did his fieldwork among the Jivaro, the fierce headhunters of Ecuador. The initiation of their boys involves a fearful struggle with a spirit being. See Michael J. Harner, *The Jivaro: People of the Sacred Waterfalls* (Garden City, N.Y.: Anchor/Doubleday, 1973).

4. Paul G. Zolbrod, *Diné bahane': The Navajo Creation Story* (Albuquerque: University of New Mexico Press, 1984), p. 83.

5. Brueder Grimm, *Hausmaerchen* (Leipzig: R. Becker, n.d.).

6. Robert Graves, *The Greek Myths*, 2 vols. (Baltimore, Md.: Penguin Books, 1955).

7. I had seen this curious painted mask in pictures reproduced in Rudolf Poertner and Nigel Davies, eds., *Alte Kulturen der Neuen Welt,* (Duesseldorf: Econ, 1980), pp. 104–105. When I later obtained colored photographs from the Historic Preservation Section of the Georgia Department of Natural Resources, where the statues are stored, the paint had deteriorated to a few unsightly brown patches.

8. THE GIFT OF HEALING

1. Felicitas D. Goodman, *Ecstasy, Ritual, and Alternate Reality: Religion in a Pluralistic World* (Bloomington: Indiana University Press, 1988), Chapter 10.

2. No one, including me, had any idea, of course, what experience this posture would mediate. As a matter of interest, I am identifying the group to which each person cited belonged. They did not know each other.

3. See my article "Spontaneous Initiation Experiences in an Experimental Setting," in *Proceedings of the Third International Conference on the Study of Shamanism and Alternate Modes of Healing*, August 30–September 1, 1986, St. Sabina Center, San Raphael, Calif. (Madison, Wis.: A-R Editions, 1987), pp. 68–73. See also Findeisen and Gehrts, *Die Schamanen*.

4. John Cawte, *Medicine Is the Law: Studies in Psychiatric Anthropology of Australian Tribal Societies* (Honolulu: University Press of Hawaii, 1974), p. 65.

9. FEMALE POWERS OF HEALING

1. The story of the discovery of the Chiltan posture is told in Holl, *Die Zweite Wirklichkeit*.

2. *Tennessee Archeologist* 4, nos. 2–3, n.d.

3. Marija Gimbutas, *The Goddesses and Gods of Old Europe* (Berkeley: University of California 'ress, 1982), pl. 145.

4. Mihály Hoppál, ed., *Shamanism in Eurasia*, 2 vols. (Goettingen: Herodot, 1984).

5. Ibid., photograph on p. 265.

6. V. N. Basilov, "The *chiltan* Spirits," in Hoppál, *Shamanism in Eurasia*, pp. 253–261.

10. CHANGING SHAPE

1. Bill Reid and Robert Bringhurst, *The Raven Steals the Light* (Seattle: University of Washington Press, 1984).

2. Karl W. Luckert, *The Navajo Hunter Tradition* (Tucson: University of Arizona Press, 1975), p. 133.

3. See Jane Goodale, *Tiwi Wives* (Seattle: University of Washington Press, 1974), p. 245; also Richard A. Gould, *Yiwara: Foragers of the Australian Desert* (New York: Scribner, 1969), p. 109.

4. Jill L. Furst and Peter T. Furst, *Mexiko: Die Kunst der Olmeken, Mayas und Azteken* (Muenchen: Hirmer, 1981), pp. 22 and 23.

11. CELEBRATIONS

1. In an Olmec rock relief in Chalcatzingo, Morelos (Mexico), phantom jaguars are scratching the chest of supine humans.

2. Gordon F. Eckholm, *A Maya Sculpture in Wood*, The Museum of Primitive Art Studies no. 4 (Greenwich, Conn.: New York Graphic Society, 1964).

3. Since then, leadership of the Buddhist Center has changed hands, and the programs are more specifically oriented toward Buddhist concerns, which has left no place for us.

12. THE PIT OF DEATH AND THE PSYCHOPOMP

1. From an exhibit catalog: *Kunst der Kykladeninseln im 3. Jahrtausend v. Chr.* (Badisches Landesmuseum, Karlsruhe, 1976).

2. I am grateful to Edith Hoppál for this information.

3. Norman Bancroft-Hunt and Werner Forman, *People of the Totem: The Indians of the Pacific Coast* (New York: Putnam, 1979), p. 39.

13. LIFE EVERLASTING

1. A. P. Okladnyikov and A. I. Martinov, *Szibériai sziklarajzok* (Budapest: Corvina, 1972). Original in Russian; the Hungarian edition enlarged and edited by Mihály Hoppál.

2. Leone Fasani, *Die illustrierte Weltgeschichte der Archaeologie* (Muenchen: Suedwest Verlag, 1978), p. 535.

3. Terence Grieder, *The Art and Archeology of Pashash* (Austin: University of Texas Press, 1978), p. 81, pl. 54.

SECTION III

1. Napoleon Chagnon, *Yąnomamö: The Fierce People* (New York: Holt, Rinehart, and Winston, 1977).

2. In the introduction to Heino Gehrts and Gabriele Lademann-Priemer, eds.,

Schamanentum und Zaubermaerchen (Kassel: Erich Roeth, 1984), Gehrts provides valuable insights into the nature of myth.

3. Alfonso Ortiz, *The Tewa World* (Chicago: University of Chicago Press, 1969).

4. Zolbrod, *Diné bahane'*.

5. Jarold Ramsey, ed., *Coyote Was Going There* (Seattle: University of Washington Press, 1977). "Coyote and the Shadow People," pp. 33–37.

6. Dennis Tedlock, trans., *Popol Vuh* (New York: Simon and Schuster, 1985).

7. G. C. Vaillant, *The Aztecs of Mexico* (Harmondsworth, Middlesex: Pelican, 1960).

8. Background material for this story was taken from Linda Schele and Mary Ellen Miller, *The Blood of Kings: Dynasty and Ritual in Maya Art* (Fort Worth: Kimbell Art Museum, 1986). There are a number of different local Maya religious traditions. See, e.g., Christian Raetsch, ed., *Chactun: Die Goetter der Maya* (Koeln: Diederichs, 1986).

The Rio Azul figurine was created between A.D. 400 and 500. While postures fell into disuse in later classical times, some local traditions still employed them ritually during that century. There is a stele in Copan from the same period on which the priest stands in the posture of the Singing Shaman. Even his mouth is open.

For the record, from the archeologist's drawer in our simile, here are the relevant original reports from the workshop in Columbus, Ohio, on November 16, 1986.

> GAYLE: I felt pushed back, and something or somebody was pulling me back by my hair. I became dark and cool and damp. Five rattles were going around, and they danced. At my left, something was pulling me, I could not tell what it was, and a pressure engulfed me. I felt warm and safe. The rattle sound turned into the distant sound of a flute. It was nice. I wanted to stay there.

> JACKIE: My body was rocking. It was a special movement; my torso described a circle. I asked, how can I hold this? And I was told, let the body do it and listen instead. There was a whispering. I saw feet and paid attention to the dance. I saw a mountain, it was hot; and I felt a power on the mountain, it felt big. I climbed the mountain, and on the mountain there was a man in this posture, and he was serious. He took out one of his eyes and gave it to me. I looked through the eye; I could see vibration, colors that merged. It was channeling energy.

> DIANE: I saw a being holding a child, rocking it to the rhythm of the rattle. The air was warm, it was dark, and a fire was burning. People were celebrating, talking in a foreign language and yelling. Acrobats were jumping into the fire, but they were not hurt. I backed away from the fire and went into the forest or jungle. I went back to the fire and tried jumping into it myself. Then I went to a hut to sleep. A deer came into the hut. I killed it and took out its heart. Then I rekindled the fire. I went back into the dark and walked in time with the rattle. It was like a dance; I was in a chain of people, and the chain was very long.

> JUDY: I felt really warm. On a screen I saw a white bird; it had the profile of an eagle. I tried to be the [clay] figure. When I got into it, I saw a huge dark pond; it was very still, stagnant, and had not moved in eons. It was very beautiful but sterile. When I got outside, I fell apart, and that made me feel happy. Something was saying, "Things can start again."

> CATHLEEN: I felt the straightness of my spine, the possession of power. I was large and was expanding, and I felt male. Then I bent back; it was like giving birth, and I held back a scream, but nothing came out.

> JILL: I thought that the posture would not hurt, but it did. I was with a lot of reptiles, iguanas, like that, and I was one of them. I thought that I will have to look at the world from their perspective. The pain was caused by a reptile going up my spine. I was in an iron cage, and I was being rolled around.

> JAN: All was hazy, then things began to clear. I was told, "Don't be afraid to expose your power center, your belly, but watch the heart." Someone was poking a sword into my belly, and that sword in my belly was being turned. My belly became transparent; it becomes fire. My body opens, my head opens, flowers come out of my head. I was no longer in the posture, but was making an X with my arms. I was rejuvenated and was giving the energy back to

the universe. We shot out; there were four others with me. We created a sun, then went back into the posture, and this was repeated twice. Very quickly I went through the moon and through the earth, and my body broke into droplets, and this too was repeated. I was a newborn star; it was an incredible feeling.

ADRIANA: All was dark blue; the rattle sounded like fire crackling, and I was being pulled from behind. Afterward I had to struggle. I must not fall asleep, I must stay alert.

SHARRON: The energy was not flowing easily. There was a light in my head. Then there is a twin in me, but we are facing in opposite directions and meet at the tongue. There is a sense of spreading out, of a chalice forming. I am being hollowed out. At the right there is a flower basket. I see the sun through a circle. I am given to understand that that's how the sun rises; we participate in it. My tongue is being pulled outward. We are waiting for the sun to be put on our tongue.

9. Viola E. Garfield and Linn A. Forest, *The Wolf and the Raven: Totem Poles of Southeastern Alaska* (Seattle: University of Washington Press, 1986). Original 1948.
10. Ibid., pp. 31–35.
11. For classical Greek myths, see Graves, *The Greek Myths*.

CONCLUSION

1. A. E. Jensen, *Die getoetete Gottheit: Weltbild einer fruehen Kultur*. Stuttgart: Kohlhammer, 1966.
2. Hans Peter Duerr, *Dreamtime*, trans. Felicitas Goodman (Oxford: Blackwell, 1984).

BIBLIOGRAPHY

Altenmueller, Hartwig. 1982. *Grab- und Totenreich der alten Aegypter*. Hamburg: Hamburgisches Museum fuer Voelkerkunde.

Badisches Landesmuseum Karlsruhe. 1976. *Kunst der Kykladeninseln im 3. Jahrtausend v. Chr.* (exhibit).

Baer, Gerhard. 1984. *Die Religion der Matsigenka: Ost-Peru*. Basel: Wepf.

Baer, G.; E. Ferst; and C. N. Dubelarr. 1984. Petroglyphs from the Urubamba and Pantiacolla Rivers, Eastern Peru. *Verhandl. Naturf. Ges. Basel* 94:287–306.

Bancroft-Hunt, Norman, and Werner Forman. 1979. *People of the Totem: The Indians of the Pacific Coast*. New York: Putnam.

Basilov, V. N. 1984. The *chiltan* Spirits. In *Shamanism in Eurasia*, Mihály Hoppál, ed. Goettingen: Herodot, pp. 253–261.

Bernal, Ignacio. 1969. *The Olmec World*. Berkeley: University of California Press.

——. 1970. *The Mexican National Museum of Anthropology*. London: Thames and Hudson.

Bounure, Vincent. 1968. *Die amerikanische Malerei*. Lausanne: Editions Rencontre.

Bourguignon, Erika. 1973. *Religion, Altered States of Consciousness, and Social Change*. Columbus: Ohio State University Press.

Budge, W. E. E. 1911. *Osiris and the Egyptian Resurrection*. New York: Dover.

Buehler, Alfred; Terry Barrow; and Charles P. Mountford. 1980. *Ozeanien und Australien: Die Kunst der Suedsee*. Baden-Baden: Holle.

Bushnell, G. H. S. 1957. *Peru*. New York: Praeger.

Campbell, Joseph. 1983. *The Way of the Animal Powers*. Vol. 1, *Historical Atlas of World Mythology*. London: Alfred van der March.

Cawte, John. 1974. *Medicine Is the Law: Studies in Psychiatric Anthropology of Australian Tribal Societies*. Honolulu: University Press of Hawaii.

Chagnon, Napoleon. 1977. *Yąnomamö: The Fierce People*. New York: Holt, Rinehart and Winston.

Charbonneaux, J.; R. Martin; and F. Villard. 1969. *Die griechische Kunst II: Das archaische Griechenland*. Muenchen: Beck-Verlag.

Cholula, Ciudad Sagrada. 1971. *Artes de México* 18, no. 140.

Coe, Ralph T. 1977. *Sacred Circles: Two Thousand Years of American Indian Art*. Exhibition, Nelson Gallery of Art-Atkins Museum of Fine Arts, Kansas City, Missouri.

Daicoviciu, Constantin, and Emil Condurachi. 1972. *Rumaenien*. Genf: Nagel.

Demarque, Pierre. 1975. *Die griechische Kunst I: Die Geburt der griechischen Kunst*. Muenchen: C. H. Beck.

Diószegi, Vilmos. 1958. *A sámánhit emlékei a magyar népi müveltségben*. Budapest: Akadémiai Kiadó.

Dockstader, Frederick J. 1973. *Indian Art in America*. New York: Promontory Press.

Doebler, Hanns Ferdinand. 1972. *Kunst- und Sittengeschichte der Welt, Magie, Mythos, Religion*. N.p.: Bertelsmann.

Duerden, Dennis. 1974. *African Art*. London: Hamlyn.

Duerr, Hans Peter. 1984. *Dreamtime*. Trans. Felicitas Goodman. Oxford: Blackwell.

——. 1982. *Satyricon*. Berlin: Karin Kramer.

——. 1984. *Sedna oder die Liebe zum Leben*. Frankfurt am Main: Suhrkamp.

Eckholm, Gordon F. 1964. *A Maya Sculpture in Wood*. The Museum of Primitive Art Studies no. 4. Greenwich, Conn.: New York Graphic Society.

Eliade, Mircea. 1964. *Shamanism: Archaic Techniques of Ecstasy.* Bollinger Series 76. Princeton: Princeton University Press.

Elkin, A. P. 1964. *The Australian Aborigines.* Garden City, N.Y.: Anchor/Doubleday.

Emerson, V. F. 1972. Can Belief Systems Influence Neurophysiology? Some Implications of Research on Meditation. *Newsletter Review,* the R. M. Bucke Memorial Society, 5:20–32.

Fasani, Leone. 1978. *Die illustrierte Weltgeschichte der Archaeologie.* Muenchen: Suedwest Verlag.

Feest, Christian. 1968. *Indianer Nordamerikas.* Museum fuer Voelkerkunde, Wien (exhibit).

Findeisen, Hans, and Heino Gehrts. 1983. *Die Schamanen: Jagdhelfer und Ratgeber, Seelenfahrer, Kuender und Heiler.* Koeln: Diederichs.

Furst, Jill L., and Peter T. Furst. 1981. *Mexiko: Die Kunst der Olmeken, Mayas und Azteken.* Muenchen: Hirmer.

Furst, Peter T., and Jill L. Furst. 1982. *North American Indian Art.* New York: Rizzoli.

Gafni, Shlomo S. 1983. *The Glory of the Old Testament.* Jerusalem: The Jerusalem Publishing House.

Garfield, Viola E., and Linn A. Forest. 1986 (original 1948). *The Wolf and the Raven: Totem Poles of Southeastern Alaska.* Seattle: University of Washington Press.

Gehrts, Heino, and Gabriele Lademann-Priemer, eds. 1984. *Schamanentum und Zaubermaerchen.* Kassel: Erich Roeth.

Gimbutas, Marija. 1982. *The Goddesses and Gods of Old Europe.* Berkeley: University of California Press.

Goodale, Jane. 1974. *Tiwi Wives.* Seattle: University of Washington Press.

Goodman, Felicitas D. 1972. *Speaking in Tongues: A Cross-Cultural Study of Glossolalia.* Chicago: University of Chicago Press.

———. 1981. *The Exorcism of Anneliese Michel.* Garden City, N.Y.: Doubleday.

———. 1988. *Ecstasy, Ritual, and Alternate Reality: Religion in a Pluralistic World.* Bloomington: Indiana University Press.

———. 1988. *How about Demons? Possession and Exorcism in the Modern World.* Bloomington: Indiana University Press.

Gottschalk, Herbert. 1982. *Lexikon der Mythologie.* Muenchen: T. B. Heyne.

Gould, Richard A. 1969. *Yiwara: Foragers of the Australian Desert.* New York: Scribner.

Graves, Robert. 1955. *The Greek Myths.* Baltimore: Penguin Books.

Grieder, Terence. 1978. *The Art and Archeology of Pashash.* Austin: University of Texas Press.

Grimm, Brueder. N.d. *Hausmaerchen.* Leipzig: R. Becker.

Guttmann, G.; F. D. Goodman; C. Korunka; H. Bauer; and M. Leodolter. 1988. DC-Potential Recordings during Altered States of Consciousness. *Research Bulletin, Psychologisches Institut der Universitaet Wien.*

Halifax, Joan. 1982. *The Wounded Healer.* London: Thames and Houston.

Die Hallstattkultur: Fruehform europaeischer Einheit. 1980. Land Oberoesterreich, Schloss Lamberg, Steyr (exhibit).

Harner, Michael J. 1973. *The Jivaro: People of the Sacred Waterfalls.* Garden City, N.Y.: Anchor/Doubleday.

———. 1980. *The Way of the Shaman: A Guide to Power and Healing.* New York: Harper and Row.

Holl, Adolf. 1980. *The Last Christian.* Garden City, N.Y.: Doubleday.

———. 1987. *Die zweite Wirklichkeit.* Wien: Ueberreuter.

Holm, E. 1969. *Felsbilder Suedafrikas.* Tuebingen.

Hoppál, Mihály, ed. 1984. *Shamanism in Eurasia.* 2 vols. Goettingen: Herodot.

Jelinek, J. 1972. *Das grosse Bilderlexikon des Menschen in der Vorzeit.* Artia: Prag.

Jensen, A. E. 1966. *Die getoetete Gottheit: Weltbild einer fruehen Kultur.* Stuttgart: Kohlhammer.

Jung, Carl G. 1938. *Wandlungen und Symbole der Libido,* 3d ed. Leipzig.

——. 1980. *Der Mensch und seine Symbole.* 6th ed. Olten: Walter.

Kooijman, Simon. N.d. *Niew Guinea: Kunst, Kunstvormen en Stijlgebieden.* Leiden: Rijksmuseum voor Volkenkunde.

Land, L. K., 1979. *Pre-Columbian Art from the Land Collection.* N.p.: California Academy of Science.

Lawrence, D. H. 1934. *Mornings in Mexico.* New York: Knopf.

Lensinger, Elsy. 1985. *Propylaen Weltgeschichte, Naturvoelker.* Wien: Propylaen Verlag.

Lincoln, Yvonne, and Egon G. Guba. 1985. *Naturalistic Inquiry.* Beverly Hills: Sage.

Lommel, Andreas. 1966. *Vorgeschichte und Naturvoelker.* Vol. 1. London: Paul Hamlyn.

Lothrop, Samuel K. 1969. *Das vorkolumbianische Amerika und seine Kunstschaetze.* Genève: Editions d'Art Albert Skira.

Luckert, Karl W. 1975. *The Navajo Hunter Tradition.* Tucson: University of Arizona Press.

Mair, L. 1969. *Witchcraft.* New York: McGraw-Hill.

Mode, Heinz. 1959. *Das fruehe Indien.* Stuttgart: Gustav Klipper.

Monti, Franco. 1969. *Precolumbian Terracottas.* London: Hamlyn.

Museum fuer Voelkerkunde Wien. N.d. *Voelker der Tundra und Taiga: Schutzgeister der Orotschen und Golden* (exhibit).

Museum fuer Vor- und Fruehgeschichte, Frankfurt am Main. 1983. *Keramik und Gold: Bulgarische Jungsteinzeit im 6. und 5. Jahrtausend* (exhibit).

Neher, Andrew. 1961. Auditory Driving Observed with Scalp Electrodes in Normal Subjects. *Electroenceph. Clin. Neurophysiol.* 13:449–451.

——. 1962. A Physiological Explanation of Unusual Behavior in Ceremonies Involving Drums. *Human Biology* 34:151–160.

Okladnyikov, A. P. and A. I. Martinov. 1972. Hungarian ed. by Mihály Hoppál. *Szibériai sziklarajzok.* Budapest: Corvina.

Oppitz, Michael. 1981. *Schamanen im Blinden Land.* Frankfurt am Main: Syndikat.

Ortiz, Alfonso. 1969. *Tewa World.* Chicago: University of Chicago Press.

Osborne, Harold. 1969. *South American Mythology.* Feltham, Middlesex: Hamlyn.

Peters, Larry G., and Douglas Price-Williams. 1983. A Phenomenological Overview of Trance. *Transcultural Psychiatric Research Review* 20:5–39.

Poertner, Rudolf, and Nigel Davies, eds. 1980. *Alte Kulturen der Neuen Welt.* Duesseldorf: Econ.

Radin, Paul. 1972 (original 1956). *The Trickster: A Study in American Indian Mythology.* New York: Schocken.

Raetsch, Christian, ed. 1986. *Chactun: Die Goetter der Maya.* Koeln: Eugen Diederichs.

Ramsey, Jarold, ed. 1977. *Coyote Was Going There: Indian Literature of the Oregon Country.* Seattle: University of Washington Press.

von Reden, Sibylle, and G. T. Best. 1981. *Auf der Spur der ersten Griechen.* Koeln: Dumon.

Reid, Bill, and Robert Bringhurst. 1984. *The Raven Steals the Light.* Seattle: University of Washington Press.

Rosenthal, Robert, and Ralph L. Rosnow, eds. 1969. *Artifact in Behavioral Research.* New York: Academic Press.

Scheffer, J. 1673. *Lapponia.* Frankfurt.

Schele, Linda, and Mary Ellen Miller. 1986. *The Blood of Kings: Dynasty and Ritual in Maya Art.* Fort Worth: Kimbell Art Museum (exhibit).

Segall, Marshall H.; Donald T. Campbell; and Melville J. Herskovitz. 1966. *The Influence of Culture on Visual Perception.* Indianapolis: Bobbs-Merrill.

Shao, Paul. 1976. *Asiatic Influences in Pre-Columbian American Art.* Ames: Iowa State University Press.
Sheldrake, Rupert. 1987. "The Habits of Nature." Manuscript.
Soustelle, Jacques. 1979. *Die Olmeken.* N.p.: Atlantis.
Striedter, Karl Heinz. 1984. *Felsbilder der Sahara.* Muenchen: Prestel.
Tarradell, M. 1978. *Regard sur l'art ibérique.* Paris: Société Française de Livre.
Tedlock, Dennis, trans. 1985. *Popol Vuh.* New York: Simon and Schuster.
Torbruegge, Walter. 1967. *Europaeische Vorzeit.* Baden-Baden: Holle.
Turnbull, Colin M. 1961. *The Forest People: A Study of the Pygmies of the Congo.* Garden City, N.Y.: Anchor/Doubleday.
Vaillant, G. C. 1960. *The Aztecs of Mexico.* Harmondsworth, Middlesex: Pelican.
Wiesner, Joseph. 1963. *Die Thraker.* Stuttgart: Kohlhammer.
Wilhelm, Manhardt. 1859. Das Brueckenspiel. *Zeitschrift fuer deutsche Mythologie und Sittenkunde* 4:301–320.
Wingert, Paul S. 1970. *African Art.* University Prints, Series N, Section I. Cambridge, Mass.: University Prints.
———. 1970. *Oceanic Art.* University Prints, Series N, Section II. Cambridge, Mass.: University Prints.
Winkelman, Michael. 1986. Trance States: A Theoretical Model and Cross-Cultural Analysis. *Ethos* 14:174–203.
Zenil, Alfonso Medellin. 1966. *Obras Maestras del Museo de Xalapa, Veracruz* (exhibit).
Zolbrod, Paul G. 1984. *Diné bahane': The Navajo Creation Story.* Albuquerque: University of New Mexico Press.

INDEX